Real-World Svelte

Supercharge your apps with Svelte 4 by mastering advanced web development concepts

Tan Li Hau

BIRMINGHAM—MUMBAI

Real-World Svelte

Group Product Manager: Rohit Rajkumar
Publishing Product Manager: Bhavya Rao
Book Project Manager: Aishwarya Mohan
Content Development Editor: Debolina Acharyya
Technical Editor: K Bimala Singha
Copy Editor: Safis Editing
Proofreader: Safis Editing
Indexer: Hemangini Bari
Production Designer: Ponraj Dhandapani
DevRel Marketing Coordinators: Nivedita Pandey, Namita Velgekar, and Anamika Singh

First published: November 2023

Production reference: 1011123

Published by Packt Publishing Ltd.

Grosvenor House
11 St Paul's Square
Birmingham
B3 1RB, UK

ISBN 978-1-80461-603-1

www.packtpub.com

To my beloved wife, Chai Ying, whose love and belief in me have been my anchor, and to my parents, Eng Swee and Sook Hwa, who have always been my guiding stars – this book is dedicated to you, my pillars of strength and inspiration.

– Tan Li Hau

Foreword

One of the hardest parts of maintaining an open source project is finding people to maintain it *with*. It's not enough for someone to be a good programmer, though that is certainly an essential ingredient. They must also be gifted at communication (working in public means constantly explaining yourself to an unseen audience), empathetic (understanding users' frustrations and needs is a large part of a maintainer's responsibility), patient (on a large-enough project, seemingly simple changes can take months to land), farsighted (anticipating how apparently unrelated things might interact with each other in future is very important), and aligned with the values and goals of the wider community. Above all, they must be fun to work with, otherwise what's the point?

Such people are exceedingly rare.

Tan Li Hau epitomizes these rare qualities. His contributions to the Svelte project are wide-ranging and significant — only two people have made more code commits to the core repository — and he has developed elegant solutions for some of the thorniest problems. Everyone who uses the framework has benefitted from his work.

And yet that's not what Li Hau is best known for, because in addition to being an excellent steward of the code base, he is a widely followed educator, whose "hello, hello" catchphrase introduces countless informative videos on every aspect of Svelte and other related tools.

As such, I can't think of anyone better qualified to write the book that you're now reading. Within these pages, you'll learn everything you need to build Svelte apps of all different shapes and sizes and gain an expert-level understanding of the underlying concepts. You've made a great choice, and we're very excited to have you as part of the Svelte community. Welcome!

Rich Harris, creator of Svelte

October 2023

Contributors

About the author

Tan Li Hau is a frontend developer at Shopee and a core maintainer of Svelte. He has delivered multiple conference talks and workshops on Svelte. Passionate about sharing his knowledge, Li Hau regularly contributes to the community through blog posts, YouTube videos, and books. He aspires to inspire others to explore and learn about Svelte and other modern web technologies.

I want to thank the people who have been close to me and supported me, especially my wife, Chai Ying, my parents, Eng Swee and Sook Hwa, and my siblings, Li Khai and Li Huey.

About the reviewer

Shareej V K has over 14 years of experience in frontend, Node.js, and full stack development and leadership. He currently works as an educator as well as a consultant, focusing on full stack development training and SvelteKit consulting.

He is a frontend and full stack framework specialist, experienced in many of the frontend frameworks, including Angular, React, Vue, and Svelte, and the full stack meta-frameworks SvelteKit and Next.js.

He has a master's degree in psychology and believes tech educators can do more if they understand the psychological aspects of learning. According to him, learning is a process that demands time and perseverance. He loves exploring and implementing effective methods for technical training.

Table of Contents

Part 1: Writing Svelte Components

1

2

3

Managing Props and State   35

4

Composing Components   53

Part 2: Actions

5

6

7

Part 3: Context and Stores

8

Context versus Stores   121

9

Implementing Custom Stores   139

10

State Management with Svelte Stores   159

11

Renderless Components   175

12

Stores and Animations   191

Part 4: Transitions

13

Using Transitions   207

14

Exploring Custom Transitions   223

15

Accessibility with Transitions   245

Preface

In today's digital age, web development is ever-evolving, with new tools and frameworks emerging almost daily. Among them, Svelte stands out, being voted in the top place as the most beloved framework in a recent developer survey (`https://survey.stackoverflow.co/2022/#section-most-loved-dreaded-and-wanted-web-frameworks-and-technologies`). Svelte brings a fresh perspective by optimizing performance and providing an intuitive design, as well as being fully featured.

While other resources out there cover Svelte's vast features, this book offers a unique lens and approach. We'll delve deep into key Svelte features, demystifying core concepts. Through hands-on, real-world examples, we'll not only teach the "how" but also the "why" behind each approach. By understanding the underlying principles and thought processes, you'll be equipped to seamlessly integrate what you learn into your Svelte projects.

Who this book is for

This book is tailored for web developers and software engineers who possess a foundational understanding of JavaScript, CSS, and general web development practices. Whether you're new to Svelte and are eager to dive deep or have dabbled with its basics but seek to elevate your expertise through real-world examples and patterns, this guide is for you. Beyond mere instruction, the content delves into the 'why' and 'how' behind each concept, ensuring readers not only grasp the material but can also effectively apply it in professional contexts and diverse projects. If you're ready to not just learn about Svelte but to master its intricacies and practical applications, then this book is your next essential read.

What this book covers

Chapter 1, *Lifecycles in Svelte*, provides an overview of Svelte's lifecycles, their respective functions, the rules for invoking them, and strategies to reuse and compose these lifecycle functions.

Chapter 2, *Implementing Styling and Theming*, dives into six unique methods to style Svelte components. You will also learn the essentials of theming Svelte components, from defining themes to enabling user customization.

Chapter 3, *Managing Props and State*, deepens your understanding of props and state within Svelte. This chapter demystifies props, state, and bindings, and discusses the distinctions between one-way and two-way data bindings. It also showcases deriving state from props.

Chapter 4, Composing Components, provides techniques to control content within child components from their parent components. You will explore the `<slot>` element and various Svelte special elements, such as `<svelte:self>` and `<svelte:fragment>`.

Chapter 5, Custom Events with Actions, kickstarts your exploration of Svelte actions over three chapters. This chapter starts by exploring the idea of creating custom events using Svelte actions.

Chapter 6, Integrating Libraries with Actions, provides a hands-on guide to integrating a third-party JavaScript library into Svelte using actions.

Chapter 7, Progressive Enhancements with Svelte Actions, unpacks the concept of progressive enhancements and helps you understand how Svelte actions can be leveraged to progressively enhance your Svelte application.

Chapter 8, Context versus Stores, delves into Svelte context and stores. You'll learn how and when to use Svelte context and stores.

Chapter 9, Implementing Custom Stores, teaches you how to implement custom Svelte stores through a practical step-by-step guide, going through multiple real-world examples along the way.

Chapter 10, State Management with Svelte Stores, arms you with practical tips on managing application state in Svelte applications. You will also learn how to use third-party state management libraries in Svelte.

Chapter 11, Renderless Components, explores the concept of the renderless component, a type of reusable component that does not render any HTML elements of its own. We will systematically go through implementing such a component.

Chapter 12, Stores and Animations, explores the built-in `tweened` and `spring` stores. You'll learn how to apply them in your Svelte application, and how to customize the interpolation for these animating stores.

Chapter 13, Using Transitions, provides a comprehensive understanding of transitions in Svelte. You'll learn how to use transitions in Svelte, when and how transitions are played, and how they work under the hood.

Chapter 14, Exploring Custom Transitions, explores the idea of writing a custom transition in Svelte. You'll learn about the Svelte transition contract, and with practical examples, you'll be guided step by step through creating a custom transition in Svelte.

Chapter 15, Accessibility with Transitions, sheds light on accessibility considerations in transitions, particularly for users with vestibular disorders. You'll gain insights into crafting responsible transitions that respect user preferences and cater to all.

To get the most out of this book

You will need to have basic knowledge of web development and a basic understanding of JavaScript, CSS, and HTML.

Software/hardware covered in the book	Operating system requirements
Svelte 4	Windows, macOS, or Linux
JavaScript	

If you are using the digital version of this book, we advise you to type the code yourself or access the code from the book's GitHub repository (a link is available in the next section). Doing so will help you avoid any potential errors related to the copying and pasting of code.

Download the example code files

You can download the example code files for this book from GitHub at https://github.com/PacktPublishing/Real-World-Svelte. If there's an update to the code, it will be updated in the GitHub repository.

We also have other code bundles from our rich catalog of books and videos available at https://github.com/PacktPublishing/. Check them out!

Conventions used

There are a number of text conventions used throughout this book.

`Code in text`: Indicates code words in text, database table names, folder names, filenames, file extensions, pathnames, dummy URLs, user input, and Twitter handles. Here is an example: "Mount the downloaded `WebStorm-10*.dmg` disk image file as another disk in your system."

A block of code is set as follows:

```
const folder = [
  { type: 'file', name: 'a.js' },
  { type: 'file', name: 'b.js' },
  { type: 'folder', name: 'c', children: [
    { type: 'file', name: 'd.js' },
  ]},
];
```

When we wish to draw your attention to a particular part of a code block, the relevant lines or items are set in bold:

```
<!-- filename: JsonTree.svelte -->
<script>
  export let data;
</script>
<ul>
  {#each Object.entries(data) as [key, value]}
    <li>
      {key}:
      {#if typeof value === 'object'}
        <svelte:self data={value} />
      {:else}
        {value}
      {/if}
    <li>
  {/each}
</ul>
```

Bold: Indicates a new term, an important word, or words that you see onscreen. For instance, words in menus or dialog boxes appear in **bold**. Here is an example: "When you have a `<form>` element, by default when you hit the **Submit** button, it will navigate to the location indicated by the `action` attribute, carrying along with it the value filled in the `<input>` elements within the `<form>` element."

> Tips or important notes
> Appear like this.

Get in touch

Feedback from our readers is always welcome.

General feedback: If you have questions about any aspect of this book, email us at `customercare@packtpub.com` and mention the book title in the subject of your message.

Errata: Although we have taken every care to ensure the accuracy of our content, mistakes do happen. If you have found a mistake in this book, we would be grateful if you would report this to us. Please visit `www.packtpub.com/support/errata` and fill in the form.

Piracy: If you come across any illegal copies of our works in any form on the internet, we would be grateful if you would provide us with the location address or website name. Please contact us at `copyright@packt.com` with a link to the material.

If you are interested in becoming an author: If there is a topic that you have expertise in and you are interested in either writing or contributing to a book, please visit `authors.packtpub.com`.

Share Your Thoughts

Once you've read, we'd love to hear your thoughts! Scan the QR code below to go straight to the Amazon review page for this book and share your feedback.

`https://packt.link/r/1804616036`

Your review is important to us and the tech community and will help us make sure we're delivering excellent quality content.

Download a free PDF copy of this book

Thanks for purchasing this book!

Do you like to read on the go but are unable to carry your print books everywhere?

Is your eBook purchase not compatible with the device of your choice?

Don't worry, now with every Packt book you get a DRM-free PDF version of that book at no cost.

Read anywhere, any place, on any device. Search, copy, and paste code from your favorite technical books directly into your application.

The perks don't stop there, you can get exclusive access to discounts, newsletters, and great free content in your inbox daily

Follow these simple steps to get the benefits:

1. Scan the QR code or visit the link below

https://packt.link/free-ebook/9781804616031

2. Submit your proof of purchase
3. That's it! We'll send your free PDF and other benefits to your email directly

Part 1: Writing Svelte Components

In this section, we will lay the foundation for writing Svelte components. We will kick things off by delving into the lifecycles of Svelte components. Then, we will learn how to style and theme our Svelte components. After that, we will explore the intricacies of data passing between components and finally wrap up with techniques to compose components into a cohesive Svelte application.

This part has the following chapters:

- *Chapter 1, Lifecycles in Svelte*
- *Chapter 2, Implementing Styling and Theming*
- *Chapter 3, Managing Props and State*
- *Chapter 4, Composing Components*

1
Lifecycles in Svelte

Svelte is a frontend framework. You can use Svelte to build websites and web applications. A Svelte application is made up of components. You write a Svelte component within a file with `.svelte` extension. Each `.svelte` file is one Svelte component.

When you create and use a Svelte component, the component goes through various stages of the component lifecycle. Svelte provides lifecycle functions, allowing you to hook into the different stages of the component.

In this chapter, we will start by talking about the various lifecycles and the lifecycle functions in Svelte. With a clear idea of lifecycles in mind, you will then learn the basic rule of using the lifecycle functions. This is essential, as you will see that this understanding will allow us to use the lifecycle functions in a lot of creative ways.

This chapter contains sections on the following topics:

- What are Svelte lifecycle functions?
- The rule of calling lifecycle functions
- How to reuse and compose lifecycle functions

Technical requirements

Writing Svelte applications is very easy and does not require any paid tools. Despite the added value of most paid tools, we decided to use only free tools to make the content of this book available to you without any limitations.

You will require the following:

- Visual Studio Code as the integrated development environment (`https://code.visualstudio.com/`)
- A decent web browser (Chrome, Firefox, or Edge, for instance)
- Node.js as the JavaScript runtime environment (`https://nodejs.org/`)

All the code examples for this chapter can be found on GitHub at: `https://github.com/PacktPublishing/Real-World-Svelte/tree/main/Chapter01`

Code for all chapters can be found at `https://github.com/PacktPublishing/Real-World-Svelte`.

Understanding the Svelte lifecycle functions

When using a Svelte component, it goes through different stages throughout its lifetime: mounting, updating, and destroying. This is similar to a human being. We go through various stages in our lifetime, such as birth, growth, old age, and death, throughout our lifetime. We call the different stages lifecycles.

Before we talk about lifecycles in Svelte, let's look at a Svelte component.

```
<script>
  import { onMount, beforeUpdate, afterUpdate, onDestroy } from
'svelte';
  let count = 0;
  onMount(() => { console.log('onMount!'); });
  beforeUpdate(() => { console.log('beforeUpdate!'); });
  afterUpdate(() => { console.log('afterUpdate!'); });
  onDestroy(() => { console.log('onDestroy!'); });
</script>
<button on:click={() => { count ++; }}>
  Counter: {count}
</button>
```

Can you tell me when each part of the code is executed?

Not every part of the code is executed at once; different parts of the code are executed at different stages of the component lifecycle.

A Svelte component has four different lifecycle stages: initializing, mounting, updating, and destroying.

Initializing the component

When you create a component, the component first goes through the initialization phase. You can think of this as the setup phase, where the component sets up its internal state.

This is where lines 2–7 are being executed.

The count variable is declared and initialized. The onMount, beforeUpdate, afterUpdate, and onDestroy lifecycle functions are called, with callback functions passed in, to register them at the specific stages of the component lifecycles.

After the component is initialized, Svelte starts to create elements in the template, in this case, a <button> element and text elements for "Counter: " and {count}.

Mounting the component

After all the elements are created, Svelte will insert them in order into the **Document Object Model (DOM)**. This is called the mounting phase, where elements are mounted onto the DOM.

If you add Svelte actions to an element, then the actions are called with the element:

```
<script>
   function action(node) {}
</script>
<div use:action>
```

We will explore Svelte actions in more depth in *Chapter 5* to *7*.

If and when you add event listeners to the element, this is when Svelte will attach the event listeners to the element.

In the case of the preceding example, Svelte attaches the click event listener onto the button after it is inserted into the DOM.

When we add bindings to an element, the bound variable gets updated with values from the element:

```
<script>
   let element;
</script>
<div bind:this={element} />
```

This is when the element variable gets updated with the reference to the <div> element created by Svelte.

If and when you add transitions to an element, this is when the transitions are initialized and start playing.

The following snippet is an example of adding a transition to an element. You can add a transition to an element using the `transition:`, `in:`, and `out:` directives. We will explore more about Svelte transitions in *Chapter 13* to *15*:

```
<div in:fade />
```

After all the directives, `use:` (actions), `on:` (event listeners), `bind:` bindings, `in:`, `transition:` (transitions), are processed, the mounting phase comes to an end by calling all the functions registered in the `onMount` lifecycle functions.

This is when the function on line 4 is executed, and you will see `"onMount!"` printed in the logs.

Updating the component

When you click on the button, the `click` event listener is called. The function on line 9 is executed. The `count` variable is incremented.

Right before Svelte modifies the DOM based on the latest value of the `count` variable, the functions registered in the `beforeUpdate` lifecycle function are called.

The function on line 5 is executed, and you will see the text `"beforeUpdate!"` printed in the logs.

At this point, if you attempt to retrieve the text content within the button, it would still be `"Counter: 0"`.

Svelte then proceeds to modify the DOM, updating the text content of the button to `"Counter: 1"`.

After updating all the elements within the component, Svelte calls all the functions registered in the `afterUpdate` lifecycle function.

The function on line 6 is executed, and you will see the text `"afterUpdate!"` printed in the logs.

If you click on the button again, Svelte will go through another cycle of `beforeUpdate`, and then update the DOM elements, and then `afterUpdate`.

Destroying the component

A component that is conditionally shown to a user will remain while the condition holds; when the condition no longer holds, Svelte will proceed to destroy the component.

Let's say the component in our example now enters the destroy stage.

Svelte calls all the functions registered in the `onDestroy` lifecycle function. The function on line 7 is executed, and you will see the text `"onDestroy!"` printed in the logs.

After that, Svelte removes the elements from the DOM.

Svelte then cleans up the directives if necessary, such as removing the event listeners and calling the destroy method from the action.

And that's it! If you try to recreate the component again, a new cycle starts again.

The Svelte component lifecycle starts with initializing, mounting, updating, and destroying. Svelte provides lifecycle methods, allowing you to run functions at different stages of the component.

Since the component lifecycle functions are just functions exported from `'svelte'`, can you import and use them anywhere? Are there any rules or constraints when importing and using them?

Let's find out.

The one rule for calling lifecycle functions

The only rule for calling component lifecycle functions is that you should call them during component initialization. If no component is being initialized, Svelte will complain by throwing an error.

Let's look at the following example:

```
<script>
  import { onMount } from 'svelte';
  function buttonClicked() {
    onMount(() => console.log('onMount!'));
  }
</script>
<button on:click={buttonClicked} />
```

When you click on the button, it will call `buttonClicked`, which will call `onMount`. As no component is being initialized when `onMount` is being called, (the component above has initialized and mounted by the time you click on the button), Svelte throws an error:

```
Error: Function called outside component initialization
```

Yes, Svelte does not allow lifecycle functions to be called outside of the component initialization phase. This rule dictates when you can call the lifecycle functions. What it does not dictate is where or how you call the lifecycle functions. This allows us to refactor lifecycle functions and call them in other ways.

Refactoring lifecycle functions

If you look carefully at the rule for calling lifecycle functions, you will notice that it is about when you call them, and not where you call them.

It is not necessary to call lifecycle functions at the top level within the `<script>` tag.

In the following example, the `setup` function is called during component initialization, and in turn calls the `onMount` function:

```
<script>
  import { onMount } from 'svelte';
  setup();
  function setup() {
    onMount(() => console.log('onMount!'));
  }
</script>
```

Since the component is still initializing, this is perfectly fine.

It is also not necessary to import the `onMount` function within the component. As you see in the following example, you can import it in another file; as long as the `onMount` function is called during component initialization, it is perfectly fine:

```
// file-a.js
import { onMount } from 'svelte';
export function setup() {
  onMount(() => console.log('onMount!'));
}
```

In the preceding code snippet, we've moved the `setup` function we defined previously to a new module called `file-a.js`. Then, in the original Svelte component, rather than defining the `setup` function, we import it from `file-a.js`, shown in the following code snippet:

```
<script>
  import { setup } from './file-a.js';
  setup();
</script>
```

Since the `setup` function calls the `onMount` function, the same rule applies to the `setup` function too! You can no longer call the `setup` function outside component initialization.

Which component to register?

Looking at just the `setup` function, you may be wondering, when you call the `onMount` function, how does Svelte know which component's lifecycle you are referring to?

Internally, Svelte keeps track of which component is initializing. When you call the lifecycle functions, it will register your function to the lifecycle of the component that is being initialized.

So, the same `setup` function can be called within different components and registers the `onMount` function for different components.

This unlocks the first pattern in this chapter: reusing lifecycle functions.

Reusing lifecycle functions in Svelte components

In the previous section, we learned that we can extract the calling of lifecycle functions into a function and reuse the function in other components.

Let's look at an example. In this example, after the component is added to the screen for 5 seconds, it will call the `showPopup` function. I want to reuse this logic of calling `showPopup` in other components:

```
<script>
  import { onMount } from 'svelte';
  import { showPopup } from './popup';
  onMount(() => {
    const timeoutId = setTimeout(() => {
      showPopup();
    }, 5000);
    return () => clearTimeout(timeoutId);
  });
</script>
```

Here, I can extract the logic into a function, `showPopupOnMount`:

```
// popup-on-mount.js
import { onMount } from 'svelte';
import { showPopup } from './popup';
export function showPopupOnMount() {
  onMount(() => {
    const timeoutId = setTimeout(() => {
      showPopup();
    }, 5000);
    return () => clearTimeout(timeoutId);
  });
}
```

And now, I can import this function and reuse it in any component:

```
<script>
  import { showPopupOnMount } from './popup-on-mount';
  showPopupOnMount();
</script>
```

You may be wondering, why not only extract the callback function and reuse that instead?

```
// popup-on-mount.js
import { showPopup } from './popup';
export function showPopupOnMount() {
  const timeoutId = setTimeout(() => {
    showPopup();
  }, 5000);
  return () => clearTimeout(timeoutId);
}
```

Over here, we extract only `setTimeout` and `clearTimeout` logic into `showPopupOnMount`, and pass the function into `onMount`:

```
<script>
  import { onMount } from 'svelte';
  import { showPopupOnMount } from './popup-on-mount';
  onMount(showPopupOnMount);
</script>
```

In my opinion, the second approach of refactoring and reusing is not as good as the first approach. There are a few pros in extracting the entire calling of the lifecycle functions into a function, as it allows you to do much more than you can otherwise:

- *You can pass in different input parameters to your lifecycle functions.*

  Let's say you wish to allow different components to customize the duration before showing the popup. It is much easier to pass that in this way:

  ```
  <script>
    import { showPopupOnMount } from './popup-on-mount';
    showPopupOnMount(2000); // change it to 2s
  </script>
  ```

- *You can return values from the function.*

  Let's say you want to return the `timeoutId` used in the `onMount` function so that you can cancel it if the user clicks on any button within the component.

  It is near impossible to do so if you just reuse the callback function, as the value returned from the callback function will be used to register for the `onDestroy` lifecycle function:

  ```
  <script>
    import { showPopupOnMount } from './popup-on-mount';
    const timeoutId = showPopupOnMount(2000);
  </script>
  <button on:click={() => clearTimeout(timeoutId)} />
  ```

See how easy it is to implement it to return anything if we write it this way:

```js
// popup-on-mount.js
export function showPopupOnMount(duration) {
  let timeoutId;
  onMount(() => {
    timeoutId = setTimeout(() => {
      showPopup();
    }, duration ?? 5000);
    return () => clearTimeout(timeoutId);
  });
  return timeoutId;
}
```

- *You can encapsulate more logic along with the lifecycle functions.*

Sometimes, the code in your lifecycle functions callback function does not work in a silo; it interacts with and modifies other variables. To reuse lifecycle functions like this, you must encapsulate those variables and logic into a reusable function.

To illustrate this, let's look at a new example.

Here, I have a counter that starts counting when a component is added to the screen:

```svelte
<script>
  import { onMount } from 'svelte';
  let counter = 0;
  onMount(() => {
    const intervalId = setInterval(() => counter++, 1000);
    return () => clearInterval(intervalId);
  });
</script>
<span>{counter}</span>
```

The counter variable is coupled with the onMount lifecycle functions; to reuse this logic, the counter variable and the onMount function should be extracted together into a reusable function:

```js
import { writable } from 'svelte/store';
import { onMount } from 'svelte';
export function startCounterOnMount() {
  const counter = writable(0);
  onMount(() => {
    const intervalId = setInterval(() => counter.update($counter
=> $counter + 1), 1000);
    return () => clearInterval(intervalId);
  });
  return counter;
}
```

In this example, we use a `writable` Svelte store to make the `counter` variable reactive. We will delve more into Svelte stores in *Part 3* of this book.

For now, all you need to understand is that a Svelte store allows Svelte to track changes in a variable across modules, and you can subscribe to and retrieve the value of the store by prefixing a $ in front of a Svelte store variable. For example, if you have a Svelte store named `counter`, then to get the value of the Svelte store, you would need to use the `$counter` variable.

Now, we can use the `startCounterOnMount` function in any Svelte component:

```
<script>
  import { startCounterOnMount } from './counter';
  const counter = startCounterOnMount();
</script>
<span>{$counter}</span>
```

I hope I've convinced you about the pros of extracting the calling of lifecycle functions into a function. Let's try it out in an example.

Exercise 1 – Update counter

In the following example code, I want to know how many times the component has gone through the update cycle.

Using the fact that every time the component goes through the update cycle, the `afterUpdate` callback function will be called, I created a counter that will be incremented every time the `afterUpdate` callback function is called.

To help us measure only the update count of a certain user operation, we have functions to start measuring and stop measuring, so the update counter is only incremented when we are measuring:

```
<script>
  import { afterUpdate } from 'svelte';

  let updateCount = 0;
  let measuring = false;
  afterUpdate(() => {
    if (measuring) {
      updateCount ++;
    }
  });
  function startMeasuring() {
    updateCount = 0;
    measuring = true;
  }
  function stopMeasuring() {
```

```
        measuring = false;
    }
</script>
<button on:click={startMeasuring}>Measure</button>
<button on:click={stopMeasuring}>Stop</button>
<span>Updated {updateCount} times</span>
```

To reuse all the logic of the `counter:` – the counting of update cycles and the starting and stopping of the measurement – we should move all of it into a function, which ends up looking like this:

```
<script>
    import { createUpdateCounter } from './update-counter';
    const { updateCount, startMeasuring, stopMeasuring } =
createUpdateCounter();
</script>
<button on:click={startMeasuring}>Measure</button>
<button on:click={stopMeasuring}>Stop</button>
<span>Updated {$updateCount} times</span>
```

The update counter returns an object that contains the `updateCount` variable and the `startMeasuring` and `stopMeasuring` functions.

The implementation of the `createUpdateCounter` function is left as an exercise to you, and you can check the answer at `https://github.com/PacktPublishing/Real-World-Svelte/tree/main/Chapter01/01-update-counter`.

We've learned how to extract a lifecycle function and reuse it, so let's take it up a notch and reuse multiple lifecycle functions in the next pattern: composing lifecycle functions.

Composing lifecycle functions into reusable hooks

So far, we've mainly talked about reusing one lifecycle function. However, there's nothing stopping us from grouping multiple lifecycle functions to perform a function.

Here's an excerpt from the example at `https://svelte.dev/examples/update`. The example shows a list of messages. When new messages are added to the list, the container will automatically scroll to the bottom to show the new message. In the code snippet, we see that this automatic scrolling behavior is achieved by using a combination of `beforeUpdate` and `afterUpdate`:

```
<script>
    import { beforeUpdate, afterUpdate } from 'svelte';
    let div;
    let autoscroll;
    beforeUpdate(() => {
        autoscroll = div && (div.offsetHeight + div.scrollTop) > (div.
```

```
    scrollHeight - 20);
    });
    afterUpdate(() => {
      if (autoscroll) div.scrollTo(0, div.scrollHeight);
    });
</script>
<div bind:this={div} />
```

To reuse this `autoscroll` logic in other components, we can extract the `beforeUpdate` and `afterUpdate` logic together into a new function:

```
export function setupAutoscroll() {
    let div;
    let autoscroll;
    beforeUpdate(() => {
      autoscroll = div && (div.offsetHeight + div.scrollTop) > (div.
scrollHeight - 20);
    });
    afterUpdate(() => {
      if (autoscroll) div.scrollTo(0, div.scrollHeight);
    });
    return {
    setDiv(_div) {
    div = _div;
      },
    };
}
```

We can then use the extracted function, `setupAutoScroll`, in any component:

```
<script>
    import { setupAutoscroll } from './autoscroll';
    const { setDiv } = setupAutoscroll();
    let div;
    $: setDiv(div);
</script>
<div bind:this={div} />
```

In the refactored `setupAutoscroll` function, we return a `setDiv` function to allow us to update the reference of the `div` used within the `setupAutoscroll` function.

As you've seen, by adhering to the one rule of calling lifecycle functions during component initialization, you can compose multiple lifecycle functions into reusable hooks. What you've learned so far is sufficient for composing lifecycle functions, but there are more alternatives on the horizon. In the upcoming chapters, you'll explore Svelte actions in *Chapter 5* and the Svelte store in *Chapter 8*, expanding your options further. Here's a sneak peek at some of these alternatives.

An alternative implementation could be to make div a writable store and return it from the setupAutoscroll function. This way, we could bind to the div writable store directly instead of having to call setDiv manually.

Alternatively, we could return a function that follows the Svelte action contract and use the action on the div:

```
export function setupAutoscroll() {
  let div;
  // ...
  return function (node) {
    div = node;
    return {
      destroy() {
        div = undefined;
      },
    };
  };
}
```

setupAutoscroll now returns an action, and we use the action on our div container:

```
<script>
  import { setupAutoscroll } from './autoscroll';
  const autoscroll = setupAutoscroll();
</script>
<div use:autoscroll />
```

We will discuss the Svelte action contract in more detail later in the book.

We've seen how we can extract lifecycle functions into a separate file and reuse it in multiple Svelte components. Currently, the components call the lifecycle functions independently and function as standalone units. Is it possible to synchronize or coordinate actions across components that uses the same lifecycle functions? Let's find out.

Coordinating lifecycle functions across components

As we reuse the same function across components, we can keep track globally of the components that use the same lifecycle function.

Let me show you an example. Here, I would like to keep track of how many components on the screen are using our lifecycle function.

To count the number of components, we can define a module-level variable and update it within our lifecycle function:

```
import { onMount, onDestroy } from 'svelte';
import { writable } from 'svelte/store';
let counter = writable(0);
export function setupGlobalCounter() {
  onMount(() => counter.update($counter => $counter + 1));
  onDestroy(() => counter.update($counter => $counter - 1));
  return counter;
}
```

As the `counter` variable is declared outside the `setupGlobalCounter` function, the same `counter` variable instance is used and shared across all the components.

When any component is mounted, it will increment the `counter`, and any component that is referring to the `counter` will get updated with the latest counter value.

This pattern is extremely useful when you want to set up a shared communication channel between components and tear it down in `onDestroy` when the component is being destroyed.

Let's try to use this technique in our next exercise.

Exercise 2 – Scroll blocker

Usually, when you add a pop-up component onto the screen, you want the document to not be scrollable so that the user focuses on the popup and only scrolls within the popup.

This can be done by setting the `overflow` CSS property of the body to `"hidden"`.

Write a reusable function used by pop-up components that disables scrolling when the pop-up component is mounted. Restore the initial `overflow` property value when the pop-up component is destroyed.

Do note that it is possible to have more than one pop-up component mounted on the screen at once, so you should only restore the `overflow` property value when all the popups are destroyed.

You can check the answer at `https://github.com/PacktPublishing/Real-World-Svelte/tree/main/Chapter01/02-scroll-blocker`.

Summary

In this chapter, we went through the lifecycles of a Svelte component. We saw the different stages of a component lifecycle and learned when the lifecycle function callbacks will be called.

We also covered the rule of calling lifecycle functions. This helps us to realize the different patterns of reusing and composing lifecycle functions.

In the next chapter, we will start to look at the different patterns for styling and theming a Svelte component.

2

Implementing Styling and Theming

Without styling, an h1 element within a component will look the same as another h1 element from another component. Svelte allows you to use **Cascading Style Sheets** (**CSS**), a language used for styling and formatting web content, to style your elements, giving them a different look and feel.

In this chapter, we will start by talking about different ways to style a Svelte component. We will then see some examples, including integrating a popular CSS framework, **Tailwind CSS**, into Svelte.

Following that, we will talk about themes. When you have a set of styles consistently applied throughout Svelte components, you'll see an overall styling theme in your components. We will talk about how to synchronize the styles across components, as well as how to let users of the components customize them.

By the end of the chapter, you will have learned various methods of styling and will be comfortable in choosing the right approach and applying the right methods, depending on the scenario.

This chapter includes sections on the following:

- Ways to style a Svelte component
- Ways to style a Svelte component with Tailwind CSS
- Applying themes to Svelte components

Technical requirements

You can find the code used in this chapter on GitHub: `https://github.com/PacktPublishing/Real-World-Svelte/tree/main/Chapter02`.

Styling Svelte components in six different ways

In a Svelte component, you have elements that define the structure and content. With styling, you can change the look and feel of the elements beyond the browser default.

Svelte components can be styled in six different ways. Let's explore the different ways to apply a style to elements within a Svelte component.

Styling with the style attribute

Firstly, you can add inline styles to an element with the `style` attribute:

```
<div style="color: blue;" />
```

The preceding snippet will turn the color of the text within `div` to blue.

Similar to the `style` attribute in HTML elements, you can add multiple CSS styling declarations:

```
<div style="color: blue; font-size: 2rem;" />
```

The syntax of adding multiple CSS styling declarations in Svelte is the same as you would do in HTML. In the preceding snippet, we change the text within `div` to be blue in color and 2 rem in size.

The value of the `style` attribute is a string. You can form the `style` attribute with dynamic expressions:

```
<div style="color: {color};" />
```

Sometimes it gets messy when you have multiple CSS styling declarations within the `style` attribute:

```
<div style="color: {color}; font-size: {fontSize}; background:
{background}; border-top: {borderTop};" />
```

Using style: directives

Svelte provides `style:` directives, which allow you to split the `style` attribute into several attributes, which is hopefully more readable after adding line breaks and indentations:

```
<div
  style:color={color}
  style:font-size={fontSize}
  style:background={background}
  style:border-top={borderTop}
/>
```

The `style:` directive follows the following syntax:

```
style:css-property-name={value}
```

The CSS property name can be any CSS property, including CSS custom properties:

```
<div style:--main-color={color} />
```

And if the name of the style matches the name of the value it depends on, then you can use the shorthand form of the style: directive:

```
<div
   style:color
   style:font-size={fontSize}
   style:background
   style:border-top={borderTop}
/>
```

A style declared in the style: directive has higher priority than the style attribute. In the following example, the h1 text color is red instead of blue:

```
<div style:color="red" style="color: blue;" />
```

Besides adding inline styles to style an element one by one, the next approach allows us to write CSS selectors to target multiple elements and style them together.

Adding the <style> block

In each Svelte component, you can have one top-level <style> block.

Within the <style> block, you can have CSS rules, targeting elements within the component:

```
<div>First div</div>
<div>Second div</div>
<style>
   div {
      color: blue;
   }
</style>
```

This approach is useful when you want to apply the same style across multiple elements within the component.

In the preceding code, would the CSS rule turn all the div elements in the document to blue?

No. The CSS rules within the <style> block are scoped to the component, meaning the CSS rules will only be applied to the elements within the component, and not div elsewhere in your application.

So you do not have to worry about the CSS rule inside the <style> block changing elements outside the component.

But, how does this work? How does Svelte make sure that the CSS rules only apply to the element within the same component?

Let's explore that.

How Svelte scopes CSS rules within a component

Let's digress for a bit to understand how Svelte makes sure that the CSS rules within a component are scoped.

When Svelte compiles a component, the Svelte compiler goes through each CSS rule and attempts to match each element with the selector of the CSS rule:

```
<div>row</div>
<style>
  div { color: red; }
</style>
```

Whenever an element matches the selector, the Svelte compiler will generate a CSS class name that is unique to the component and apply it to the element. At the same time, Svelte limits the scope of the elements being selected by the CSS rule by including a class selector of the generated class name in the selector.

The transformation of the element and the CSS rule looks like this:

```
<div class="svelte-q5jdbb">row</div>
<style>
  div.svelte-q5jdbb { color: red; }
</style>
```

Here, `"svelte-g5jdbb"` is the unique CSS class name that is generated by calculating the hash value of the CSS content. The hash value will be different when the CSS content changes. Since the Svelte compiler only applies the CSS class name to the elements within the component, it is unlikely that the style will be applied to other elements outside the component.

This transformation happens during compilation by default. There's nothing additional that you need to do. The example here is more for illustration purposes only.

Knowing that the CSS rules within the `<style>` block are scoped, when you want to apply styles to all of the elements of the same node name, using the CSS type selector for your CSS rule is sufficient most of the time. However, if you want to style only some of the elements, say only the second `div` element in the preceding example, you can add a `class` attribute to the second `div` element to differentiate between other `div` elements.

And yes, adding a `class` attribute is our next way of styling our Svelte component.

Adding the class attribute

The CSS class selector in CSS works the same way in Svelte.

When you add a `class` attribute to an element, you can target it using the CSS class selector.

In the following example, we added the `highlight` class to the second `div`, and thus only the second `div` has a yellow background:

```
<div>First div</div>
<div class="highlight">Second div</div>
<style>
  .highlight {
    background-color: yellow;
  }
</style>
```

The value of the `class` attribute can be a string or a dynamic expression.

You can conditionally apply classes to the element:

```
<div class="{toHighlight ? "highlight" : ""} {toBold ? "bold" : ""}"
/>
```

In the preceding example, when the value of both `toHighlight` and `toBold` is `true`, the `class` attribute value evaluates to `"highlight bold"`. Thus, two classes, `highlight` and `bold`, are applied to the `div` element.

This pattern of conditionally applying classes to an element based on a variable is so common that Svelte provides the `class:` directive to simplify it.

Simplifying the class attribute with the class: directive

In the previous example, we conditionally applied the `highlight` class when the `toHighlight` variable was truthy, and `bold` when the `toBold` variable was truthy.

This can be simplified with the `class:` directive, where you have the following:

```
class:class-name={condition}
```

To simplify the previous example with the `class:` directive, we have the following:

```
<div class:highlight={toHighlight} class:bold={toBold} />
```

Just like the `style:` attribute, you can further simplify to a `class:` directive shorthand if the name of the class is the same as the name of the variable for the condition.

If the condition for adding the `highlight` class is instead a variable named `highlight`, then the preceding example can be rewritten as follows:

```
<div class:highlight />
```

Putting all of them together, in the following code example, the `div` element has a yellow background when the `highlight` variable is `true`, and a transparent background otherwise:

```
<script>
  export let highlight = true;
</script>
<div class:highlight />
<style>
  .highlight {
    background-color: yellow;
  }
</style>
```

All the approaches of applying styles to an element that we've explored so far have the CSS declarations written within the Svelte component. However, it is possible to define styles outside of the Svelte component.

Applying styles from external CSS files

Let's say you add a style element to the HTML of your application, like so:

```
<html>
  <head>
    <style>.title { color: blue }</style>
  </head>
</html>
```

Alternatively, you could include external CSS files in the HTML of your application, like so:

```
<html>
  <head>
    <link rel="stylesheet" href="external.css">
  <head>
</html>
```

In both cases, the CSS rules written in them are applied globally to all elements in the application, including elements within your Svelte component.

If you are using build tools such as webpack, Rollup, or Vite to bundle your application, it is common to configure your build tools to import CSS files using the `import` statement, just like importing any JS files (some tools, such as Vite, even have been configured to allow importing CSS files such as any JS files by default!):

```
import './style.css';
```

Importing CSS Modules

In Vite, when you name your CSS files ending with `.module.css`, the CSS file is considered a **CSS Modules** file. A CSS Module is a CSS file where all the class names defined within the file are locally scoped:

```
/* filename: style.module.css */
.highlight {
  background-color: yellow;
}
```

This means that the CSS class names specified within a CSS Module will not conflict with any class names specified elsewhere, even with class names that have the same name.

This is because the build tool will transform the class names within CSS Modules to something unique that is unlikely to have conflicts with any other names.

The following is an example of how the CSS rules in the preceding CSS Modules would turn out after the build:

```
/* the class name 'highlight' transformed into 'q3tu41d' */
.q3tu41d {
  background-color: yellow;
}
```

When importing a CSS Module from a JavaScript module, the CSS Module exports an object, containing the mapping of the original class name to the transformed class name:

```
import styles from './style.module.css';
styles.highlight; // 'q3tu41d'
```

In the preceding snippet, the imported `styles` module is an object, and we can get the transformed class name, `'q3tu41d'`, through `styles.highlight`.

This allows you to use the transformed class name in your Svelte component:

```
<script>
   import styles from './style.module.css';
</script>
<div class="{styles.highlight}" />
```

We've seen six different ways of styling a Svelte component, but how do you choose when to use which one?

Choosing which method to style Svelte components

Each method that we've seen so far has its pros and cons. Most of the time, choosing which method to style your Svelte component is up to personal preference and convenience.

Here are some of my personal preferences when choosing the method to style my Svelte component:

- <style> block over inline styles:

  Most of the time, I find that the style I am writing has less to do with the logic of showing the elements, and more with how the elements look. So, I find it clutters my flow of reading the component when having the styles in line along with the elements. I prefer to have all my styles in one place in the `<style>` block.

- Controlling styles using the `style:` directive and the `class:` directive:

  When the style property of an element is dependent on a variable, I would use the `style:` directive or the `class:` directive instead of the `style` attribute or the `class` attribute. I find this cleaner to read, as well as finding it a strong signal telling me that the style of the element is dynamic.

  When I am changing only one style property based on one variable, I would use the `style:` directive. However, when changing more than one style property with the same variable, I prefer declaring a CSS class to group all the styles together and controlling it via the `class:` directive.

- CSS Modules for reusing CSS declarations in multiple Svelte components:

  At the time of writing this book, there's no built-in method in Svelte to share the same CSS declarations in multiple Svelte components. So, you might want to share the CSS declarations through CSS Modules.

  However, more often than not, when you need the same CSS declarations for elements across multiple Svelte components, you have a less-than-perfect component structure. It may be possible to abstract the elements out into a Svelte component.

We've seen how we can define our own styles within and outside of a Svelte component; however, sometimes it's much easier to adopt styles written by others, rather than designing our own styles.

In the next section, we are going to explore using a popular CSS framework, Tailwind CSS, in Svelte.

Styling Svelte with Tailwind CSS

Tailwind CSS is a utility-first CSS framework. It comes with predefined classes, such as `flex`, `pt-4`, and `text-center`, which you can use directly in your markup:

```
<div class="flex pt-4 text-center" />
```

We are going to use Vite's Svelte template as a base to set up Tailwind CSS. If you are not familiar with setting up Vite's Svelte template, here are the quick steps to set it up:

1. Run the Vite setup tool:

    ```
    npm create vite@latest my-project-name -- --template svelte
    ```

    This will generate a new folder named `my-project-name` containing the basic files necessary for a Svelte project.

2. Step into the `my-project-name` folder and install the dependencies:

    ```
    cd my-project-name
    npm install
    ```

3. Once the dependencies are installed, you can start the development server:

    ```
    npm run dev
    ```

With the Svelte project up and running, let's look at what we need to do to set up Tailwind CSS.

Setting up Tailwind CSS

Tailwind CSS has come up with a `tailwindcss` CLI tool that has made the setup so much easier. Follow these steps:

1. To set up Tailwind CSS in a Svelte + Vite project, we first install the dependencies that are needed:

    ```
    npm install -D tailwindcss postcss autoprefixer
    ```

    PostCSS is a tool that transforms CSS files. PostCSS supports plugins, which extend the functionality of PostCSS to perform different transformations. Tailwind CSS is a PostCSS plugin that will transform the `@tailwind` directive – a Tailwind CSS directive, which you'll see later.

2. After `tailwindcss` is installed, run the command to generate `tailwind.config.js` and `postcss.config.js`:

    ```
    npx tailwindcss init -p
    ```

The `tailwind.config.js` file keeps the configuration for Tailwind CSS. Tailwind CSS works by scanning template files for class names and generating the corresponding styles into a CSS file.

3. Specify the location of where our Svelte components are in `tailwind.config.js` so that Tailwind CSS knows where to scan Svelte components for class names:

```
module.exports = {
  content: [
    // all files ends with .svelte in the src folder
    "./src/**/*.svelte"
  ],
};
```

The `postcss.config.js` file keeps the configuration for PostCSS. The default configuration generated is good for now.

4. Create a CSS file in `./src/main.css` to add the Tailwind directives:

```
@tailwind base;
@tailwind components;
@tailwind utilities;
```

5. Import the newly created `./src/main.css` in the `./src/main.js` file:

```
import './src/main.css';
```

This is similar to importing external CSS files, which we saw earlier on.

6. Start the Vite `dev` server:

```
npm run dev
```

And you can start using Tailwind CSS!

Try adding the `text-center` and `text-sky-400` Tailwind CSS classes onto the elements in your Svelte component.

For example, head over to `./src/App.svelte` and add the following: `<h1 class="text-center text-sky-400">Hello World</h1>`

You just created an `<h1>` element with two Tailwind CSS classes applied: `text-center` and `text-sky-400`. This will make the text in the `<h1>` element center-aligned and in a sky-blue color. As you use Tailwind CSS utility class names in your Svelte component, the style declarations for those classes are generated and replace the `@tailwind utilities` directive.

Tailwind CSS is able to extract class names from both the `class` attribute and the `class:` directive, allowing you to statically or conditionally apply the Tailwind CSS styles to the elements:

```
<script>
  export let condition = false;
```

```
</script>

<h1 class="text-center">Center aligned title</h1>
<h1 class:text-center={condition}>
  Conditionally center aligned
</h1>
```

Tailwind CSS comes with a lot of utility classes: you can learn more about Tailwind CSS at `https://tailwindcss.com/`.

Since Tailwind CSS classes are globally available, you can apply the same CSS classes to maintain the same look and feel across Svelte components within the same application. However, if you are doing so with your own style declarations, you may have to re-specify the same colors or dimensions in the style declarations across components to maintain the same look. Changing the value in the future would also be a problem, as we would have to search for usages by the value and update them.

CSS custom properties are a solution for this. They allow us to define a value in one place and then reference it in multiple other places. Let's look at how we can use CSS custom properties in Svelte components.

Theming Svelte components with CSS custom properties

Let's take a quick knowledge check on CSS custom properties:

- You define CSS custom properties like any other CSS properties, except that the name of the CSS custom property starts with two dashes:

  ```
  --text-color: blue;
  ```

- To reference the CSS custom property, use the `var()` function:

  ```
  color: var(--text-color);
  ```

- CSS custom properties cascade like any other CSS properties:

  ```
  .foo {
    --text-color: blue;
  }
  div {
    --text-color: red;
  }
  ```

  The value of the `--text-color` CSS custom property for `<div>` elements is red, except for the `<div>` elements with a class named `foo`.

- The value of CSS custom properties is inherited from their parent:

```
<div>
  <span />
</div>
```

If the value of --text-color for <div> in the preceding example is red, then without other CSS rules applied to <span>, the value of --text-color for <span> is also red.

Defining CSS custom properties

To specify a set of dimensions and colors for the Svelte components, we can define them as CSS custom properties at the root component of our application:

```
<div>
 <ChildComponent />
</div>
<style>
 div {
   --text-color: #eee;
   --background-color: #333;
   --text-size: 14px;
 }
</style>
```

In the preceding example, we define the CSS custom property at the root element of the component, the <div> element. As a CSS custom property value inherits from a parent, the child elements and elements within the child components inherit the value from the <div> element.

As we are defining the CSS custom property at the <div> element of the component, elements that are not the descendant of the <div> element will not be able to access the value.

If, instead, you would like to define the variable for all elements, even elements that are not the descendant of the root element of our root component, you can define the CSS custom property at the root of the document using the :root selector:

```
<style>
  :root {
    --text-color: #eee;
    --background-color: #333;
    --text-size: 14px;
  }
</style>
```

You do not need to use the :global() pseudo-selector for :root, as it will always refer to the root of the document, and never be scoped to the component.

The :global() pseudo-selector is used in CSS Modules to define styles that apply globally, outside the local module scope. In Svelte, when used within a component's <style> block, it allows you to define CSS rules that won't be scoped to the component, making them available and applicable to elements across the entire Svelte application.

As an alternative to defining the CSS custom properties in the <style> block, you can define them directly on the element itself through the style attribute:

```
<div style="--text-color: #eee; --background-color: #333; --text-size:
14px;">
   <ChildComponent />
</div>
```

As you may recall, doing so with the style: directive makes the code look tidier:

```
<div
   style:--text-color="#eee"
   style:--background-color="#333"
   style:--text-size="14px">
   <ChildComponent />
</div>
```

To reference the value in the child component, you use the var() function:

```
<style>
   div {
     color: var(--text-color);
   }
</style>
```

The great thing about using the CSS custom property is that we could dynamically change the value of the CSS custom property, and the element's style referencing the CSS custom property will be updated automatically.

For example, I can specify the value of --text-color of <div> to be #222 or #eee, based on a condition:

```
<script>
   export let condition = false;
</script>
<div style:--text-color={condition ? '#222' : '#eee'} >
   <ChildComponent />
</div>
```

When the condition is true, the value of var(--text-color) is #222, and the value changes to #eee when the condition changes to false.

As you can see, CSS custom properties make it much easier to synchronize the style of elements.

Now, let's look at a real-world example of using CSS custom properties: creating a dark/light theme mode.

Example – implementing a dark/light theme mode

Dark mode is a color scheme where you have light-colored text on a dark-colored background. The idea behind dark mode is that it reduces the light coming from the screen while maintaining color contrast ratios so that the content is still readable. Less light coming from the device makes it more comfortable to read, especially in a low-light environment.

Most operating systems allow users to set their preference on whether to use a dark or light theme, and major browsers support a media query, `prefers-color-scheme`, to indicate a user's system preference:

```
@media (prefers-color-scheme: dark) {
  /* Dark theme styles go here */
}
@media (prefers-color-scheme: light) {
  /* Light theme styles go here */
}
```

Before we start, let's decide on the variables needed.

To simplify things, we only change the background color and text color, so that would be `--background-color` and `--text-color`.

It is possible that your application has other colors, such as accent colors, shadow colors, and border colors, which would need to have different colors for dark and light themes.

Since these colors are going to be applied everywhere, we are going to define that on the root element with the `:root` pseudo-class:

```
<style>
  @media (prefers-color-scheme: dark) {
    :root {
      --background-color: black;
      --text-color: white;
    }
  }
  @media (prefers-color-scheme: light) {
    :root {
      --background-color: white;
      --text-color: black;
    }
```

```
    }
</style>
```

Now, in our Svelte components, we will need to start setting the color of the text to use `var(--text-color)`:

```
<style>
  * {
    color: var(--text-color);
  }
</style>
```

And that's it; the color of the text will be white when the system preference is on the dark theme, and black when it is on the light theme.

With the inheriting nature of CSS custom properties, the value of the CSS custom property will be determined by the closest parent element that has set the value.

This opens the door to allowing component users to specify the style of a component without having to override style declarations through CSS rules of higher specificity.

Allowing users to change the styles of a component

Let's say you style your component with CSS in the `<style>` block, like so:

```
<p>Hello World</p>
<style>
  p {
    color: red;
  }
</style>
```

If you want to modify the color of the p element from outside of the component, you'll need to know the following:

- **The CSS selector that has a higher specificity to override the styles**:

  Here, we attempt to use the `div :global(p)` selector to override the color; however, without knowing the implementation detail of the component, we do not know for sure whether our selector has a higher specificity:

  ```
  <div>
    <Component />
  </div>
  <style>
  ```

```
    div :global(p) {
       color: blue;
    }
</style>
```

- **The element structure of the component:**

  To know which element's color to override, we would have to know the element structure of the component and whether the element containing the text whose color we would like to change is a paragraph element.

The CSS rules and element structure of a component should not be part of the component's public API. Overriding the style of a component via a higher specificity CSS rule is not recommended. Small tweaks on the CSS rules or element structure will most likely break our CSS rule overrides.

A better approach is to expose a list of CSS custom properties that can be used to override the styles of the component:

```
<p>Hello World</p>
<style>
  p {
    color: var(--text-color, red);
  }
</style>
```

The `var()` function accepts an optional second parameter, which is the fallback value if the variable name in the first parameter does not exist.

If you use the component without defining `--text-color`, then the color of the paragraph will fall back to red.

The color of the paragraph in the following code snippet is red:

```
<div>
  <Component />
</div>
```

However, if `--text-color` is set, then the value of `--text-color` is used instead:

```
<div style:--text-color="blue">
  <Component />
</div>
```

In the preceding code snippet, the color of the paragraph is blue instead of red.

Setting CSS custom properties outside of a component is so common that Svelte provides a shorthand to pass CSS custom properties into a component directly, without needing to create a `div` element to wrap the component yourself:

```
<Component --text-color="blue" />
```

This is equivalent to the following:

```
<div style="display:contents;--text-color:blue;">
  <Component />
</div>
```

Here, "display:contents" is to make sure that the extra div does not participate in the layout of the contents of <Component />.

If we are specifying a fallback value whenever we are using the CSS custom properties, we may find ourselves repeating the fallback value a few more times. It would be a hassle if we are going to change the fallback value. Let's see how we can align the fallback value.

Aligning the fallback value

If we are using var(--text-color, red) across elements, you may quickly realize that we should also define a CSS custom property for the fallback value, lest we will be repeating the value multiple times, and it will potentially be troublesome to find and replace all of them in the future.

To define another CSS custom property, you will have to define it at the root element of your component. If the value is local to your component and its descendent components only, then you should not define the CSS custom property at the document root element via :root:

```
<p>Hello World</p>
<style>
  p {
    --fallback-color: red;
    color: var(--text-color, var(--fallback-color));
  }
</style>
```

This approach, however, requires us to use var(--fallback-color) wherever we are using var(--text-color).

A slightly better approach is to define a new CSS custom property that will have the value of --text-color if defined, or red as a fallback:

```
<style>
  p {
    --internal-text-color: var(--text-color, red);
    color: var(--internal-text-color);
  }
</style>
```

This way, the value of var(--internal-text-color) will always be defined, and it is more convenient to use just one CSS custom property for elements thereafter.

Summary

In this chapter, we went through six different methods to style a Svelte component. So, do you know which method you are going to use to style your Svelte component? You should now know to choose the approach that is best suited for the scenario.

We then saw how to use Tailwind CSS in a Svelte project. It takes some initial setup to get Tailwind up and running at the beginning, but CSS frameworks such as Tailwind CSS usually come with predefined CSS classes, and most of the time, you use a `class` attribute or the `class:` directive to apply them.

Finally, we covered how we can use the CSS custom property to theme Svelte components and how to allow component users to customize the style of a component. You can now create and share Svelte components while allowing others to have different styling than the default styles that you've created.

In the next chapter, we will look at how to manage the props and states of a Svelte component.

3
Managing Props and State

In the world of web development, managing data effectively is crucial. Whether it's the information that flows between components or the internal state of a component, proper data management is the backbone of a functional and responsive web application.

In this chapter, we will delve into the core concepts of managing props and state within a Svelte application. First, we'll clarify what props and states in Svelte are, laying the groundwork for understanding more advanced topics. We then explore the concept of bindings, a feature in Svelte for keeping state and element values or component props in sync.

We'll then explore data flow within components, highlighting the differences between one-way data flow and two-way data flow and why they matter. Moving on, we'll discuss how to derive state from props using Svelte's reactive declarations. To conclude, we'll offer tips for managing complex derived states and explain how to update props based on those derived states.

By the end of the chapter, you'll have a solid understanding of how to manage data within a Svelte component, being equipped with practical tips and strategies to tackle common challenges effectively.

In this chapter, you will learn the following:

- Defining props and state
- Understanding bindings
- One-way versus two-way data flow
- Deriving states from props with a reactive declaration
- Managing complex derived states
- Updating props using derived states

Before we start to talk about props and state, let's first define what props and state are in Svelte.

Technical requirements

You can find all the code samples used in this chapter on GitHub at `https://github.com/PacktPublishing/Real-World-Svelte/tree/main/Chapter03`

Defining props and state

In Svelte, both props and state are used to manage data within components. Props are a way to pass data from a parent component to a child component. This makes the child component flexible and reusable, as it can get different data from the parent as needed.

On the other hand, state is data that is initialized and managed internally within a component, unlike props, which are received from an external source. State allows a component to be self-contained and modular.

Defining props

Let's start with props. Props in Svelte are defined using the `export` keyword. When you export a variable in a Svelte component, it becomes a prop that you can pass data to from a parent component.

Here is a simple example:

```
<!-- file: Child.svelte -->
<script>
  export let message;
</script>
<h1>{message}</h1>
```

In the preceding code snippet, we defined a Svelte component in a file named `Child.svelte`. In the Svelte component, `message` is a prop. You can pass data to `message` from a parent component like so:

```
<!-- file: Parent.svelte -->
<script>
  import Child from './Child.svelte';
</script>
<Child message="Hello, World!" />
```

In the preceding code snippet, we define another Svelte component in a file named `Parent.svelte`. In the component, we import and use the `Child` component from `Child.svelte`. As the `Parent` component includes the `Child` component, the `Parent` component is considered the parent component of the imported `Child` component.

In the parent component, you can set the `message` props of the child component to the value `"Hello, World!"` by passing `"Hello, World!"` through the `message` attribute of the `<Child />` component, as shown in the preceding code snippet.

In summary, props are defined using the `export` keyword, and their values are passed from the parent component to the child component.

Defining state

Next, let's look at the state. State is any data that is used and managed within a component. It is not passed in from a parent component like props. Instead, it is defined within the component itself.

Here's an example that illustrates state:

```
<!-- file: Counter.svelte -->
<script>
  let count = 0;
  function increment() {
    count += 1;
  }
</script>

<button on:click={increment}>Click me</button>
<p>{count}</p>
```

In this example, `count` is a state variable. It's not passed in as a prop but is defined and managed within the `Counter` component. When you click the button, the `increment` function is called, which modifies the `count` state.

In summary, props are variables that are passed into a component from a parent component, whereas the state is data that is managed within a component itself.

Props versus state

If you look closely, both props and state represent data. The difference between them depends on the context of the component you are considering.

For example, let's consider two components, component A and component B.

Let's begin with component A:

```
<!-- A.svelte -->
<script>
  export let height;
</script>
```

In component A, we define a props called height.

Now take a look at component B:

```
<!-- B.svelte -->
<script>
  import A from './A.svelte';
  let height = 0;
</script>
<A height={height} />
```

In component B, we define a state called height and pass its value as a prop to component A.

From the perspective of component B, height is considered a state, but from the viewpoint of component A, it's considered a prop. Whether a variable is a prop or a state depends on the context of the component in which it is being viewed. At their core, they are essentially the same thing.

In this example, due to the way JavaScript passes primitive variables by value, it may not be immediately obvious that the height variable in both component A and component B refers to the same thing.

However, if we define an object as state and pass it to another component through props, it becomes clear that both the state in one component and the props in the other component refer to the same object reference.

Let's modify our example to illustrate this point:

```
<!-- A.svelte -->
<script>
  export let height;
  setInterval(() => console.log('A:', height), 1000);
</script>
<!-- B.svelte -->
<script>
  import A from './A.svelte';
  let height = { value: 100 };
  setInterval(() => console.log('B:', height), 1000);
</script>
<A height={height} />
```

In this code snippet, I've added a setInterval function to print out the value of the height variable every second in both components. In component B, I've modified the state height to be an object. Because objects in JavaScript are passed by reference, the state height in component B that is passed as a prop to component A is passed by reference as well. This means the height prop in component A is referencing the same object as the state height in component B.

If we add a `<button>` element in component B to mutate the `height` object, as shown here, you'll be able to see that both component A and component B print out the same updated value of the `height` variable in the console. This is because they are printing out the value of the same object reference:

```
<button on:click={() => { height.value += 10; }} />
```

Clicking on the button from the preceding code snippet will result in the console printing out A: { value: 110 } and B: { value: 110 }. This demonstrates that the `height` variable in both components A and B refer to the same object reference. When `height.value` is changed to `110` in component B, the change is also reflected in the `height` variable in component A.

Now that we understand what props and state are in Svelte, let's talk about bindings next.

Understanding bindings

Bindings in Svelte allow you to keep the value of a component's state in sync with the value of an `<input />` element. If the state changes, the input updates; conversely, if the input changes, the state updates as well.

The following code snippet is an example of creating a binding in Svelte:

```
<script>
    let name = "John";
</script>
<input bind:value={name} />
```

Bindings are created through the `bind:` directive. In the preceding code snippet, the input element's value is bound to the `name` variable. When you type in the input, the `name` variable will update automatically. Conversely, when you change the value of the `name` variable, the input element's value will also automatically update.

As demonstrated, bindings create a two-way data flow, enabling data changes to propagate from the element to the component state, and from the component state into the element.

The previous example demonstrates binding on elements, but bindings can also work on components. You can use the `bind:` directive to link the props of a component with your component's state, as shown in the following code:

```
<script>
    import Profile from './Profile.svelte';
    let name = "John";
</script>
<Profile bind:username={name} />
```

In the preceding code snippet, we bind the username props of the `<Profile>` component to the name state variable. When you update the name state variable, the value of the username prop will automatically reflect the new value; conversely, if you update the value of the username prop from within the `<Profile>` component, the value of the name state variable will automatically update to match.

To further demonstrate this behavior, let's make a slight modification to the code. Here's the updated version of the component:

```
<script>
  import Profile from './Profile.svelte';
  let name = "John";
</script>
<p>Name from App: {name}</p>
<Profile bind:username={name} />
<button on:click={() => name = "Svelte"}>Update from App</button>
```

In this code snippet, we've added a `<p>` element and a `<button>` element. The `<p>` element shows the value of the name state variable, and the `<button>` element, when clicked, updates the value of the name state variable to `Svelte`. Due to the binding, when the button is clicked, it will also update the username props in the `<Profile>` component.

Here's the updated version of the `<Profile>` component:

```
<script>
  export let username;
</script>
<p>Name in Profile: {username}</p>
<button on:click={() => username = "World"}>Update from Profile</
button>
```

In this code snippet, we are looking at the `<Profile>` component. This component receives a prop called username, whose value is displayed inside a `<p>` element. We've also added a button, and when clicked, it will update the value of the username prop to `"World"`.

Because of the binding we established in the parent component, any change to the username prop in this `<Profile>` component will also update the name state variable in the parent component.

Indeed, if you click on the button in the parent component, both the name state variable in the parent component and the username prop in the `<Profile>` component will update to `"Svelte"`. On the other hand, if you click on the button in the `<Profile>` component, both the name state variable in the parent component and the username prop in the `<Profile>` component will change to `"World"`. This is the power of two-way binding in Svelte, allowing you to easily synchronize data between parent and child components.

When we talk about binding in Svelte, we often refer to *two-way data binding*. But what exactly does *two-way* mean? And is there such a thing as *one-way* data binding? Let's delve deeper into the concept of data flow to clarify these terms.

One-way versus two-way data flow

When you pass data from one component to another component either through props or binding, data flows from one component to another component. The term data flow refers to how data is passed or transmitted between components or elements within a web application.

Understanding data flow is important when designing an application's architecture, as it helps to establish clear lines of communication between components and determine how information is shared and updated throughout the system.

Data flow can be unidirectional (one-way) or bidirectional (two-way), depending on how data is transferred between components.

In one-way data flow, data moves in a single direction, from a parent to a child component, or from a component to a DOM element. This unidirectional flow is achieved through component props or DOM element attributes.

For example, consider the following code snippets featuring two components, component A and component B.

In component B, we define a prop named `value`:

```
<!-- filename: B.svelte -->
<script>
  export let value;
</script>
```

In component A, we import component B and pass the value of a variable named `data` to the prop of component B:

```
<!-- filename: A.svelte -->
<script>
  import B from './B.svelte';
  let data;
</script>
<B value={data} />
```

Here, the value of `data` in component A is passed to the `value` prop in component B, illustrating the data flow from component A to component B.

If you draw up the data flow in a diagram, this is what a one-way data flow looks like:

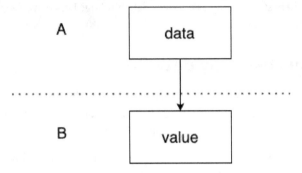

Figure 3.1: One-way data flow

The boxes show the data state and value prop, and the arrow shows how changing one value will affect another.

In one-way data flow, changes to data in the parent component automatically propagate to the child component, but the reverse is not true.

Building on the example with component A and component B, if the value of the data variable in component A changes, this change would automatically update the value props in component B. However, any changes made directly to the value props in component B would not affect the data variable in component A. Data changes only flow from component A to component B, but not in the reverse direction.

Having a one-way data flow makes the application easier to reason about and debug, as data changes follow a predictable path. For example, when the data variable in component A changes unexpectedly, isolating the issue becomes more straightforward. Because of the one-way data flow, we know that any changes to the data variable in component A will only originate from component A, not from component B.

On the other hand, two-way data flow allows data to flow in both directions, enabling automatic updates between the parent and child components, or between a component and DOM elements. Two-way data flow in Svelte is achieved through component or DOM element bindings.

For example, consider the following code snippets featuring two components, component C and component D.

In component D, we define a prop named value:

```
<!-- filename: D.svelte -->
<script>
  export let value;
</script>
```

In component C, we import component D and bind the value of a variable named data to the prop of component D:

```
<!-- filename: C.svelte -->
<script>
  import D from './D.svelte';
  let data;
</script>
<D bind:value={data} />
```

Here, the value of data in component C is bound to the value prop in component D, illustrating the two-way data flow between component C to component D.

Here is a diagram showing how the data flows in a two-way data flow:

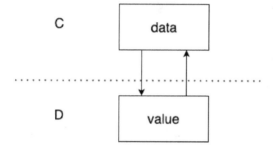

Figure 3.2: Two-way data flow

In a two-way data flow, when you change the data in the parent component, the child component is automatically updated; conversely, changing the data in the child component automatically updates the parent.

Building on the example with component C and component D, if the value of the data variable in component C changes, this change would automatically update the value props in component D. Conversely, unlike one-way data flow, any changes made directly to the value props in component D would update the data variable in component C. Data changes flow from component C to component D as well as from component D to component C.

While this bidirectional flow of data can make it easier to keep data in different components synchronized, it can also introduce complexity and make the application harder to debug, since data changes can originate from multiple sources.

For example, when the data variable in component C changes unexpectedly, isolating the issue becomes more complex. Because of two-way data flow, any changes to the data variable in component C could originate from component C, as well as from component D. This complexity can escalate further if the value prop of component D is also bound to the prop of another component.

In summary, one-way data flow offers predictability and easier debugging, while two-way data flow makes it much easier to synchronize data across multiple components but at the cost of added complexity.

Now that we've delved into both one-way and two-way data flows via props, let's explore how to create state variables that derive their values from props.

Deriving states from props with a reactive declaration

It's common in Svelte to create new state variables based on the values of props.

For instance, a `<DateLabel />` component might accept a `date` value as a prop and display a formatted date inside a `<label>` element. To use the `<DateLabel>` component, you might write the following:

```
<DateLabel date={new Date(2023,5,5)} />
```

To display the date as formatted text, you could first define a variable named `label`, deriving its value from the `date` prop:

```
<!-- filename: DateLabel.svelte -->
<script>
  export let date;
  // Deriving the 'label' variable from the 'date' prop
  let label = date.toLocaleDateString();
</script>
<label>{label}</label>
```

In this code snippet, we defined a variable called `label` and derived its value from the `date` prop using the `toLocaleDateString()` method. This variable is then used inside a `<label>` element to display the formatted date.

In the preceding code snippet, the `label` variable is initialized when the `<DateLabel>` component is first created. However, if the `date` prop changes after the component has been initialized, the `label` variable won't update to reflect the new value. This is not the intended behavior, as the `<DateLabel>` component should always display the most up-to-date formatted date based on the latest `date` prop.

To solve this issue, you can use Svelte's reactive declarations to keep the `label` variable updated whenever the `date` prop changes.

Svelte's reactive declarations utilize a special $: syntax to mark a statement as reactive. This means that whenever the variables used in that statement change, the statement itself will be re-run.

Let's modify our component code to use Svelte's reactive declaration:

```
<!-- filename: DateLabel.svelte -->
<script>
```

```
    export let date;
    // Deriving the 'label' variable from the 'date' prop
    $: label = date.toLocaleDateString();
</script>
```

In this code snippet, by modifying the declaration of `label` to a reactive declaration, the component will automatically re-compute the `label` variable whenever the `date` prop is modified, ensuring that the `<DateLabel>` component is always displaying the most current formatted date.

So, how does Svelte know when a reactive declaration statement should be re-run?

Svelte re-runs a reactive declaration statement whenever any of its dependent variables change. The Svelte compiler identifies these dependencies by analyzing the statement.

For example, in the reactive declaration `$: label = date.toLocaleDateString();`, Svelte recognizes that the dependency for this statement is the `date` variable. Therefore, whenever the `date` changes, the statement will re-run and update the value of the `label` variable.

A good rule of thumb for identifying dependencies in a reactive declaration is to look for any variable on the right side of the equal sign (`=`). These variables are considered dependencies of the reactive declaration.

You can include multiple dependencies within a single reactive declaration. For instance, let's say we want to add a new `locale` prop to the `<DateLabel>` component. To use this new prop, you might write something like this:

```
<DateLabel date={new Date(2023, 5, 5)} locale="de-DE" />
```

In this code snippet, we pass in a new `locale` prop with the value `de-DE` to format the date in German. To accommodate this new `locale` prop, we'll need to modify our `<DateLabel>` component as follows:

```
<script>
    export let date;
    export let locale;
    // Reactive declaration with multiple dependencies
    $: label = date.toLocaleDateString(locale);
</script>
<label>{label}</label>
```

In this updated code, the reactive declaration `$: label = date.toLocaleDateString(locale);` now has two dependencies: `date` and `locale`. Svelte will automatically re-run this statement whenever either of these variables changes, ensuring that the `label` value stays up to date with the latest `date` and `locale` props.

Now that we've covered the basics of props, bindings, states, and derived states, it's crucial to note that as components become more complex, managing these elements can quickly become overwhelming. In the next section, we'll explore some tips for effectively managing complex derived states to keep them manageable.

Managing complex derived states

As your Svelte application grows more complex, it will likely involve a greater number of interconnected components with multiple props and derived states. When dealing with this complexity, tracking updates and changes can become a complex task. Each prop or state change can affect other parts of your component, making it challenging to manage and predict how your component will behave.

To make this easier, here are some guidelines to consider:

- *Maintain one-way data flow for derived states*

  While it's possible to derive state from props and other states, it's crucial to maintain a one-way data flow to simplify both debugging and understanding. Consider the following Svelte example:

  ```
  <script>
    export let valueA;
    export let valueB;
    $: valueC = valueA + 5;
    $: valueD = valueB + valueC;
    $: valueC = Math.min(valueC, valueD / 2);
  </script>
  ```

  This code snippet won't compile in Svelte due to a cyclical dependency detected by the compiler. Though workarounds may exist to circumvent this compile error, the code is purposely flawed to highlight the issue.

  Upon observing the data flow, we can see that `valueC` depends on `valueA`, `valueD` depends on both `valueB` and `valueC`, and then `valueC` in turn depends on `valueD`. Consequently, it's unclear how `valueC` is actually calculated, it could be either `valueA + 5` or the minimum of `valueC` and `valueD / 2`. Such complexity makes the code hard to understand and increases the likelihood of bugs.

- *Group similar logic together*

  Consider this tip a stylistic suggestion. When dealing with multiple reactive declarations, it's beneficial to group those that are related together. Utilize blank lines to create a visual separation between unrelated reactive declarations. This not only improves readability but also aids in code maintenance.

  It is worth noting that the Svelte compiler takes care of execution order based on dependencies regardless of how you arrange your declarations. For example, the following two code snippets will behave identically due to Svelte's handling of dependencies:

```
<script>
  export let a;
  $: b = a * 2;
  $: c = b * 2;
</script>
```

In the preceding snippet, b is declared reactively before c. However, it behaves identically to the following snippet, where c is declared before b. Let's look at the next one:

```
<script>
  export let a;
  $: c = b * 2;
  $: b = a * 2;
</script>
```

The Svelte compiler analyzes the dependencies of each declaration and executes them in the correct order. In this case, it evaluates b = a * 2 before c = b * 2 since the latter depends on the value of b, established by the former declaration.

- *Avoid reassigning props directly*

  It might be tempting to modify the value of a prop directly, especially when you want to transform its value or provide a default fallback. For example, you might consider writing something like this to set a default value for an undefined prop:

```
<script>
  export let data;
  $: data = data ?? 100;
</script>
```

  While this code snippet may seem to work as intended, directly reassigning prop values within a component can introduce confusion and make data flow unpredictable. This practice can muddy the waters when you're trying to trace the origin of data changes, making it unclear whether the alteration occurred within the component itself or came from the parent component.

  Instead, it's better to declare a new state variable to manage this behavior:

```
<script>
  export let data;
  $: dataWithDefault = data ?? 100;
</script>
```

  In this improved example, we introduce a new variable, dataWithDefault, which takes on either the value of the data prop or a default value of 100 if data is undefined. This approach makes the component's behavior more transparent and easier to debug.

- *Be cautious when updating derived states*

  Modifying a derived state directly can introduce inconsistencies, particularly when that state is based on props or other state variables.

  Consider the following example:

  ```
  <script>
    export let value;
    $: double = value * 2;
    $: triple = value * 3;
  </script>
  <input bind:value={double} type="number" />
  <input bind:value={triple} type="number" />
  ```

  In this example, we have a single prop named `value` and two derived states, `double` and `triple`, which are two and three times the value of the `value` prop respectively. The component features two input boxes, each bound to `double` and `triple` using two-way binding.

  Here, `triple` can be modified in two ways: either by updating the `value` prop, which will keep `triple` at three times the value of `value`, or by directly changing the value in the input box, thereby directly altering `triple`.

  If you type into the input box bound to `triple`, you'll find that its value diverges from being strictly three times the `value` prop. This inconsistency arises because `triple` is now subject to changes from multiple sources, causing it to go *out of sync* with the original `value`.

  If you were to map out a diagram illustrating the data flow between `value double` and `triple`, you'd get the following diagram:

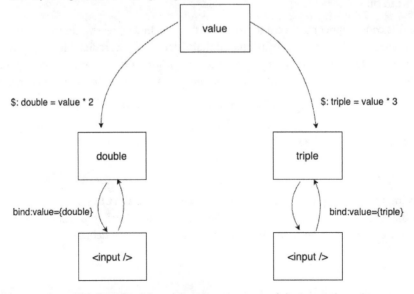

Figure 3.3: Data flows between props, states, and the input elements

Notice that both `double` and `triple` have two incoming arrows, suggesting multiple pathways for changing their values. Conversely, `value` has no incoming arrows, indicating that modifying `triple` alone would cause `value` and `double` to go out of sync.

Therefore, it is recommended to refrain from manually updating derived states, as this complicates debugging and makes the component's behavior harder to reason about.

If you wish to modify the input while maintaining the synchrony between `value`, `double`, and `triple`, a solution will be discussed in the following section.

By keeping these tips in mind, you can better manage complex derived states and make your components more maintainable and easier to understand.

In our last tip, we highlighted that updating the derived states can lead to inconsistencies between states and props and noted that there's a solution to modify the input while keeping everything in sync. That solution is what we will explore next.

Updating props using derived states

In an attempt to synchronize the `value` prop with changes to the input bound to `triple`, one might be tempted to add another reactive declaration. This declaration would update the `value` prop to be one-third of `triple` whenever `triple` changes. Here is the proposed modification:

```
<script>
  export let value;
  $: double = value * 2;
  $: triple = value * 3;
  $: value = double / 2;
  $: value = triple / 3;
</script>
<input bind:value={double} type="number" />
<input bind:value={triple} type="number" />
```

As we discussed earlier, it's best practice to maintain a one-way data flow for derived states to simplify debugging and data management. Indeed, the Svelte compiler flags the preceding code snippet for cyclical dependencies. This is because `double` is derived from `value`, and `value` is in turn dependent on `double`.

However, Svelte's compiler determines dependency relationships based solely on the reactive declarations. By refactoring the code to make these relationships less obvious, you can bypass the compiler's cyclical dependency check. Here's a refactored version of the code that does just that:

```
<script>
  export let value;
  $: double = value * 2;
  $: triple = value * 3;
```

```
  $: updateValueFromDouble(double);
  $: updateValueFromTriple(triple);
  function updateValueFromDouble(double) {
    value = double / 2;
  }
  function updateValueFromTriple(triple) {
    value = triple / 3;
  }
</script>
<input bind:value={double} type="number" />
<input bind:value={triple} type="number" />
```

In the provided code snippet, we've shifted the equations value = double / 2 and value = triple / 3 into separate functions named updateValueFromDouble and updateValueFromTriple. This change lets us evade Svelte's compiler warning about cyclical dependencies.

However, there's a catch. If you try altering the triple input, it updates value but doesn't refresh double. This happens because Svelte avoids infinite update loops. Changing triple would set off a chain reaction—updating value, then double, then back to value, and so on.

This is how the data flow looks right now:

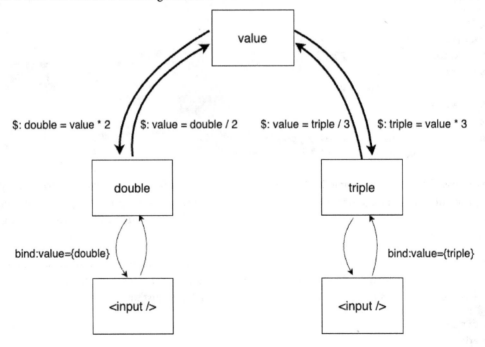

Figure 3.4: Data flows between props, states, and the input elements

As you can see in the diagram, we update the value of `value`, `double`, and `triple` through reactive declarations, creating a loop in the data flow, indicated by the bold arrows.

Therefore, using derived states to update their original properties via reactive declarations isn't advisable.

A better approach to keep `value`, `double`, and `triple` in sync is to establish value as the single source of truth. Since both `double` and `triple` are derived from `value`, any changes to the input should first update `value`. This, in turn, triggers the reactive declarations to automatically recalculate `double` and `triple`.

Here's the updated code:

```
<script>
  export let value;
  $: double = value * 2;
  $: triple = value * 3;
  function updateValueFromDouble(double) {
    value = double / 2;
  }
  function updateValueFromTriple(triple) {
    value = triple / 3;
  }
</script>
<input value={double} type="number" on:change={e =>
updateValueFromDouble(e.target.value)} />
<input value={triple} type="number" on:change={e =>
updateValueFromTriple(e.target.value)} />
```

In the preceding code snippet, we've shifted our approach to focus on `value` as the sole source of truth. Instead of binding the input elements directly to `double` and `triple`, we've added event listeners that update `value` based on user input. This change automatically updates `double` and `triple` through reactive declarations, which then refresh the displayed values in the input fields.

With the updated code, the data flow is now streamlined, as shown in the following diagram:

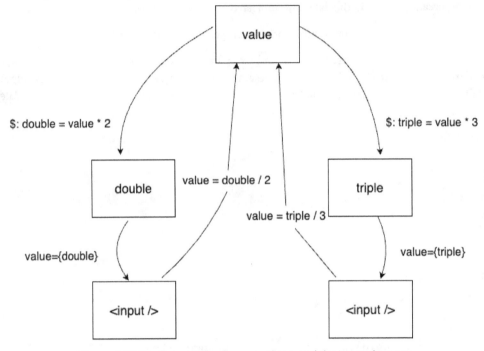

Figure 3.5: Data flows between props, states, and the input elements

The values for `double` and `triple` are directly derived from `value`, which then populates the input fields. When you modify the input, it alters `value` directly, which in turn automatically updates both `double` and `triple`, as well as the input fields themselves.

So, this is how you maintain synchronized states for `value`, `double`, and `triple`, by focusing on the data flow and keeping a single source of truth.

Summary

Understanding how to handle props and state effectively is crucial for creating robust Svelte apps. This chapter has shown you how Svelte uses props, bindings, and reactive declarations to facilitate data passing and state changes across components.

It's crucial to keep an eye on data flow within a component. Having a unified and organized data flow makes the code easier to follow and debug. Good data management paves the way for building more intricate and dynamic apps with ease.

In the next chapter, we'll explore how to compose Svelte components to construct more complex applications.

4

Composing Components

As your application grows, cramming all the logic into a single component becomes impractical. You'll need to split your app into smaller, modular components and assemble them to form a more complex application.

In this chapter, we'll explore various techniques to combine components effectively. We'll start by examining how to inject custom content into a component using slots. Then, we'll discuss how to conditionally render different HTML elements within a component. We'll also delve into recursive components, useful for displaying nested or hierarchical data.

We'll guide you through each topic with hands-on examples, ensuring the techniques you learn are both practical and applicable in real-world scenarios. By the end of this chapter, you'll have a richer set of strategies to compose components in your Svelte applications.

In this chapter, you will learn the following:

- Manipulating how a child component looks from the perspective of its parent
- Passing dynamic content through slots
- Rendering different HTML element and component types
- Creating recursive components for recursive data
- The Container/Presentational pattern

Let's kick things off by exploring the various ways we can manipulate and control the content of a child component.

Technical requirements

All the code in this chapter can be found at https://github.com/PacktPublishing/Real-World-Svelte/tree/main/Chapter04.

Manipulating how a child component looks

When you're combining multiple components, you'll need to manage how each child component appears and behaves. Even though a child component handles its own display and logic, it still offers controls to tweak its appearance and behavior. From the perspective of the parent component, you'll want to coordinate these child components to achieve the desired overall functionality.

In this section, we'll explore various ways to control the look of child components, ranging from the most to the least commonly used methods. Understanding these options will equip you with the tools to make your components both versatile and effective.

The list of options to control how the child component looks includes the following:

- **Controlling through props**: This is perhaps the most straightforward way to influence the behavior and appearance of a child component. By passing props from a parent component to a child, you can make your child component highly dynamic and responsive to external changes.

  To demonstrate how a parent component can control content using props in Svelte, consider the following code example:

  ```
  <script>
     import Child from './Child.svelte';
     let message = 'Hello from Parent';
  </script>
  <Child message={message} />
  ```

  In the code snippet, we imported the `Child` component and passed the `message` prop to it. The child component, implemented in the following code snippet, then uses this `message` prop to display text within a `<p>` element:

  ```
  <script>
     export let message;
  </script>
  <p>{message}</p>
  ```

  As you can see, the parent component has the ability to dictate the text shown in the `Child` component by modifying the `message` prop's value. Controlling props is a simple yet effective way to manipulate a child component's content. If you're interested in learning more about props, we covered the topic extensively in *Chapter 3*.

- **Controlling through context**: Svelte's context API allows components to share state without explicitly passing props through every layer of the component tree. This is particularly useful when you have deeply nested components.

  Here's an example of a `parent` component:

  ```
  <script>
     import Child from './Child.svelte';
  ```

```
    import { setContext } from 'svelte';
    setContext('message', 'Hello from parent');
  </script>
  <Child />
```

In the previous code, we established a context named `message` with the `'Hello from parent'` value, using `setContext`. Then, we imported and used the `Child` component without sending any props to it.

The following is the code for the `Child` component:

```
  <script>
    import { getContext } from 'svelte';
    const message = getContext('message');
  </script>
  <p>{message}</p>
```

Here, `getContext` is used to read the `message` context value, which is then displayed within a `<p>` element. As demonstrated, the parent component can influence the text in the child component's `<p>` element by changing the context value.

For a deeper dive into Svelte's context feature, you can refer to *Chapter 8*, where we will explore the topic in greater detail.

- **Controlling the styles**: Manipulating a child component's appearance isn't solely about controlling the data passed to it. It also involves tweaking or modifying its styles.

  You can modify a component style through CSS custom properties. This approach allows for greater design flexibility, and it ensures that child components can adapt to various contexts or themes within the parent component or the broader application.

  For an in-depth discussion on how to alter a component's style using CSS custom properties, feel free to refer to *Chapter 2*.

- **Passing dynamic content through slot**: Svelte's slot feature allows you to insert custom content into specific areas of a child component. This provides a flexible way to have greater control over a component's content without modifying its internal behavior.

  We will talk about slots and how to use them in the following section.

As you can see, there are various ways to shape a child component's appearance and behavior. When we compose different components within a parent component, the goal is to make them work together in a coordinated way. You can use a combination of the approaches discussed to achieve this.

Most of these methods will be covered in separate chapters, and in the following section, we'll focus on how to dynamically alter a child component's look by passing content through slots.

Passing dynamic content through slots

When building complex applications, one size doesn't always fit all. Balancing between a component's modularity and a component's flexibility for customization is crucial.

Take a generic `Card` component, for example. You might sometimes want to include special headlines, unique lists, or custom footers for specific use cases. It's nearly impossible to anticipate every requirement, so it's essential to design components that are both modular and maintainable, yet still open to customization.

This is where Svelte's slot feature shines. **Slots** enable you to inject dynamic content into your components, making them incredibly versatile. Instead of designing a `Card` component that tries to include every possible feature, aim for a simple, clean base that can be enhanced through composition. This approach allows you to piece together more complex, customized components as your needs evolve.

In a Svelte component, a `<slot>` element is a placeholder within your component where you can inject any type of content from a parent component. Here's how you can define a slot inside a Svelte component:

```
<!-- filename: Card.svelte -->
<div class="card">
  <slot></slot>
</div>
```

In the preceding code snippet, we defined a `<slot>` element inside a `<div>` element. Any dynamic content from the parent component will be inserted into the `<div>` element.

Now, to pass dynamic content from a parent component into the slot of a child component, you need to place that content between the opening and closing tags of the child component:

```
<script>
  import Card from './Card.svelte';
</script>
<Card>
  <h1>Special headline</h1>
</Card>
```

In this code snippet, we passed in a `<h1>` element between the opening and closing tags of the `<Card>` component. This effectively replaces the `<slot>` element in the `Card` component with the `<h1>` element we provide.

There may be instances where you don't need to pass dynamic content from a parent component to a child component's slot. For these cases, Svelte allows you to define default content within the `<slot>` element, providing a fallback when no custom content is supplied by the parent.

Providing default slot content

To provide default content for your `<slot>` element, you can place them inside the `<slot>` element, like so:

```
<div class="card">
  <slot>
    <div>this is the default content</div>
  </slot>
</div>
```

In the preceding code snippet, we defined `<div>`, containing the text `This is the default content` within the `<slot>` element. This serves as the default content for the slot.

When you use this `Card` component in a parent component and don't provide content for the slot, as shown in the following code snippet, the default text will automatically appear:

```
<script>
  import Card from './Card.svelte';
</script>
<Card />
```

By utilizing the default content in slots, you can create more flexible Svelte components that offer sensible fallbacks when no custom content is provided.

In the examples we've seen so far, we've been limited to inserting dynamic content from the parent component into just one spot. But what if we wanted multiple insertion points for dynamic content? Let's explore how to achieve that.

Having multiple slots with named slots

Slots are amazing, and you are not limited to a single slot either. You can define multiple slots in a component and name them to target specific areas for dynamic content.

You can use the `name` attribute on the `<slot>` element to give the slot a name, as shown in the following code:

```
<!-- filename: Card.svelte -->
<div class="card">
  <header>
    <slot name="header"></slot>
  </header>
  <footer>
    <slot name="footer"></slot>
  </footer>
</div>
```

In the previous code snippet, we defined two named slots, one named `"header"` and another named `"footer"`.

To target the dynamic content into these named slots, you will need to use the `<svelte:fragment>` element in the parent component:

```
<script>
  import Card from './Card.svelte';
</script>
<Card>
  <svelte:fragment slot="header">
    <h1>Special headline</h1>
  </svelte:fragment>
  <svelte:fragment slot="footer">
    Custom footer
  </svelte:fragment>
</Card>
```

Here, we pass two `<svelte:fragment>` elements into the Card component. The first has a slot attribute set to `"header"`, and the second slot attribute is set to `"footer"`.

The name specified in the `slot` attribute will correspond with the named slots within the Card component. The content within `<svelte:fragment slot="header">` replaces the `<slot name="header">` in the Card component. Similarly, the content within `<svelte:fragment slot="footer">` takes the place of `<slot name="footer">` in the component.

Sometimes, you will want the dynamic content from the parent component to be aware of the data within the child component. To handle this scenario, Svelte offers a feature known as slot props, which allows you to pass data from the child component to the content in the slot. Let's explore how this works.

Passing data through slot props

You can pass data from the child component back to the dynamic content in the parent component using slot props, like so:

```
<!-- filename: Card.svelte -->
<div class="card">
  <header>
    <slot name="header" width={30} height={50}></slot>
  </header>
</div>
```

In the code example, we passed in two additional attributes to the `<slot>` element besides the name attribute, which is used to name the slot. These additional attributes, `width` and `height`, serve as slot props; their values can be accessed in the parent component when you create dynamic content.

Here is an example of how you can use these slot prop values when using `<svelte:fragment>`:

```
<script>
  import Card from './Card.svelte';
</script>
<Card>
  <svelte:fragment slot="header" let:width let:height>
    <h1>Dimension: {width} x {height}</h1>
  </svelte:fragment>
</Card>
```

In the preceding code snippet, you can see that we use `let:width` and `let:height` within the `<svelte:fragment>` element. These are called `let:` bindings.

The `let:` bindings allow us to access the `width` and `height` slot props provided by the child `Card` component. The values for the width and height are then used within an `<h1>` element to display the dimensions. This way, we can dynamically adjust content in the parent component, based on data originating from the child component.

Now that we have covered how to pass dynamic content through slots, how to define multiple-named slots, and how to pass data from a child component to the dynamic slot content in a parent component, you are well equipped to create more versatile and reusable Svelte components.

Renderless component

One of many common patterns to compose components using slots is the Renderless component pattern. This technique allows you to build components that are purely functional, leaving the presentation details to the parent component. We have dedicated *Chapter 11* to delving into this fascinating topic.

Now that we've explored how to pass dynamic content through slots, let's dive into another exciting feature of Svelte that lets you dynamically render different element or component types.

Rendering different HTML element or component types

In any dynamic application, there comes a time when you need even more flexibility than what static components or elements offer. What if you don't know the type of element or component you'll need to render until runtime?

Let's imagine that you're building a form generator, and the type of form field – whether it's `<Input>`, `<Checkbox>`, or `<Select>` – is determined by dynamic data. How could you switch between these components seamlessly, especially when they share the same set of props?

One straightforward approach is to use Svelte's {#if} blocks to conditionally render the component you need. Here is an example code snippet:

```
<script>
  import Input from './Input.svelte';
  import Checkbox from './Checkbox.svelte';
  import Select from './Select.svelte';
  let type = "input"; // Could be "checkbox" or "select"
</script>
{#if type === "input"}
  <Input value={value} onChange={onChange} />
{:else if type === "checkbox"}
  <Checkbox value={value} onChange={onChange} />
{:else}
  <Select value={value} onChange={onChange} />
{/if}
```

In the code snippet, we use the {#if} blocks to choose among three different component types, passing the same prop values to each. If you find yourself needing to manage more component types, this could lead to a lengthy and hard-to-maintain series of conditional blocks.

Is there a more efficient way to handle this?

Svelte provides two specialized elements, `<svelte:element>` and `<svelte:component>`, precisely for this. The `<svelte:element>` element lets you create different HTML element types dynamically, based on variable data, whereas the `<svelte:component>` element lets you dynamically render different Svelte component types.

Here's how you can rewrite the previous example using `<svelte:component>`:

```
<script>
  import Input from './Input.svelte';
  import Checkbox from './Checkbox.svelte';
  import Select from './Select.svelte';
  let type = "input"; // Could be "checkbox" or "select"
  let DynamicComponent;
  if (type === "input") {
    DynamicComponent = Input;
  } else if (type === "checkbox") {
    DynamicComponent = Checkbox;
  } else {
    DynamicComponent = Select;
  }
</script>
<svelte:component
```

```
   this={DynamicComponent}
   value={value}
   onChange={onChange}
 />
```

In the preceding code snippet, the DynamicComponent variable is used to hold the type of component that will be rendered. This component type is then passed to the this attribute within the <svelte:component> element. The <svelte:component> element also accepts other props such as value and onChange.

With the preceding code, what happens is that <svelte:component> renders the designated component stored in the this attribute, simultaneously forwarding any props passed to <svelte:component> to this dynamically rendered component. For example, if the value of DynamicComponent is the Select component, then the preceding code is effectively the same as this code:

```
<Select value={value} onChange={onChange} />
```

By using <svelte:component>, we simplify the code and make it more maintainable. It's also easier to extend; adding another form element type would only require an additional condition and assignment.

Now that we've explored the use of <svelte:component>, let's look at <svelte:element>, which follows a similar pattern. The following is a sample code snippet that demonstrates the usage of <svelte:element>:

```
<script>
  let type = 'button'; // could be 'div', 'p', 'a', etc.
</script>
<svelte:element this={type}>
  Click Me
</svelte:element>
```

In the preceding code snippet, the type variable holds the type of HTML element we want to render – in this example, it's button. The <svelte:element> tag dynamically creates an HTML element of the type specified by type. So, if type is 'button', this will render as a <button> element, containing the text "Click Me".

This approach is particularly useful when you want to switch the type of an HTML element, based on some condition, without having to rewrite the entire block of code. All you need to do is change the value of type.

To summarize, <svelte:element> and <svelte:component> offer a more efficient and maintainable way to handle dynamic rendering needs. They provide a robust alternative to multiple {#if} blocks, making your Svelte applications more flexible and easier to manage.

Sometimes, when designing Svelte components for data visualization, we encounter recursive data structures. In such cases, we need to build components that can recursively render themselves. Let's delve into how we can accomplish this next.

Creating recursive components for recursive data

A **recursive data structure** is a data structure that is defined in terms of itself, meaning that it can be composed of smaller instances of the same type of structure. Recursive data is everywhere – think of a comment section where replies can have their own sub-replies, or a filesystem with nested folders. Creating a component to display them in a frontend application can be challenging.

Imagine we have a variable called `folder`, which is an array containing either files or additional folders. In this example, the `folder` variable could look like this:

```
const folder = [
  { type: 'file', name: 'a.js' },
  { type: 'file', name: 'b.js' },
  { type: 'folder', name: 'c', children: [
    { type: 'file', name: 'd.js' },
  ]},
];
```

Currently, our `folder` variable is two levels deep. To represent this structure in a Svelte component, you might think to use nested `{#each}` blocks:

```
<script>
  export let folder;
</script>
<ul>
  {#each folder as item}
    <li>
      {#if item.type === 'file'}
        <div>File: {item.name}</div>
      {:else}
        <div>Folder: {item.name}</div>
        <ul>
          {#each item.children as child}
            <li>
              {#if child.type === 'file'}
                <div>File: {child.name}</div>
              {:else}
                ...
              {/if}
            </li>
```

```
        {/each}
      </ul>
    {/if}
  </li>
{/each}
</ul>
```

In the preceding code snippet, we used an {#each} block to iterate over the items in the `folder` variable, rendering either a file or a folder based on `item.type`. If `item.type` is a folder, we use another nested {#each} block to go through its contents.

However, here's the catch – the inner folder could also contain files or additional folders, making it recursive. As a result, we end up with repeated code for the inner and outer {#each} blocks. This works fine for a folder structure that's only two levels deep, but what if it's more complex? How can we avoid duplicating the same code for each level of nesting?

Svelte offers an elegant solution to handle such recursive structures with the `<svelte:self>` element. The `<svelte:self>` element allows a component to embed itself within its own markup, thus making it easier to handle recursive data.

Here's the updated code using the `<svelte:self>` element:

```
<script>
  export let folder;
</script>
<ul>
  {#each folder as item}
    <li>
      {#if item.type === 'file'}
        <div>File: {item.name}</div>
      {:else}
        <div>Folder: {item.name}</div>
        <svelte:self folder={item.children} />
      {/if}
    </li>
  {/each}
</ul>
```

In the updated code snippet, we replaced the nested {#each} block with `<svelte:self folder={item.children} />`. This effectively re-renders the current component, passing `item.children` as the `folder` prop.

The beauty of this is that it eliminates the need to initiate a new `<ul>` element and duplicate {#each} blocks for each nesting level. Instead, the component simply reuses itself, making it capable of handling nested structures of any depth.

When comparing this with the previous code snippet, you can immediately see the advantage – it's much cleaner and avoids repetitive code, making it easier to read and maintain, and it scales naturally to handle any level of nested folders.

Now that we've discussed how to tackle recursive data with `<svelte:self>`, let's look at a practical example in the following section, where we will create a Svelte-based JSON tree viewer.

Example – a JSON tree viewer

In this section, we will walk you through building a JSON tree viewer component in Svelte. The JSON tree viewer component helps you visualize JSON data in a tree-like format. Along the way, we'll make use of some of the advanced Svelte features we've covered in this chapter, including `<svelte:self>`, `<svelte:component>`, and slots.

Before we start, let's think about what our JSON Tree Viewer should look like and how it should behave. Essentially, a JSON object is made up of key-value pairs, where the values can be either primitives, arrays, or other nested objects. Our goal is to display these key-value pairs in a way that clearly represents the hierarchical structure of the JSON object.

So, let's create a `JsonTree` component for our JSON tree viewer:

```
<!-- filename: JsonTree.svelte -->
<script>
  export let data;
</script>
<ul>
  {#each Object.entries(data) as [key, value]}
    <li>{key}: {value}<li>
  {/each}
</ul>
```

In the preceding code snippet, we defined a `JsonTree` component that accepts data as a prop. Inside this component, we utilize Svelte's `{#each}` block to generate a list of `<li>` elements. Each element displays a key-value pair from the `data` object.

However, these values can vary. They could be primitive types or nested objects. Take the following example:

```
data = {
  name: 'John Doe',
  address: {
    street: '123 Main St'
  },
}
```

In the preceding `data` object, the `name` key has a primitive string value, while the value for the `address` key is an object. For nested objects like this, we will need to use our `JsonTree` component recursively to render that nested object. This is where `<svelte:self>` comes into play.

Here's the updated code:

```
<!-- filename: JsonTree.svelte -->
<script>
  export let data;
</script>
<ul>
  {#each Object.entries(data) as [key, value]}
    <li>
      {key}:
      {#if typeof value === 'object'}
        <svelte:self data={value} />
      {:else}
        {value}
      {/if}
    <li>
  {/each}
</ul>
```

In this updated code snippet, we introduced an `{#if}` block that renders differently based on whether the value is a primitive type or a nested object. For nested objects, we recursively render another `JsonTree` component using `<svelte:self>`. This allows us to elegantly handle JSON objects of any depth.

Now, in our current implementation, we haven't made distinctions between different types of primitive values. Suppose you'd like to render various primitive types using specialized Svelte components. In that case, you could dynamically switch between different component types using `<svelte:component>`.

Let's assume you have three separate Svelte components – `StringValue` for strings, `NumberValue` for numbers, and `JsonValue` for others (such as Booleans, `null`, and `undefined`). Here is how you can update the code to use `<svelte:component>`:

```
<script>
  import StringValue from './StringValue.svelte';
  import NumberValue from './NumberValue.svelte';
  import JsonValue from './JsonValue.svelte';

  export let data;
  function getComponent(type) {
    if (type === 'string') return StringValue;
    if (type === 'number') return NumberValue;
```

```
    return JsonValue;
  }
</script>
<ul>
  {#each Object.entries(data) as [key, value]}
    <li>
      {key}:
      {#if typeof value === 'object'}
        <svelte:self data={value} />
      {:else}
        <svelte:component this={getComponent(typeof value)}
value={value} />
      {/if}
    </li>
  {/each}
</ul>
```

In the updated code snippet, we created a utility function named getComponent to determine which component to render, based on the type of the primitive value. We then used `<svelte:component this={getComponent(typeof value)} />` to dynamically load the appropriate component for each primitive type, allowing our JsonTree component to switch to different components for different types of data.

Lastly, to make our JSON tree viewer more versatile, we can introduce named slots to customize the appearance of keys and values. By doing so, users can easily tailor the look of these elements according to their needs, while keeping our current design as the default fallback. Let's update the code to add the two named slots:

```
<ul>
  {#each Object.entries(data) as [key, value]}
    <li>
      <slot name="obj-key" key={key}>{key}:<slot>
      {#if typeof value === 'object'}
        <svelte:self data={value} />
      {:else}
        <slot name="obj-value" value={value}>
          <svelte:component this={getComponent(typeof value)}
value={value} />
        </slot>
      {/if}
    </li>
  {/each}
</ul>
```

In the updated code, we added two named slots – one to customize keys, called `"obj-key"`, and another to customize values, called `"obj-value"`. These slots receive the current `key` and `value` as slot props, enabling you to tailor their appearance in the parent component.

For instance, if you wish to change how keys and values are displayed, here's how you can write in your parent component:

```
<JsonTree data={{a: 1, b: 2}}>
  <svelte:fragment slot="obj-key" let:key>
    <em>{key}</em>
  </svelte:fragment>
  <svelte:fragment slot="obj-value" let:value>
    <u>{value}</u>
  </svelte:fragment>
</JsonTree>
```

Here, we use Svelte's `<svelte:fragment>` special element to target the named slots, `"obj-key"` and `"obj-value"`, in our `JsonTree` component. The `let:key` and `let:value` syntax allows us to access the current key and value being rendered, respectively.

In the `<svelte:fragment>` element, we wrapped the key in an `<em>` tag and the value in a `<u>` tag, offering custom styling for these elements. This customization overrides the default rendering provided by the `JsonTree` component. If you don't specify any custom content, the component will fall back to its default rendering, offering both robustness and flexibility.

By combining `<svelte:self>` for recursion, `<svelte:component>` for dynamic behavior, and slots for customization, we have created a flexible and powerful JSON tree viewer. This not only demonstrates Svelte's capability to handle complex UI patterns but also serves as a practical example of component composition in Svelte.

You can find the complete code for this exercise here: `https://github.com/PacktPublishing/Real-World-Svelte/tree/main/Chapter04/06-exercise-svelte-json-tree`.

Before we wrap up this chapter, let us take a moment to discuss a helpful common pattern to organize our components, the Container/Presentational pattern.

The Container/Presentational pattern

As your application scales in complexity, you may find it beneficial to adopt specific design patterns or guidelines to structure components. One such approach is the **Container/Presentational pattern**, which divides a component into two categories, the Container component and the Presentational component:

- *Container components* focus on functionality. They handle data fetching, state management, and user interactions. While they usually don't render **Document Object Model** (**DOM**) elements themselves, they wrap around Presentational components and supply them with data and actions.

- *Presentational components* are all about the user interface. They get their data and event-handling functions exclusively through props, making them highly reusable and straightforward to test.

A common scenario where you'll see this pattern in action is when using a UI component library. In this case, the library's components serve as the presentational elements, focusing solely on how things look. Meanwhile, the components you create that utilize these library elements act as Container components, managing data and handling interactions such as clicks, typing, and dragging.

The Component/Presentational pattern is useful in a few aspects:

- **Simplicity**: Separating behavior from appearance makes your codebase easier to understand and maintain

- **Reusability**: Since Presentational components are agnostic about data sources or user actions, you can reuse them in different parts of your application

- **Collaboration**: With this division, designers can work on the Presentational components while developers focus on the Container components, streamlining development

As you come to appreciate the benefits of the Component/Presentational pattern, there are specific situations where I think you should consider using it, such as the following:

- **When your application starts to grow**: Managing everything in a single component can become confusing as complexity increases

- **When you find yourself repeating the same UI patterns**: Creating reusable Presentational components can save time in the long run

- **When your team scales**: As your development team grows, having a standardized way of building components can reduce learning curves and prevent code conflicts

While the Container/Presentational pattern offers a structured approach to organizing your components, it's not always the best fit – especially for smaller applications, where it might be overkill. Hopefully, with the insights provided, you'll be better equipped to make informed decisions.

Summary

In this chapter, we delved into various strategies for component composition in Svelte, each offering its own set of advantages and applicable scenarios. Mastering these techniques will equip you to build Svelte applications that are not only more dynamic but also easier to maintain and scale.

We kicked off by discussing multiple ways to influence a child component. These ranged from controlling props or using Svelte's context to customizing styles via CSS custom properties, and even dynamically passing content through slots.

Then, we turned our attention to some of Svelte's special elements. We explored `<svelte:element>` and `<svelte:component>` to dynamically render various HTML elements and Svelte components. We also learned about `<svelte:self>`, which allows a component to reference itself, thereby facilitating the creation of recursive UI structures. We then applied these newfound skills to build a JSON tree viewer as an illustrative example.

Finally, we touched upon a popular design pattern – the Container/Presentational pattern. We examined its advantages and considered scenarios where it would be beneficial to employ this approach.

Armed with these advanced techniques, you are now better prepared to tackle complex challenges in your Svelte projects. As we conclude our four-chapter exploration of writing Svelte components, we'll shift our focus in the upcoming chapter to another fundamental feature of Svelte – Svelte actions.

Part 2: Actions

In this part, we embark on a journey to learn about Svelte actions. Across three chapters, we will delve into three different use cases of Svelte actions. Starting with the creation of custom events using actions, we'll progress to integrating third-party JavaScript libraries with Svelte via actions. Finally, we'll unveil techniques to progressively enhance our applications, harnessing the power of Svelte actions.

This part has the following chapters:

- *Chapter 5, Custom Events with Actions*
- *Chapter 6, Integrating Libraries with Actions*
- *Chapter 7, Progressive Enhancements with Svelte Actions*

Custom Events with Actions

Actions are one of the most powerful features of Svelte.

They are a lightweight alternative to a component that encapsulates logic and data into a reusable unit. They help us reuse the same logic on different elements.

While components have life cycle methods such as `onMount` and `onDestroy` that run when all the elements within the component are added to or removed from the DOM, actions are designed to handle the logic for individual elements, running only when that specific element is added to or removed from the DOM.

While components can receive and react to prop changes, you can pass data to actions from a parent component to a child component. The actions will react when the data is changed and you can specify how the action should react when that data changes.

Actions are simple yet amazingly versatile. You can use them for various things. In this and the following chapters, we are going to explore some of the use cases of actions.

One of the many use cases of actions is to manage elements' event listeners. Event listeners are very common in web applications as they allow us to implement specific behaviors in response to user actions. This makes our application more interactive and dynamic. So, it will be interesting to see how Svelte actions can be used to help us manage event listeners.

In this chapter, we will start by looking at how we can use actions to help manage event listeners for elements. We will follow that up with examples and exercises to reinforce the idea.

This chapter includes sections on the following:

- Managing event listeners with actions
- Creating custom events with actions

Technical requirements

You can find the projects of the chapter here: `https://github.com/PacktPublishing/Real-World-Svelte/tree/main/Chapter05`

Defining actions

Before we start to talk about using Svelte actions to create custom events, let's quickly recap how to define an action in Svelte.

In Svelte, an action is nothing but a function that follows an action contract. This means if a function follows a specific function signature, it is considered an action. Here is the function signature of an action:

```
function action(node) {
  return {
    destroy() {}
  };
}
```

It is a function that optionally returns an object that has a `destroy` method.

In this case, since the `action` function follows the action contract, it is a Svelte action.

To use the Svelte action on an element, you can use the `use:` directive:

```
<div use:action />
```

Here, we used the Svelte action named `action` on the `div` element.

So, what will happen to the `div` element with a Svelte action?

When the `<div>` element is mounted to the DOM, Svelte will call the `action` function with the reference to the `<div>` element:

```
const action_obj = action(div);
```

When the element is removed from the DOM, Svelte will call the `destroy` method from the object returned from calling the `action` function:

```
if (action_obj && action_obj.destroy) action_obj.destroy();
```

We can customize the behavior of a Svelte action by using parameters. We can pass in an extra parameter to the `action` function:

```
function action(node, parameter) {
  return {
    update(parameter) {},
```

```
      destroy() {},
    };
  }
```

Also, you can add another method to the returning object, `update`, which will be called when the value of the parameter changes:

```
action_obj.update(new_value);
```

To pass in an additional parameter, you can specify it in a similar syntax as the `value` attribute:

```
<div use:action={value} />
```

Now that we know how to use and define an action in Svelte, let's take a look at our first use case of actions.

Reusing DOM event logic with custom events

Before we start talking directly about actions, let's look at an example of using the `mousedown` and `mouseup` events to create a long-press behavior. We shall see how this simple example will lead us on to Svelte actions:

```
<script>
  let timer;
  function handleMousedown() {
    timer = setTimeout(() => {
      console.log('long press!');
    }, 2000);
  }
  function handleMouseup() {
    clearTimeout(timer);
  }
</script>
<button
  on:mousedown={handleMousedown}
  on:mouseup={handleMouseup}
/>
```

In the preceding example, we tried to implement a long-press behavior in a button. The idea is to press and hold the button for more than two seconds and then perform some action. As we detect it's a long press, we print `'long press!'` into the console.

To implement the long-press behavior, I attached two event listeners: `mousedown` and `mouseup`. The two event listeners work together. `mousedown` starts counting down using `setTimeout` for two seconds, and `mouseup` clears the countdown using `clearTimeout`. If the user did not hold onto the button for long enough, the timeout would not be triggered and it would not be considered a long press. Note that to coordinate the timers between the two event listeners, the `timer` variable is shared across the event listeners.

As you can see, to implement a long-press behavior, you will need two event listeners and one shared variable.

Now, what if you need to have this long-press behavior on another button?

You can't really share the same event listener and the variable, as you might want a different duration to be considered as a timeout or a different behavior when a long press happens.

So, you would have to redeclare them again and remember to pair the right event with the right event listener.

Encapsulating logic into a component

A way to recreate a different long-press button is to encapsulate it as a component, putting all the long-press button logic into a component and reusing the component as a means to reuse the logic.

When you define a component, you define the logic as well as the elements in the component. This means that if we put both the long-press logic and the `button` element into the component, we have to use the long-press logic together with the `button` element and no other elements.

If you want to customize the element, maybe by using a different element, having a different style, showing a different text content, or adding more event listeners, you would have to define the styles, text contents, or event listeners as props of the component and pass them into the `button` element in the component:

```
<!-- LongPressButton.svelte -->
<button
  // besides the longpress behavior
  on:mousedown={handleMousedown}
  on:mouseup={handleMouseup}
  // you need to pass down props as attributes
  {...$$props}
  // and also forward events up
  on:click
  on:dblclick
>
  <slot />
</button>
```

In the preceding code, we passed in extra attributes from the props into the `button` element along with forwarding two events, `click` and `dblclick`, from the button element out to the component.

The point I am trying to make here is that if you wish to reuse event listener logic via components, you will find yourself having to take care of other attributes that go along with the element in the component.

We can do much more with a component, but if we are trying to reuse just the long-press behavior, then reusing it by defining it in a component is a bit overkill, and it can grow unmanageable rather quickly.

So, what other options do we have?

Encapsulating logic into an action

A better option is to use an action to encapsulate the long-press behavior.

Let's just do that and then I'll explain why using an action is a better approach:

```
function longPress(node) {
  let timer;
  function handleMousedown() {
    timer = setTimeout(() => {
      console.log('long press!');
    }, 2000);
  }
  function handleMouseup() {
    clearTimeout(timer);
  }
  node.addEventListener('mousedown', handleMousedown);
  node.addEventListener('mouseup', handleMouseup);
  return {
    destroy() {
      node.removeEventListener('mousedown', handleMousedown);
      node.removeEventListener('mouseup', handleMouseup);
    }
  }
}
```

With the action defined (as shown in the preceding code), we can use the action over multiple elements:

```
<button use:longPress>Button one</button>
<button use:longPress>Button two</button>
```

You can apply the action to a different type of element:

```
<span use:longPress>Hold on to me</span>
```

You can also use it alongside other attributes or event listeners:

```
<button use:longPress class="..." on:click={...} />
```

I hope you can see that the `longPress` action encapsulates only the long-press behavior. Unlike the `LongPressButton` component, the `longPress` action can easily be reused in any element.

So, as a rule of thumb, when abstracting logic from an element, if you are abstracting it together with the elements, it is okay to use a component. But if you only need to abstract the logic behavior from an element, use actions.

Actions are a great tool for abstracting out element-level logic. But there is still one missing piece of the puzzle: how should we add a different long-press handler for a different element? We'll see how next.

Passing parameters to an action

So, how do we customize the behavior of our `longPress` action?

You could have probably guessed the answer since you've seen it in the previous section. We can customize the behavior of an action by passing parameters into the action.

For example, if we want to have a different function to handle a long-press action on different `button` elements, we can pass a different function into the action through action parameters:

```
<button use:longPress={doSomething1} />
<button use:longPress={doSomething2} />
```

We will then receive this function within the second argument of the action function:

```
function longPress(node, fn) {
  // ...
}
```

We call the function passed in when it is considered a long press:

```
fn();
```

We can similarly pass in other parameters, such as the duration to be considered as a long press.

In Svelte actions, you can only pass in one parameter. To pass in multiple parameters, you will have to turn them into an object and pass them in as one parameter.

Over in our `longPress` action, we want to pass the function to be called when the `longPress` action is detected, as well as the duration to be considered a long press, into the `longPress` action. To pass both the function and the duration in, we create an object that has them as object values and pass the object as the action parameter:

```
<button
  use:longPress={{
    onLongPress: doSomething1,
```

```
      duration: 5000
   }} />
```

Some of the parameters in the object could be optional, so we might need to provide a default value when reading them within the action:

```
function longPress(node, { onLongPress, duration = 1000 }) {
   // if not specified, the default duration is 1s
}
```

At this stage, you might wonder, can the onLongPress be optional too?

It does not make much sense in our case since the main goal of our action is to detect a long press and call the onLongPress function.

However, this is a good question.

In some other actions, you may have function handlers that are optional.

For example, what if we have a gesture action that can detect different gestures performed on the element? In that case, each gesture callback function can be optional since you may only be interested in one of the gestures:

```
function gesture(node, { onSwipe, onDrag, onPinch }) { }
```

The onSwipe, onDrag, and onPinch function handlers in this gesture action are optional and could be undefined.

Instead of creating an empty function as a fallback, we should instead check whether the function is defined before calling it:

```
if (typeof onSwipe === 'function') onSwipe();
```

This way, we don't have to create a function unnecessarily.

However, this gets messier when you have multiple callback functions and you need to check whether each of them has been defined before calling them.

Is there a better way to handle this?

Yes, there is.

In fact, a more idiomatic Svelte way of having an action to notify or call a function when something happens is to dispatch a custom event.

For example, to know whether the user has long-pressed the <button> element, it would be natural to listen to the 'longpress' custom event on the <button> element:

```
<button on:longpress={doSomething1} />
```

However, there's no native event called `'longpress'`.

But no worries, we can create a custom `'longpress'` event.

Luckily, we have the `longPress` action to determine when the user long-presses a button. What we need to create a custom `'longpress'` event is to trigger the `'longpress'` event after determining the user has long-pressed a button in our `longPress` action. And so, in the line of code where we have determined that the user is long-pressing the button, we can dispatch a custom event from the button:

```
node.dispatchEvent(new CustomEvent('longpress'));
```

Let's listen to the `longpress` custom event and create the custom `'longpress'` event in our action. Here is the final code:

```
<script>
  function longPress(node, { duration = 1000 } = {}) {
    let timer;
    function handleMousedown() {
      timer = setTimeout(() => {
        node.dispatchEvent(new CustomEvent('longpress'));
      }, duration);
    }
    function handleMouseup() {
      clearTimeout(timer);
    }
    node.addEventListener('mousedown', handleMousedown);
    node.addEventListener('mouseup', handleMouseup);
    return {
      destroy() {
        node.removeEventListener('mousedown', handleMousedown);
        node.removeEventListener('mouseup', handleMouseup);
      }
    }
  }
</script>
<button use:longPress on:longpress={() => {/* do something */}} />
```

Putting it in words, we add a `longPress` action to the `button` element, which adds logic to determine whether the button is being long-pressed. When the button is long-pressed, the `longPress` action dispatches a custom event called `'longpress'` on the element. To react to and trigger specific behaviors when the custom `'longpress'` event is dispatched on the element, we can listen to the event by using `on:longpress` with an event handler.

It may feel like a roundabout way to call a function from an action by dispatching an event, but doing it this way has a few pros:

- Whether we listen to the `'longpress'` event on the button or not, the action could still dispatch the `'longpress'` custom event. So, with this approach, we don't need to check whether the handler is defined or not.

- Listening to the `'longpress'` event using `on:` instead of passing the function directly into the action would mean that you could use other Svelte features that come with Svelte's `on:` directive. For example, to only listen to the `'longpress'` event once, you can use the `|once` event modifier, for example, `on:longpress|once`.

Another way of describing what we have done with the `longPress` action is that the `longPress` action enhances the button element and provides a new event, `'longpress'`, that can be listened to on the element.

Now that we've learned how we can define Svelte actions, and how we can use actions to create new events that we can listen to on an element, let's look at a few more examples that use this technique.

Example – validating form inputs with custom events

The example that we are going to explore is using actions to validate form inputs.

When you add an input element to your form, you can add attributes such as `required`, `minlength`, and `min` to indicate that the input value has to pass the constraint validation or else would be considered invalid.

However, by default, such a validation check is only done during form submission. There's no real-time feedback on whether your input is valid as you type.

To make the input element validate as you type, we need to add an `'input'` event listener (which will be called on every keystroke as we type in the input element) and call `input.checkValidity()` to validate the input. Now, let's do just that:

```
<input on:input={ (event) => event.target.checkValidity() } />
```

As you call the `checkValidity()` method, if the input is indeed invalid, then it will trigger the `'invalid'` event:

```
<input
  on:input={ (event) => event.target.checkValidity() }
  on:invalid={ (event) => console.log(event.target.validity) }
/>
```

Unfortunately, there's no `'valid'` event. So, there's no way to tell whether the input has passed the validation.

It would be great if there were an event called `'validate'` in which within the event details, we can tell whether the input is valid or not. If it isn't, we could get an error message about why the input is invalid.

Here's an example of how we could use the `'validate'` event:

```
<input on:validate={(event) => {
  if (event.detail.isValid) {
    errorMessage = '';
  } else {
    errorMessage = event.detail.errorMessage;
  }
}} />
```

There isn't an event called `'validate'`, but we can create this custom event ourselves. So, why not create an action to create this custom event for us?

This logic is well suited to be written as an action for the following reasons:

- It can be reused in other input elements.

- This logic itself is not involved in creating or updating elements. If it were, it would probably be better suited to be a component.

Let us write this action:

1. Firstly, this action involves listening to the `'input'` event listener. So, in the code, as shown, we are going to add an event listener at the start of the action and remove the `'input'` event listener in the `destroy` method. This means that whenever an element that uses this action is added to the DOM, it will listen to the `'input'` event, and when it is removed from the DOM, the event listener will be automatically removed:

```
function validateOnType(input) {
  input.addEventListener('input', onInput);
  return {
    destroy() {
      input.removeEventListener('input', onInput);
    }
  };
}
```

2. Next, within the input handler, we are going to call `checkValidity()` to check whether the input is valid. If the input is invalid, then we will read `input.validity` and determine the error message:

```
function validateOnType(input) {
  function onInput() {
```

```
    const isValid = input.checkValidity();
    const errorMessage = isValid ? '' : getErrorMessage(input.
validity);
  }
  // ...
}
```

3. Finally, we will dispatch the custom `'validate'` event with `isValid` and `errorMessage` as event details:

```
function validateOnType(input) {
  function onInput() {
// ...
input.dispatchEvent(
  new CustomEvent(
    'validate',
    { detail: { isValid, errorMessage } }
  )
);
  }
  // ...
}
```

4. Now, with this action completed, we can enhance the `<input>` element by adding a new `'validate'` event, which will be called as-you-type, letting you know whether the input is currently valid or invalid. It will also show the corresponding error message:

```
<input
  use:validateOnType
  on:validate={(event) => console.log(event.detail)}
/>
```

To make the validation results more useful to the user, you can use the result from the `'validate'` event to modify element styles, such as setting the input border color to red when the validation result is invalid, as shown in the following snippet:

```
<script>
  let isValid = false;
</script>
<input
  class:invalid={!isValid}
  use:validateOnType
  on:validate={(event) => isValid = event.detail.isValid}
/>
<style>
```

```
      .invalid { border: red 1px solid; }
   </style>
```

Are you getting the hang of writing actions that create custom events?

Let's try the next one as an exercise. This time, we'll tackle one of the most common user interactions, drag and drop.

Exercise – creating a drag-and-drop event

A drag-and-drop behavior means clicking on an element, moving the mouse while holding down the click to drag the element across the screen to the desired location, and then releasing the mouse click to drop the element in the new location.

A drag-and-drop behavior thus involves coordination between multiple events, namely, `'mousedown'`, `'mousemove'`, and `'mouseup'`.

As we perform the drag-and-drop motion, what we are interested in knowing is when the dragging starts, how far the element is dragged, and when the dragging ends.

These three events can be translated into three custom events: `'dragStart'`, `'dragMove'`, and `'dragEnd'`.

Let us try to implement the drag-and-drop behavior as an action that will create these three custom events:

```
<div
   use:dragAndDrop
   on:dragStart={...}
   on:dragMove={...}
   on:dragEnd={...}
/>
```

You can check the answer to this exercise here: `https://github.com/PacktPublishing/Real-World-Svelte/tree/main/Chapter05/03-drag-and-drop`.

Summary

In this chapter, we saw how to define an action. We talked about one of the common patterns of actions, which is to create custom events. This allows us to encapsulate DOM event logic into custom events and reuse them across elements.

In the next chapter, we will look at the next common pattern of actions, which is integrating third-party libraries.

6

Integrating Libraries with Actions

There are a lot of JavaScript UI libraries out there on the internet. However, at the time of writing this book, Svelte is relatively new. Not all the UI libraries out there are written using Svelte and written specifically for Svelte. But that does not mean that we can't use them in our Svelte component.

There are many ways to integrate third-party JavaScript UI libraries into Svelte. In this chapter, we are going to explore how we can do it using Svelte actions.

We will start by integrating an imaginary UI library, slowly building up our case for why Svelte actions are suitable for the job. Along the way, I will explain how to use Svelte actions for different scenarios and show you where Svelte actions fall short. I'll discuss my reasonings and personal opinions on when to choose Svelte actions and when to choose otherwise.

Following that, I will show you some real-world UI library examples. After that, we will explore integrating UI libraries written in other frameworks, such as React and Vue, with a few more examples.

By the end of this chapter, you will see that you are not limited to using only UI libraries written in Svelte in your Svelte application – you can reuse any UI library that is available on the internet.

This chapter covers the following topics:

- Integrating JavaScript UI libraries into Svelte
- Why we should use actions to integrate UI libraries and other alternatives
- Integrating UI libraries written in other frameworks into Svelte

Technical requirements

You can find the examples and code for this chapter here: https://github.com/PacktPublishing/Real-World-Svelte/tree/main/Chapter06.

Integrating vanilla JavaScript UI libraries into Svelte

First, we will explore UI libraries that are written in vanilla JavaScript. When we use the phrase *vanilla JavaScript*, we're referring to plain JavaScript, or JavaScript in the absence of frameworks or libraries.

There are many reasons a UI library is written in vanilla JavaScript:

- Performance reasons – it would be much easier to optimize without the abstractions from the web framework
- The library author's personal preference to be framework-agnostic
- The library was created predating any modern web frameworks

For us, vanilla JavaScript UI libraries are great because they do not depend on any specific framework runtime, which is an extra overhead on top of the UI library itself.

For example, if we use a calendar component library that is implemented in React, then besides installing the calendar component library, we would need to install React's framework as well.

This additional dependency leads to an increased bundle size and potential conflicts with Svelte. Therefore, when using a component library in Svelte, it is generally preferable to choose a library that does not depend on any specific framework.

Now that we have learned about why vanilla JavaScript UI libraries are great, let's discuss how we can integrate them into Svelte. In this chapter, we will explore integrating libraries in Svelte using Svelte actions, which begs the question, why do we choose to use Svelte actions to integrate a UI library?

Why use Svelte actions to integrate a UI library?

In the previous chapter, we explored how Svelte actions are useful for adding custom event handlers. At the same time, Svelte actions function as element-level life cycle functions, making them very useful for interfacing with third-party libraries. Now, let's explore why that's the case.

Let's take a calendar component library as an example. For simplicity's sake and to not get bogged down by implementation details, let's imagine the library as an imaginary library instead of using any real-life calendar component library. This allows us to focus on the general problem itself rather than the specific library's implementation details.

We will look at some real-life UI libraries afterward.

To decide where the calendar component will be added to the DOM, component libraries usually require us to specify a container element to house the library component.

For example, here, `ImaginaryCalendar` requires us to pass the container element as part of the argument for the constructor:

```
new ImaginaryCalendar({ container: containerElement })
```

To get the reference to an element in Svelte, we can use bind:this:

```
<script>
  let containerElement;
</script>
<div bind:this={containerElement} />
```

The containerElement variable is only updated with the reference of the element after the element is mounted, so it can only be referred to in onMount:

```
<script>
  import { onMount } from 'svelte';
  let containerElement;
  let calendar;
  onMount(() => {
    calendar = new ImaginaryCalendar({ container: containerElement });
    return () => calendar.cleanup();
  });
</script>
```

Note that we are keeping the reference of the calendar instance because we can use it to call calendar methods to get or set values:

```
calendar.setDate(date);
```

Also, we call calendar.cleanup() when the component unmounts for cleanup purposes.

> **Note**
>
> The calendar library is just an imaginary example. However, most UI libraries will provide similar APIs or methods to retrieve or modify the component instance's internal state and clean up when they are no longer in use.

We need to be extra careful when we are using the calendar instance here. We want to avoid referencing the calendar instance before it is initialized to prevent encountering a reference error as the calendar instance is only declared and initialized after onMount:

To be safe, we should check whether the calendar instance is defined before calling any of its methods. In the code example below, we verify if the calendar instance is defined, before calling the calendar.setDate() method.

```
if (calendar) calendar.setDate(date).
```

The need for this extra level of cautiousness is more obvious when the calendar is conditionally created:

```
<script>
  import { onMount } from 'svelte';
  let containerElement;
  let calendar;
  onMount(() => {
    if (containerElement) {
      calendar = new ImaginaryCalendar({ container: containerElement
});
      return () => calendar.cleanup();
    }
  });
</script>
{#if someCondition}
  <div bind:this={containerElement} />
{/if}
```

In the preceding code, you can see that `<div>` is conditionally created based on `someCondition`. That is why in `onMount`, we need to check whether `containerElement` is available before we create `ImaginaryCalendar` using `containerElement` as a container. And the `calendar` instance is only available if `ImaginaryCalendar` is created, and thus only available if `someCondition` is `true`.

The preceding code illustrates one of the many possibilities where the `calendar` instance could be undefined.

One thing to note about this code is that it is not behaviorally correct as it does not attempt to create `ImaginaryCalendar` whenever the value of `someCondition` turns from `false` to `true` and does cleanup whenever it turns back to `false`.

This is where Svelte actions shine.

Using Svelte actions

By altering the preceding code so that it uses actions, you will see that we do not need the extra check to ensure that `containerElement` is available before instantiating `ImaginaryCalendar`.

The following code shows how such an action could be implemented. Here, the name of our Svelte action is `calendar`:

```
<script>
  function calendar(containerElement) {
    const calendar = new ImaginaryCalendar({ container:
containerElement });
    return {
```

```
        destroy() {
          calendar.cleanup();
        }
      };
    }
</script>
{#if someCondition}
   <div use:calendar />
{/if}
```

This is because, when using Svelte actions, the action function will only be called with the reference of the element whenever the element is created and mounted onto the DOM.

When the condition changes to such that the `<div>` element is removed from the DOM, the `destroy` method of the action will be called to clean things up.

Using Svelte actions, we can now create as many `ImaginaryCalendar` instances as we want within one component by adding the action to different HTML elements:

To prove my point, in the code snippet below, in addition to the original `<div>` element you've seen in the previous examples, I am adding another `<div>` element and three more `<div>` elements using the `{#each}` block. I am then applying the calendar actions to all four `<div>` elements to create four more calendars, and we do not run into any errors for having multiple calendars at once.

```
{#if someCondition}
   <div use:calendar />
{/if}
<!-- Look we can have as many calendars as we want -->
<div use:calendar />
{#each [1, 2, 3] as item}
   <div use:calendar />
{/each}
```

If we were to use `bind:this` and `onMount`, we would have to repeat ourselves multiple times by declaring multiple `containerElement` variables multiple times and instantiate `ImaginaryCalendar` with each of the `containerElement` variables.

Now, with the `calendar` instance encapsulated within the action, how should we call the `calendar` instance method to update the `calendar` state from the outside?

That's what the action data is for!

Adding data to Svelte actions

In the previous section, we created a `calendar` action and instantiated an `ImaginaryCalendar` instance inside that action. If we want to call an instance method of `ImaginaryCalendar` outside the `calendar` action, such as calling `calendar.setDate(date)` to set the date of the calendar, what should we do?

There's no way to call `calendar.setDate(date)` outside of the `calendar` action since the `calendar` instance is defined within the `calendar` action. A workaround is to pass `date` through action data – that is, we can provide `date` as action data and call `calendar.setDate(date)` with the date passed in.

For example, in the following code snippet, we're passing `date` into the `calendar` action:

```
<div use:calendar={date} />
```

In the `calendar` action, we call `calendar.setDate(date)` with the date passed in. In addition to that, we define an `update` method in the action, such that whenever the date that's passed to the calendar action changes, Svelte will call `calendar.setDate(date)`:

```
<script>
  function calendar(containerElement, date) {
    const calendar = new ImaginaryCalendar({ container:
containerElement });
    calendar.setDate(date);
    return {
      update(newDate) {
        calendar.setDate(newDate);
      },
      destroy() {
        calendar.cleanup();
      }
    };
  }
</script>
<div use:calendar={new Date(2022, 10, 5)} />
```

Here, we can pass different dates to the different `calendar` instances:

```
{#each dates as date}
  <div use:calendar={date} />
{/each}
```

That's great!

Now, what if you want to call a different `calendar` instance method, such as `calendar.setMode()`, whenever the mode changes?

You could pass both `date` and `mode` into the action:

```
<div use:calendar={{ date, mode }} />
```

In that case, the `calendar` action would need to handle both `date` and `mode`:

```
function calendar(node, { date, mode }) {
  const calendar = new ImaginaryCalendar({ container: containerElement
}) ;
  calendar.setDate(date);
  calendar.setMode(mode);
  return {
    update({ date: newDate, mode: newMode }) {
      calendar.setDate(newDate);
      calendar.setMode(newMode);
    },
    destroy() { ... }
  };
}
```

The `update` method of the `calendar` action will be called whenever either `date` or `mode` changes. This means that in the preceding code, we are calling both `calendar.setDate()` and `calendar.setMode()` whenever either `date` or `mode` changes. This may not have any apparent consequences, but we may be doing an unnecessary job.

A workaround for this is to keep track and always check whether `date` or `mode` have changed in the `update` method. This is how we can do this:

```
function calendar(node, { date, mode }) {
  const calendar = new ImaginaryCalendar({ container: containerElement
}) ;
  calendar.setDate(date);
  calendar.setMode(mode);
  return {
    update({ date: newDate, mode: newMode }) {
      if (date !== newDate) {
        calendar.setDate(newDate);
        date = newDate;
      }
      if (mode !== newMode) {
        calendar.setMode(newMode);
        mode = newMode;
      }
```

```
    },
    destroy() { ... }
  };
}
```

In the preceding code, we're checking if `newDate` is different from the current `date`, and if it is different, then we call the `calendar.setDate()` method and update our current reference of `date`. We do a similar thing for `mode`.

This works. However, as you can see, it is more code and more complex than what we set up when we first started creating the `calendar` action.

And what if you want to call a `calendar` instance method that is not tied to any data, such as `calendar.refreshDates()`?

This is where using actions falls short.

An alternative to Svelte actions

Remember the previous example, where we used `bind:this` and `onMount` to initialize `ImaginaryCalendar`?

We said that the approach is not versatile enough and falls short if we need to do the following:

- Conditionally render the container and create `ImaginaryCalendar`
- Have multiple calendars within the same component

These drawbacks are all true, but there's a use case in which it is perfectly fine to use `bind:this` and `onMount` to initialize `ImaginaryCalendar`. This is when the conditions we mentioned previously are never true:

- We do not need to conditionally render the container
- We do not need to have multiple calendar instances within the same component (this is not exactly true, but we will come back to this)

I'm not sure whether you are thinking the same thing right now but allow me to cut the suspense.

This is when we want to use `ImaginaryCalendar` as a Svelte component.

Within the `ImaginaryCalendar` Svelte component itself, we will have only one container element, and it will always be available:

```
<!-- ImaginaryCalendarComponent.svelte -->
<script>
  import { onMount } from 'svelte';
  let containerElement;
```

```
  let calendar;
  onMount(() => { ... });
</script>
<div bind:this={containerElement} />
```

You can then use this component conditionally:

```
<script>
  import ImaginaryCalendarComponent from './
ImaginaryCalendarComponent.svelte';
</script>
{#if someCondition}
  <ImaginaryCalendarComponent />
{/if}
```

Alternatively, you can use it however many times as you like:

```
{#if someCondition}
  <ImaginaryCalendarComponent />
{/if}
<!-- Look we can have as many calendars as we want -->
<ImaginaryCalendarComponent />
{#each array as item}
  <ImaginaryCalendarComponent />
{/each}
```

Here, we've swapped out elements using actions, `<div use:calendar />`, with Svelte components, `<ImaginaryCalendarComponent />`.

This is perfectly normal.

In the previous chapter, we contemplated between abstracting logic through components or abstracting through actions.

In this scenario, we are looking at abstracting the logic of instantiating a UI library using an element as a container, and we could abstract it into a Svelte action or a Svelte component.

Both options are equally fine.

Both options are designed for this.

So, which options should you choose? Let's find out.

Choosing between Svelte actions and Svelte components

Here are my personal preferences when faced with a choice between either option.

Choose a Svelte action to integrate with a UI library when you are looking for an option that provides the following aspects:

- Is more lightweight. A Svelte component has slightly more overhead compared to a Svelte action.
- Only passes zero to one data into the UI library component instance. If you were to pass in two or more pieces of data into the action, then the update method of the action will be called whenever any part of the data changes.

You should choose a Svelte component if you are looking for an option that provides the following:

- Allows more room for optimization and finer control
- Allows you to call UI library component instance methods directly
- Allows you to pass in child content into the UI component library

We did not discuss this much, but integrating a UI library as a component opens up the possibility of passing additional content into the UI component library through slots:

```
<ImaginaryCalendarComponent>
  <!--Customize how each cell of the calendar looks -->
  <svelte:fragment sl"t="c"ll" let:date>
    {date}
  </svelte:fragment>
</ImaginaryCalendarComponent>
```

If you are interested in learning more about slots and how to compose components in Svelte, read *Chapter 4*, where we explored this topic extensively. Now that we've covered how we could integrate a UI library using Svelte actions, why we should use Svelte actions, as well as the alternatives and considerations, let's take a look at a real-world example, Tippy.js.

Example – integrating Tippy.js

Tippy.js is a tooltip, popover, dropdown, and menu library.

I do not have any affiliation with the Tippy.js library, and the reason I chose Tippy.js as an example is purely by chance. Nonetheless, Tippy.js has a nice and simple API, making it a good candidate for an example.

First, let's look at the Tippy.js documentation: `https://atomiks.github.io/tippyjs/`.

After installing the `tippy.js` library using a package manager of our choice, we can then import Tippy.js into our code:

```
import tippy from 'tippy.js';
import 'tippy.js/dist/tippy.css';
```

Now, we can initialize `tippy` with the following constructor function:

```
tippy('#id');
tippy(document.getElementById('my-element'));
```

Here, we pass in the element where Tippy.js should provide a tooltip.

You can specify any customizations of the tooltip's content through the data attributes of the element, which Tippy.js will pick up as it initializes:

```
<button data-tippy-content="hello" />
```

Alternatively, you can pass this in the constructor:

```
tippy(element, { content: 'hello' });
```

To update the content after initialization, call the Tippy.js `setContent` method:

```
tooltipInstance.setContent("bye");
```

To permanently destroy and clean up the tooltip instance, Tippy.js provides the `destroy` method:

```
tooltipInstance.destroy();
```

Here, we have all we need to create a `tippy` action. We have methods to do the following:

- Create the `tippy` tooltip – `tippy(...)`
- Clean up the `tippy` tooltip – `tooltipInstance.destroy()`
- Update the `tippy` tooltip – `tooltipInstance.setContent(...)`

Let's take a look at what the `tippy` action should look like.

Here is how I want it to look:

```
<div use:tippy={tooltipContent} />
```

In the preceding code snippet, we applied our `tippy` action to a `<div>` element. The content within the tooltip created by Tippy.js should be passed into the `tippy` action as action data, represented by the `tooltipContent` variable. Whenever `tooltipContent` changes, the action should react to it and update the tooltip.

So, let's write our `tippy` Svelte action. Here's the scaffolding for an action:

```
function tippy(element, content) {
  // TODO #1: initialize the library
  return {
    update(newContent) {
```

```
      // TODO #2: do something when action data changes
    },
    destroy() {
      // TODO #3: clean up
    }
  };
}
```

As you can see, we created the `tippy` action based on the Svelte action contract: a function that returns an object with `destroy` and `update` methods.

I left three TODOs in the code, each marking different stages of Svelte actions. Let's go through each one and fill them up. The first TODO is where the action will be called after the element is created and mounted onto the DOM. Here, we are given the element the action is applied to and the action data, and we should use it to initialize the Tippy.js tooltip:

```
// TODO #1: initialize the library
const tooltipInstance = tippy(element, { content });
```

The second TODO is inside the `update` method. This method will be called every time the action data changes. Here, we need to call the Tippy.js tooltip instance to reflect the dataset in the Svelte component:

```
// TODO #2: do something when action data changes
tooltipInstance.setContent(newContent);
```

The third TODO is inside the `destroy` method. This method will be called after the element is removed from the DOM. Here, we need to do the cleanup on the Tippy.js tooltip instance that we created in the action:

```
// TODO #3: clean up
tooltipInstance.destroy();
```

And that's it – we now have a working `tippy` action that integrates the Tippy.js tooltip and will show a tooltip with customizable content whenever we hover over the element.

You can find the complete code on GitHub: `https://github.com/PacktPublishing/Practical-Svelte/tree/main/Chapter06/01-tippy`.

Let's look at one more example, through which I want to show you one more thing that you can do with actions when integrating with UI libraries.

The UI library we are going to look at next is CodeMirror.

Example – integrating CodeMirror

CodeMirror is a code editor component that has many great features for editing, such as syntax highlighting, code folding, and more.

You can find the CodeMirror documentation at `https://codemirror.net/`.

At the time of writing, CodeMirror is currently at version 5.65.9.

After installing the `codemirror` library using the package manager of our choice, we can import `codemirror` into our code:

```
import CodeMirror from 'codemirror';
import 'codemirror/lib/codemirror.css';
```

Now, we can initialize CodeMirror with the following constructor function:

```
const myCodeMirror = CodeMirror(document.body);
```

Here, we pass in the element where we want the CodeMirror code editor to be.

Before I continue, at this point, note that we are looking for the same set of things from CodeMirror:

- Methods to initialize CodeMirror

- Any method needed to clean up a CodeMirror instance

- Any method to update a CodeMirror instance

I am going to leave it to you to complete the checklist and figure it out.

However, allow me to draw your attention to one particular API from the CodeMirror instance:

```
myCodeMirror.on('change', () => { ... });
```

The on method from CodeMirror allows the CodeMirror instance to listen to events and react to them.

So, if we want to add event listeners to the CodeMirror instance from outside of the action, how should we do it?

In the previous chapter, we saw that we could create custom events on the element using actions.

This means that we can allow users to listen to the `'change'` event from the element that uses the `codemirror` action:

```
<div use:codemirror on:change={onChangeHandler} />
```

To make this happen, you can dispatch an event from within the action:

```
function codemirror(element) {
  const editor = CodeMirror(element);
  editor.on('change', () => {
    // trigger 'change' event on the element
    // whenever the editor changes
    element.dispatchEvent(new CustomEvent('change'));
  });
}
```

Remember to check whether you need to clean up or unlisten to any event in the `destroy` method so that you don't cause any unwanted behavior.

And that's it!

The rest of the action is left to you as an exercise.

You can find the complete code on GitHub: `https://github.com/PacktPublishing/Real-World-Svelte/tree/main/Chapter06/02-codemirror`.

In this section, we learned how to integrate vanilla UI libraries into Svelte. However, not all UI libraries are implemented independently without any framework. Sometimes, the library you are looking for might be implemented in a different framework, such as React or Vue. In such cases, how can you integrate them into a Svelte application? That is what we will explore next.

Using UI libraries written in other frameworks

It is not impossible to use components from other frameworks in Svelte.

However, doing so will introduce the framework's runtime and other overheads that come along with the framework. The runtime usually includes code to handle reactivity and normalize browser APIs and events. Each framework usually ships its own code for this logic and does not share it with other frameworks. The runtime for React version 18.2.0 weighs 6.4 kB when minified, which is additional code you need to include when you want to use a React component within Svelte.

So, this is not recommended unless it is necessary.

The reason this section has been included in this book is more for educational purposes and to demonstrate that this is possible, as well as what needs to be done to make it happen.

Creating components in various frameworks

Each framework usually provides an API that takes in a container element and the framework component as the root of the application.

In this section, we're going to take a look at React and Vue, the two most popular JavaScript frameworks at the time of writing.

For example, in React 18, we use the `createRoot` API:

```
import ReactDOM from 'react-dom';
const root = ReactDOM.createRoot(container);
root.render(<h1>Hello, world</h1>);
```

The preceding code uses the JSX syntax, which is not part of the standard JavaScript language syntax. It is syntactic sugar for `jsx`:

```
import { jsx } from 'react/jsx-runtime';
const root = ReactDOM.createRoot(container)
root.render(jsx('h1', { children: 'Hello, world' }));
```

You will have to write the preceding code if you do not configure any transpiling process in your code to turn JSX syntax into valid JavaScript.

On the other hand, In Vue 3, there is the `createApp` API:

```
import { createApp } from 'vue'
import App from './App.vue'
const app = createApp(App);
app.mount(container);
```

The Vue framework uses the word *application* in the documentation, mentioning that the `createApp` method is used to create a new application instance. The word *application* is aptly used as integrating component libraries written in other frameworks is very much like starting a new sub-application within our Svelte application.

You may have also started to notice the similarity between the APIs from these frameworks and other UI libraries that we've seen so far – all of them take in a container element so that they know where to render the content or apply changes.

Similar to integrating UI libraries using actions, after figuring out what APIs we can use to render a component within a container element, the next thing we must check is whether there is any API to clean up when it is no longer needed.

Cleaning up the components in various frameworks

Depending on the underlying framework of the component library, different APIs are provided to clean up whenever the component is no longer needed.

In React, there is a method for this called `unmount`:

```
root.unmount();
```

In Vue, it is also called unmount:

```
app.unmount();
```

The next thing we need to check is whether there is any API to pass data into our component and API so that they can be updated later.

Updating the component in various frameworks

Similar to different frameworks having different APIs for cleaning up, frameworks provide different APIs to update the component with new data.

If you are familiar with React, you can pass data into a React component through props:

```
<Component prop_name={value} />
```

This is akin to the props in a Svelte component.

The preceding code desugars into the following:

```
jsx(Component, { prop_name: value });
```

To update the props of the component, React allows us to call `root.render` again with the same component but with a different prop value:

```
root.render(jsx(App, { prop_name: 123 }));
// some time later
root.render(jsx(App, { prop_name: 456 }));
```

React will reconcile this internally and figure out how to update the DOM.

On the other hand, in Vue, you can pass data through props in the `createApp` API:

```
const app = createApp(Component, { prop_name: value });
```

However, to the best of my knowledge, there's no straightforward way to update the props' value from the outside.

However, you could use a Vue Composition API, such as `ref()`, to create a reactive and mutable ref. With that, you could modify the ref instead of updating the props directly:

```
const value = ref(123);
const app = createApp(Component, { prop_name: ref });
// some time later
value.value = 456;
```

It is okay if you are not familiar with how React and Vue work. This book is for Svelte, not for React or Vue.

The most important thing to take home from this is that when integrating a UI library, whether it is in vanilla JavaScript, React, or Vue, we look for three things:

- A method to create the component with a container element
- A method to clean up the component instance
- A method to pass in data and update the data

If you are familiar with a framework, you will be able to figure out a way to do all these things.

With that out of the way, let's take a look at a real-world example, where we will integrate a React calendar library, `react-calendar`.

Integrating react-calendar into Svelte

The `react-calendar` library is a calendar component library written in React.

You can read more about it here: `https://projects.wojtekmaj.pl/react-calendar/`.

The `react-calendar` library takes in various props for customization purposes. But for demonstration purposes, we are only going to focus on two props, `value` and `onChange`, which allow us to control the selected date of the library.

We pass the selected date through a prop named `value`. The `onChange` prop, on the other hand, is used to pass in an event handler that will be called when the value changes from within the calendar component. We saw how we could handle event handlers in a UI library in the previous section when we discussed CodeMirror.

So, here is what I think using the `calendar` action would look like:

```
<div
  use:calendar={selectedDate}
  on:change={(event) => selectedDate = event.detail}
/>
```

Here, `event.detail` is the data attached to the custom `'change'` event, which would be the date value that's sent from the `react-calendar` component through the `onChange` props.

Now that we know what our `calendar` action would look like, let's write the action out.

Again, here's the scaffolding of an action:

```
function calendar(element, date) {
  // TODO #1: render the react-calendar into the element
  // TODO #2: the onChange handler to dispatch a new custom event
  return {
    update(newDate) {
```

```
            // TODO #3: re-render the calendar again when there's a new date
    value
        },
        destroy() {
            // TODO #4: clean up
        }
    };
}
```

Here, I've created a basic code structure of a Svelte action and left a few TODOs within the code. The first two TODOs are to set up the `calendar` instance with the element the action is applied to. The third TODO is to handle when a new date is passed into the action, and the last TODO is to clean up when the element is removed from the DOM.

So, let's fill up the TODOs.

For the first TODO, let's create a React root and render our `react-calendar` component:

```
import { jsx } from 'react/jsx-runtime';
import ReactDOM from 'react-dom';
function calendar(element, date) {
    # TODO #1: render the react-calendar into the element
    const app = ReactDOM.createRoot(element);
    app.render(jsx(Calendar, { value: date, onChange }));
    // ...
}
```

Here, we passed in onChange, which we have not defined yet.

Let's do this now:

```
# TODO #2: the onChange handler to dispatch a new custom event
function onChange(value) {
    element.dispatchEvent(
    new CustomEvent('change', { detail: value })
    );
}
```

In the preceding code snippet, whenever onChange is called, we will dispatch a new custom event, with `value` passed in as the detail for the custom event.

The third TODO is the content for the `update` method. Whenever a new date value is passed in from the action, we will re-render the `Calendar` component again:

```
// TODO #3: re-render the calendar again when there's a new date value
app.render(jsx(Calendar, { value: newDate, onChange }));
```

In the last TODO, in the `destroy` method, we unmount our `Calendar` component:

```
// TODO #4: clean up
app.unmount();
```

And that's it.

You can find the complete code on GitHub: `https://github.com/PacktPublishing/Real-World-Svelte/tree/main/Chapter06/03-react-calendar`.

With that, you've written a Svelte action that integrates a component library from a different framework, React, into Svelte, and you set up and updated the component's value in a controlled manner.

Summary

In this chapter, we learned how to use actions to integrate UI libraries, either written in vanilla JavaScript or any other frameworks into Svelte. We went through two real-world examples – integrating Tippy.js and `react-calendar` into Svelte using Svelte actions. In both examples, we went through a step-by-step process of writing out a Svelte action. We started by creating the structure of a Svelte action and then filled up the steps within the action for when the Svelte action is initialized as the element is created, when the data changes, and when the element is removed from the DOM. We also discussed why we choose to use Svelte actions, as well as the other alternatives and considerations when it comes to integrating UI libraries.

In the next chapter, we will look at the next common pattern of actions, which is to progressively enhance your elements.

7

Progressive Enhancement with Actions

Progressive enhancement is a design philosophy in web development that emphasizes providing content and core functionality to everyone while delivering an enhanced experience to users who can afford it.

In this chapter, we will start with a more in-depth discussion of what progressive enhancement is. There are many ways to achieve progressive enhancement in your application; we will explore one of them by using Svelte actions. I will explain my reasoning as to why I think Svelte actions are designed for this use case.

Toward the end of the chapter, we will go through a few examples of using Svelte actions to progressively enhance our application.

By the end of this chapter, you will be able to build an application that follows the principles of progressive enhancement and supports as many user devices as possible.

This chapter covers the following topics:

- What is progressive enhancement?
- Why use Svelte actions for progressive enhancement?
- Examples of progressive enhancements using Svelte actions

Technical requirements

You can find the examples and code for this chapter here: `https://github.com/PacktPublishing/Real-World-Svelte/tree/main/Chapter07`.

What is progressive enhancement?

The most important thing in *progressive enhancement* is missing from the phrase itself. Something that is implied here is where are we progressively enhancing from.

The main idea of progressive enhancement is to provide a great baseline of essential content and core functionality to everyone, regardless of the browser software, device hardware, or the quality of the internet connection. Older browser software may not support newer JavaScript syntaxes and CSS features; older device hardware may take up more time to process and render your web page; a slower internet connection may take longer to load the resources needed to display your web page.

How do we ensure our web page stays usable for as many users as possible? Think about this for a while—I will come back to it later.

For users who can afford better browsers, more powerful hardware, and higher internet bandwidth, we progressively provide an enhanced experience to them. We leverage the power of JavaScript and CSS to surprise and delight our users.

How do we differentiate between the users and decide when to deliver an enhanced experience?

There is another term that is often used to compare with progressive enhancement, and that is *graceful degradation*. Graceful degradation starts from a feature-rich baseline and gracefully handles the situation when the user browser can no longer support the feature by replacing it with a simpler alternate experience. A lot of the time, these features start with a more complex assumption, and so execution-wise, it is much harder to gracefully degrade to all kinds of users.

Progressive enhancement, on the other hand, starts from a baseline that works for most users and slowly works its way up by adding more features. So, we can be sure that when a new feature is not loaded or does not work, users will still have a basic working web page.

So, let's get back to our question: *How do we make sure that our web page is usable to all users?* We'll uncover that in the following section.

Progressively enhancing the web experience

One of the ways is to make sure that we follow the standards. HTML, CSS, and JavaScript are the main languages of the web. We make sure we only use language features that are part of the standard specifications. Features that have been part of the specifications for longer have a higher probability of being implemented by all browsers. The latest and hottest features are less likely to be available in all browsers.

So, build your web pages with standard HTML, CSS, and JavaScript.

This then leads to the next question: *How do we deliver a differentiating experience to users based on their browser, device, and network capabilities?*

There are many ways to do this.

One key idea for most approaches is to build your application layer by layer. Start with the first layer of core functionality and make sure everything works. Then, add subsequent layers to enhance the experience.

Building web pages in layers

One example of building web pages in layers is to build the base content and functionality in HTML as the base layer, then add styles, transitions, and animations using CSS as the next layer. Finally, complex interactivity is added using JavaScript as the final layer.

This aligns with how the browser loads your website.

Whenever a user visits your website, the first thing the browser downloads from your website is HTML. HTML describes your content. HTML tags such as `<p>`, `<div>`, and `<table>` describe how your content should be laid out on the screen. HTML tags such as `<form>`, `<input>`, and `<a>` describe how users can submit data and interact with your content.

With HTML, your website should already provide basic content and functionality to the user.

And if you have `<link rel="stylesheet">` within the HTML, with reference to external CSS files, the browser will then make separate requests to download the CSS resource and parse and apply the CSS styles to your document. This will, in turn, enhance the look and feel of the default browser styles. HTML can offer basic layouts, but with CSS, you can have advanced layouts, such as flex layouts, grid layouts, and so on.

On the other hand, if you have `<script>` tags in your HTML, the browser will seek them out and load the referenced JavaScript files, and as soon as the JavaScript files are downloaded, the browser will parse them and execute them. JavaScript can be used to dynamically make changes to the DOM, perform computations, and add interactivity to the website.

Without JavaScript, HTML forms alone allow users to submit data; however, upon submission, the browser will navigate to a new location based on the form action. With JavaScript, you can make an asynchronous HTTP request to send data to the server while the user can continue browsing on the same page.

So, as you can see, serving HTML as a base experience layer and adding CSS and JavaScript on top for an enhanced experience is progressive enhancement.

Users with older browsers, slower hardware, and lower internet bandwidth can still view and interact with your website with just HTML while waiting for CSS and JavaScript to be downloaded and executed for a more enhanced experience.

Hopefully, you are now convinced about the first HTML approach. But what if your website content is dynamic? How do you generate dynamic HTML for the user? Do you need to write separate code to generate dynamic HTML?

No, you don't.

Svelte supports **server-side rendering (SSR)**. What that means is that the same Svelte component can be used to render content on the browser as well as generate HTML on the server side.

You can set it up yourself (however, that's beyond the scope of this book), or you can use meta frameworks such as SvelteKit, which comprehensively sets out how everything should work.

One thing to take away from here is that no matter your setup, it is possible to write your Svelte component as is and have the same Svelte component code that you write used in both generating HTML on the server side and rendering content on the browser side.

This begs the question: Does all the code work the same way on both the server side and the browser side? Is there code that only runs on the server but not on the browser, or the other way around?

Well, not all code runs both on the server side and on the browser. Svelte actions, along with `bind:` directives and `on:` event listeners, are Svelte features that do not run on both the server side and the browser side. Svelte actions only run on the browser side and not on the server side. That's because Svelte actions run after an element is added to the DOM. Since there's no DOM when generating HTML strings on the server side, Svelte actions do not run on the server side.

This makes Svelte actions the perfect candidate for progressive enhancements.

Svelte actions for progressive enhancements

In the previous section, we learned about progressive enhancements and the concept of building web pages in layers to achieve progressive enhancements.

In this section, we will delve deeper into the role of Svelte actions, which enable us to add an extra layer of interactivity to existing HTML elements, making them a natural fit for creating progressive enhancements.

Let's begin by examining a code example in Svelte to understand how Svelte actions fit into this approach.

Now, imagine the following code:

```
<button use:enhance />
```

When rendered from the server side, you get HTML that looks like this:

```
<button></button>
```

The HTML `button` element alone should be able to do what a button element is supposed to do: be clickable and able to submit forms.

But as JavaScript is loaded and the Svelte component code is executed, the `enhance` action is run with the `button` element, allowing the action code to enhance the `button` element.

Here are some examples of what the action could do: show a helpful tooltip upon hovering, provide a loading indicator when pressed, and so on.

Users with older browsers that are having trouble running the Svelte component code on the client side might still be able to use and interact with just the default HTML button element and experience an unenhanced version of the web page.

As we have gathered from this section, Svelte actions allow us to add another layer of interactivity to existing HTML elements. They are a naturally good candidate for designing progressive enhancements.

With that, let's look at a few examples of using actions to progressively enhance HTML elements.

The first example we are going to look at is progressively enhancing the <a> element.

Example – previewing a link with a <a> element

In our first example, we will explore how to progressively enhance a <a> element to display a preview when hovered upon.

Here, the browser receives HTML that contains a <a> tag with a href attribute, like this:

```
<a href="..." />
```

It then creates a hyperlink. When you click on the hyperlink, the browser will navigate to the destination specified in the href attribute.

This is the default behavior of the <a> element.

As the user loads the JavaScript, we want to make the <a> element do more than just navigate to a new location.

We are going to enhance the <a> element by having it show the destination location when hovering over it.

To do that, we are going to create a preview action and use it on the <a> element:

```
<script>
  function preview(element) {
  }
</script>
<a href="..." use:preview>Hello</a>
```

Regardless of how the preview action is implemented when rendering the preceding code on the server side, Svelte will generate the following HTML:

```
<a href="..." />Hello</a>
```

This is because Svelte actions never run on the server side.

As soon as your user receives the HTML response, they can start clicking on the link and navigating to new locations. You now have a workable application with just the HTML.

Depending on the user's network condition, your JavaScript code, compiled from your Svelte component, may take a longer time to arrive. But that does not stop the user from using the hyperlinks to navigate away.

Only when the JavaScript is loaded and executed does Svelte run the `preview` action with the `<a>` element that is on the DOM and enhances the `<a>` element's behavior.

The point here is that, as much as possible, we make the core functionality of our application workable with just the HTML, and we add a layer of enhancement with JavaScript, which may come at a much later time depending on the user's network condition.

Enough with the progressive enhancement philosophy. Let's look at how we can implement this `preview` action.

We want the `preview` action to show a floating popup containing the content of the link when we move our mouse cursor over the link and hide it as we move our mouse cursor away.

We can achieve that with `'mouseover'` and `'mouseout'` events. Here's how:

```
function preview(element) {
    element.addEventListener('mouseover', onMouseOver);
    element.addEventListener('mouseout', onMouseOut);
    return {
        destroy() {
            element.removeEventListener('mouseover', onMouseOver);
            element.removeEventListener('mouseout', onMouseOut);
        }
    };
}
```

In the preceding code snippet, we add `'mouseover'` and `'mouseout'` event listeners at the beginning of the `preview` action. Additionally, we ensure proper cleanup by removing both the `'mouseover'` and `'mouseout'` event listeners in the `destroy` method. Before we figure out how to implement `onMouseOver` and `onMouseOut`, we need to first decide what the floating popup would look like and how would we lay it out in the DOM.

To show the content of the link target, we are going to use the `<iframe>` element, which allows us to embed another HTML page into the current one:

```
<iframe src="..." />
```

To make the `<iframe>` element float above other content instead of being part of the document flow, we will need to modify the CSS `position` property of the `<iframe>` element by using either `position: fixed` or `position: absolute`.

If we used `position: fixed` on the <iframe> element, then the <iframe> element would be positioned relative to the viewport. To place the <iframe> element right next to the <a> element, we will have to figure out the position of the <a> element relative to the viewport and calculate the top and left values to place our <iframe> element.

On the other hand, if we used `position: absolute`, then the <iframe> element would be positioned relative to the nearest positioned parent element. We could place the <iframe> element inside the <a> element and make the <a> element a positioned parent element by specifying `position: relative` on the <a> element (the `position: relative` CSS property is to be positioned relative to its current position). The <iframe> element would then be positioned relative to its parent, the <a> element.

Either approach has its pros and cons. I am going to use the second approach here, which is to use `position: absolute`. I will have to modify the content and the `position` CSS property of the <a> element, but I could get away from needing to perform calculations if I use `position: absolute` instead of `position: fixed`.

Here's what the DOM will look like after we place the <iframe> element inside the <a> element:

```
<a href="..." style="position: relative">Hello<iframe src="..."
style="position: absolute"/></a>
```

Our task now is to programmatically create and insert the <iframe> element in the onMouseOver function. The following code snippet illustrates how to do this:

```
function preview(element) {
  // make the <a> element position relative
  element.style.position = 'relative';
  let iframe;
  function onMouseOver() {
    iframe = document.createElement('iframe');
    iframe.src = element.getAttribute('href');
    iframe.style.position = 'absolute';
    iframe.style.left = 0;
    iframe.style.top = '100%';
    element.appendChild(iframe);
  }
  // ...
}
```

In the preceding code snippet, we set the CSS `position` property of the <a> element to `'relative'`. In the onMouseOver function, which will be called when the mouse is hovered over the <a> element, we programmatically create a <iframe> element, style it, and insert it into the <a> element.

In the previous code, we are using the DOM API such as `document.createElement()` and `element.appendChild()`. Since the `<iframe>` element is programmatically created, we are also programmatically modifying its `style` attribute.

Luckily, in this example, we are only creating one element, but you can imagine how this could easily grow messy if we were to create more elements.

Since we are learning Svelte here and Svelte is designed to abstract out these imperative DOM instructions into declarative Svelte syntax, why not leverage Svelte in our action?

We can replace the previous imperative code with a Svelte component, like so:

```
<!-- IframePopup.svelte -->
<script>
  export let src;
</script>
<iframe {src} />
<style>
  iframe {
    position: absolute;
    left: 0;
    top: 100%;
  }
</style>
```

The preceding code snippet shows a Svelte component that contains a `<iframe>` element. This `<iframe>` element is equivalent to the one we created programmatically in the previous code snippet. It has the same CSS styles applied.

The Svelte component exposes a prop called `src`, and the value of the `src` prop will be used to set the value of the `src` attribute of the `<iframe>` element. Now, instead of calling the DOM APIs to create the `<iframe>` element, we can instantiate our Svelte component and pass the desired `src` value as the `src` prop to the component. In Svelte, you can instantiate a component by using the new keyword along with the component's constructor, passing in any required props as part of the constructor arguments. The Svelte component will then render the `<iframe>` element with the specified `src` attribute value based on the passed prop. This simplifies the process of creating and managing a `<iframe>` element within our Svelte application:

```
import IframePopup from './IframePopup.svelte';
function preview(element) {
  // ...
  function onMouseOver() {
    iframe = new IframePopup({
      // target specifies where we want the component
      // to be inserted into
```

```
      target: element,
      // we are passing the href value into the
      // component through props
      props: { src: element.getAttribute('href') },
    });
  }
  // ...
}
```

In the preceding code snippet, we've replaced the DOM operations in the `onMouseOver` function to instantiate the `IframePopup` Svelte component.

We need to remember to remove the popup when we move our mouse away from the link. Here's how we can do that:

```
function onMouseOut() {
  iframe.$destroy();
}
```

Although we are only inserting one HTML element into the DOM through Svelte actions, we've seen that it's much more manageable to encapsulate that into a Svelte component and instantiate the Svelte component instead of manually creating HTML elements.

We can then leverage Svelte to create scoped styles, as well as add other interactive logic to the elements we are going to create.

We could also add transitions to elements; instead of appearing abruptly upon hovering, we can make the popup fade by using a `fade` transition, like so:

```
<!-- IframePopup.svelte -->
<script>
  import { fade } from 'svelte/transition';
  // ...
</script>
<iframe {src} transition:fade />
```

By default, transitions are not played when the component is first created. So, we need to pass in the `intro: true` option to play the transition:

```
iframe = new IframePopup({
  target: element,
  props: { src: element.getAttribute('href') },
  // play transition when created
  intro: true,
});
```

In the preceding code snippet, we pass in `intro: true` to the `IframePopup` constructor.

We now have a link that shows a preview in a popup that fades in upon hovering. Try simulating loading the page with a slow network. Most browsers provide developer tools to simulate network speed. For example, if you are using Google Chrome, then you can open the **Developer Tools**, find the **Network conditions** tab, look for the **Network throttling** section, and choose the **Slow 3G** preset.

Try reloading your page, and you'll find that once you see the link (albeit the JavaScript file is still loading), the link is immediately working; clicking it will navigate you to the destination. As the JavaScript is finally loaded into the browser, your link is now enhanced, and you are now able to hover over the link and see a preview.

With our link preview action done, let's look at another common component in a web app, forms, and see how we can progressively enhance a form element.

Example – progressively enhancing a form

A `<form>` element is a section of a document that can contain inputs that will be used to submit information.

By default, when you submit a form, the browser will navigate to a URL to process the form submission. This means that the user will lose the state they are in as they navigate away from the current page when they submit the form.

However, with the ability to make asynchronous requests through the browser `fetch` API, we can now submit data through API requests without leaving the current page, and stay where we are.

This means that if the site is playing music, video, or animation, they will still be playing while we make asynchronous API calls.

Our task now is to create an action to enhance the form element so that the enhanced form will not navigate to a new location, but rather submit the form data asynchronously.

For lack of a better name, I am going to call this enhancing action `enhance`.

Before we proceed to implement the `enhance` action, let's recap on the default form behavior.

The default form behavior

When you have a `<form>` element, by default when you hit the **Submit** button, it will navigate to the location indicated by the `action` attribute, carrying along with it the value filled in the `<input>` elements within the `<form>` element.

For example, imagine you have the following form:

```
<form action="/foo">
  <input name="name" />
```

```
    <input name="address" />
    <button>Submit</button>
  </form>
```

When you hit the **Submit** button, the browser will navigate to `/foo?name=xxx&address=yyy`, carrying the form data via query parameters.

A `<form>` element can define the HTTP method to use to submit the form, by specifying the `method` attribute.

For example, the following form will navigate to `/foo` via a POST request:

```
  <form action="/foo" method="post">...</form>
```

Form data will be sent as a request body for the POST request.

Depending on the server's implementation for the `/foo` endpoint, the server can choose how to process the data and what to show on the `/foo` page. Sometimes, the server may decide to redirect back to the current page after processing the data. In that case, having an action that can replace the default form action and submit the form data asynchronously instead would be very useful, since we will eventually come back to the same page.

Now we know the default form behavior, let's figure out what we need to implement the `enhance` action.

Implementing the enhance action

Let's break the problem down.

First, we need to figure out how to know when a user submits a form. Then, we need to prevent the default form behavior and then make an asynchronous API call to submit the form asynchronously, and finally reset the form to the initial state, similar to what you would see after the server redirects back to the same page.

To figure out when the user submits a form, we could listen to the `'submit'` event on the `<form>` element:

```
  form.addEventListener('submit', handleSubmit);
```

To prevent the default form behavior, we call `event.preventDefault()` on the `'submit'` event listener to prevent the default submit behavior:

```
  function handleSubmit(event) {
    event.preventDefault();
  }
```

To make the API call to submit the form asynchronously, we need to first find out where we are submitting the form. We can get this information from reading the `action` property of the `form` instance:

```
form.action; // "https://domain/foo"
```

We can also determine the preferred HTTP request method from the `form` instance:

```
form.method // "post"
```

To get the form data submitted, we can use the `FormData` interface:

```
const data = new FormData(form);
```

With the URL, request method, and data, we can use the `fetch` API to submit the form:

```
fetch(form.action, {
  method: form.method,
  body: new FormData(form),
});
```

Finally, to reset the form, we can use the `reset()` method:

```
form.reset()
```

Putting everything together, we have the following:

```
<script>
  function enhance(form) {
    async function handleSubmit(event) {
      event.preventDefault();
      const response = await fetch(form.action, {
        method: form.method,
        body: new FormData(form),
      });
      form.reset();
    }
    form.addEventListener('submit', handleSubmit);
    return {
      destroy() {
        form.removeEventListener('submit', handleSubmit);
      }
    };
  }
</script>
<form action="/foo" method="post" use:enhance>...</form>
```

Now, try to submit the form after the JavaScript is loaded. You'll notice that a network request is made to submit the form, while you remain on the same page without navigating away.

Try to disable the JavaScript or simulate a slow network speed. You'll notice that you can still submit the form, while the JavaScript is still being loaded. However, this time round, you submit through the default browser behavior, which will navigate you away from the page.

Here we have it—a workable form by default, but progressively enhanced to submit form data without leaving the page if the JavaScript is being loaded.

There's a lot that can be improved on the `enhance` action. I'll leave that as an exercise:

- Modify the `enhance` action to allow passing in a callback function that will be called after the form submission is successfully made.

- What happens if the form submission fails? How should you handle such a case?

- Right now, the `enhance` action submits the form data through the request body; however, when the form method is `"get"`, form data should be passed through query parameters. Modify the `enhance` action to handle the `"get"` form method.

Summary

In this chapter, we explained what progressive enhancement is and why it is important. Following up on that, we learned how we can use Svelte actions to progressively enhance our elements.

We went through two different examples of progressive enhancements—enhancing a link to make it show a preview popup, and enhancing form elements to submit a form asynchronously.

In the past three chapters, we've seen three different patterns and use cases of Svelte actions, creating custom events, integrating UI libraries, and progressive enhancements. What you can do with Svelte actions is not limited to the three different use cases that we've discussed so far, but hopefully, these patterns have opened your imagination and made you see what is possible with Svelte actions.

With that, we are moving on to the next part of the book. We will be exploring Svelte context and stores from *Chapter 8* to *Chapter 12*, exploring their various use cases, such as in state management, creating renderless components, and using them for animations. We will start by defining and comparing Svelte contexts and Svelte stores in the next chapter.

Part 3: Context and Stores

In this part, we will dive deep into Svelte's two core features, Svelte context and Svelte stores. Over the five chapters, we will explore different scenarios for using Svelte context and stores. We'll start our exploration by defining Svelte context and stores. This will be followed by a deep dive into implementing custom stores and strategies for managing application state using Svelte stores. Following that, we will learn how to use Svelte context to create a renderless component. Finally, we will learn how to create animations using Svelte stores.

This part has the following chapters:

Context versus Stores

A Svelte application can be composed of one or many Svelte components. A Svelte component can be seen as a standalone unit, encapsulating its own reactive data and logic. In the previous chapter, we learned how two Svelte components – in particular, components in a parent and child relationship – communicate and pass data between each other. In this chapter, however, we are going to explore communication and passing data between components beyond the parent and child relationship.

Svelte provides two primitives to pass data across Svelte components – Svelte context and Svelte stores. Svelte context allows you to pass data from an ancestor to all children, while Svelte stores use the observer pattern to allow you to access reactive data across multiple unrelated Svelte components.

In the coming five chapters, we are going to explore the different use cases of Svelte context and Svelte stores. In this chapter, we will cover what Svelte context and Svelte stores are.

We will talk about when to use Svelte context and/or Svelte stores and the considerations for choosing them. We will then proceed with an example of a combination of both Svelte context and Svelte stores – a Svelte context store.

By the end of this chapter, you'll be proficient in using Svelte stores and Svelte context in your Svelte application. You will also understand when to use them effectively.

In this chapter, we will cover the following topics:

- Defining Svelte context and Svelte stores
- When to use Svelte context and Svelte stores
- Creating dynamic context using Svelte stores

Defining Svelte context

When you need to pass data from a parent component to a child component, the first thing you should think of is using props:

```
<Component props={value} />
```

What if you need to pass data from a parent component to a grandchild component? You could pass data as props from the parent component to the child component, and then from the child component to the grandchild component:

```
<!-- Parent.svelte -->
<Child props={value} />

<!-- Child.svelte -->
<script>
  export let props;
</script>
<GrandChild props={props} />
```

What if you need to pass data from a parent component to a great-grandchild component?

You could follow a process similar to what we did in the preceding code, passing the data through layers of components to reach the great-grandchild component.

This approach is called *prop drilling*. It is akin to drilling a hole through layers of components via props. This is frowned upon in most cases due to the following reasons:

- It is hard to trace where the data comes from.

    Whenever you want to trace where the data comes from in the child component, you may endlessly trace up through layers of the parent component, jumping through different Svelte component files.

    This slows you down and makes it harder to reason with the data flow.

- It is hard to trace where the data leads to.

    The data that's passed down through props into the child component is not to be used by the child component directly, but to be passed through it to its child component. You would have to step through the layer of components to find out where the data is finally being used.

    You may lose sight of where the data goes and have less confidence in making changes to the data that's passed down.

- It is hard to restructure the component hierarchy.

    When you add a new component in between the layers, you need to make sure to still pass the props through the new component from its parent to its children.

    When you move the components around, you need to make sure the child component still gets the props it needs by checking the chain of parent components.

> **Note**
>
> Keeping this in mind, when the component tree is small and simple, even with its drawback, passing props around may still be the simplest way to pass data from a parent to its child components.

So, what is the alternative to *prop drilling*? Svelte context.

Svelte context is a method that provides data to all child components, no matter how many levels down the component tree they are.

A component tree is like a family tree for components. You have a parent component at the top, and one level down its child components, and one more level down is the child components of the child components:

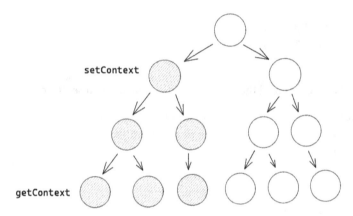

Figure 8.1: Component tree diagram

In the preceding component tree diagram, the top-left node represents where `setContext` is called, and all shaded nodes under the node can access the context value using `getContext`. To set a context value in a component, you can use `setContext()`:

```
<script>
   import { setContext } from 'svelte';
   setContext("key", value);
</script>
```

All its child components and child components' child components will be able to read the context value through `getContext()`:

```
<script>
   import { getContext } from 'svelte';
   const value = getContext("key");
</script>
```

If you paid attention to the preceding snippets, you may have noticed that we have been using strings as the context key when setting and reading context. However, you might wonder whether it is possible to use other data types as the context key. Let's look into this.

Using an object as a context key

What is the underlying mechanism of Svelte context?

Svelte context is implemented using a JavaScript Map, which means you can set values and read values out of Svelte context using a key, the same way you would with a JavaScript map.

This also means that you can set more than one key to Svelte context:

```
<script>
  setContext("item", item);
  setContext("order", order);
</script>
```

You just need to make sure you read them out using the same key you set the context with.

As I mentioned earlier, Svelte context is implemented using a JavaScript Map, and the keys of a Map can be of any type, including functions, objects, or any primitives; you are not constrained to using just a String key value:

```
<script>
  const object = {};
  setContext(object, value);
</script>
```

And just as how JavaScript Map works, if you set a context using an object, then you would need to use the same object instance to read the value out of the Svelte context.

Changing the context value

One thing to take note of when using setContext and getContext is that these functions need to be called during component initialization. Read *Chapter 1* to recap on what component initialization is.

If we can call setContext after component initialization, then this leads us to the next question – how would we change the context value?

Look at the following snippet:

```
<script>
  let itemId = 123;
  setContext("itemid", itemId);
```

```
    itemId = 456;
</script>
```

When calling `setContext` in line 3, we are passing the value of the `itemId` variable to the `setContext` function. Reassigning the `itemId` variable in line 5 would not make the context value change.

This is how JavaScript works. If you call a function with a primitive-type variable, then the value of the variable is being passed in, and reassigning the variable outside of the function would not change the value of the variable that's read from inside the function.

How about passing an object as a context value? Let's see how that works:

```
<script>
   let item = { id: 123 };
   setContext("item", item);

   item.id = 456;
</script>
```

In JavaScript, objects are passed by reference. This means that the Svelte context and the `item` variable outside of the `setContext` function are referring to the same object. Mutating the object modifies the same referenced object and thus the changes can be seen when reading the Svelte context:

```
<script>
   const item = getContext("item");
</script>
{item.id}
```

However, you may have noticed that after you render `{item.id}` onto the DOM, the value shown in the DOM does not change when you mutate it in the parent component.

This does not mean `item.id` has not changed. If you try to print out `item.id` on an interval, you will notice that `item.id` has changed, but the value in the DOM remains the same:

```
const item = getContext("item");
setInterval(() => {
   console.log(item.id);
}, 1000);
```

Why would this happen?

Svelte tracks variable mutations and reassignments within a Svelte component and instruments operations to update the DOM to reflect the changes. However, what this means is that changes that happen outside of the component are not tracked, and therefore the DOM does not reflect such changes.

So, what should we do to make Svelte aware of changes to a variable outside of the component?

This is where the Svelte store comes in.

Defining the Svelte store

To understand why Svelte reactivity is limited within a Svelte component, we must first understand how Svelte's reactivity works.

Unlike some other frameworks, Svelte reactivity works during build time. As Svelte compiles a Svelte component into JavaScript, Svelte looks at each variable and tracks the variable to see when the variable changes.

Instead of tracking all the variables throughout the application, Svelte limits itself to only analyzing and compiling one file at a time. This allows Svelte to compile multiple Svelte component files in parallel but also means that a Svelte component would not be aware of variable changes that happen in other files.

A common situation where a variable change is not tracked is when the variable is defined in a separate file and imported into the current component.

In the following code snippet, the `quantity` variable is imported from a separate file. Svelte will not track any changes to the `quantity` variable that may have occurred in that file:

```
<script>
   import { quantity } from './item';
</script>
<p>Quantity: {quantity}</p>
```

If you attempt to modify the variable outside of the Svelte component, then Svelte is not able to track that. So, Svelte has no idea when you modify the variable and therefore will not be able to update the DOM when that happens.

To make Svelte aware of the changes outside of the component and update the DOM accordingly, we will need to design a mechanism at runtime that will notify Svelte whenever a variable changes.

For this, we can draw inspiration from the **observer pattern**. The observer pattern is a design pattern that lets you define a subscription mechanism to notify multiple objects when an event happens.

Using the observer pattern

Here, instead of just importing the `quantity` variable, I am also importing a `subscribe` function, which we will define later:

```
import { quantity, subscribe } from './item';
```

The idea of the `subscribe` function is such that we can subscribe to know when `quantity` changes.

Here, we assume that `subscribe` takes in a callback function, which will be called whenever `quantity` changes. The callback function takes in a parameter that gives us the latest value of `quantity`:

```
import { quantity, subscribe } from './item';
subscribe((newQuantity) => { ... });
```

So, now, although Svelte still cannot track changes to the `quantity` variable outside of the component, we can use the `subscribe` function to tell Svelte when that happens.

As an example of how to tell Svelte this, we can define another variable called `_quantity` that initializes to be the same value as `quantity`.

Whenever `quantity` changes, the callback function that's passed into the `subscribe` function should be called with the new `quantity` value. We will use this as an opportunity to update `_quantity` to the new `quantity` value:

```
<script>
  import { quantity, subscribe } from './item';
  let _quantity = quantity;
  subscribe((newQuantity) => { _quantity = newQuantity; });
</script>
<p>Quantity: {_quantity}</p>
```

Since the `_quantity` variable is defined within the component, and we update the value of the variable within the component (in the `_quantity = newQuantity` statement), Svelte can track the update of `_quantity`. And since the `_quantity` variable tracks the changes of the `quantity` variable itself, you can see that the DOM updates whenever `quantity` changes.

However, all of this depends on the `subscribe` function, which would call the callback function whenever the value of `quantity` changes.

So, let's see how we can define the `subscribe` function.

Defining the subscribe function

There are multiple ways of defining the `subscribe` function.

Here, we are going to use an array and name it `subscribers` so that we can keep track of all the functions being called with `subscribe`. Then, when we attempt to update the value of `quantity`, we will iterate through the `subscribers` array to get each of the subscriber functions and call them one by one:

```
let subscribers = [];
function subscribe(fn) {
  subscribers.push(fn);
}
```

```
function notifySubscribers(newQuantity) {
  subscribers.forEach(fn => {
    fn(newQuantity);
  });
}
```

As an example, here, we want to update `quantity` to `20`. To make sure that the subscribers are notified of the changes, we call `notifySubscribers` with the updated value at the same time so that each `subscribers` is notified with the latest value for `quantity`:

```
quantity = 20;
notifySubscribers(quantity);
```

Take your time when connecting the implementation of the `subscribe` and `notifySubscribers` functions in the preceding code back to the Svelte component code in the previous section. You will see that whenever we call `notifySubscribers`, the callback function that's passed into the `subscribe` function will be called. `_quantity` will be updated, and the value in the DOM will be updated.

So, it doesn't matter if you are modifying `quantity` outside the Svelte component, so long as you call the `notifySubscribers` function. With the new value of `quantity`, Svelte will update the DOM elements to reflect the latest value of `quantity`.

With the observer pattern, we are now able to define and update variables across Svelte components.

You will see this pattern a lot in Svelte. Svelte encapsulates the idea of `subscribe` and `notifySubscribers` into a concept called a Svelte store. So, let's explore what it means to be a Svelte store and explore what first-class support Svelte is providing for Svelte stores.

Defining a Svelte store

A Svelte store is any object that follows the Svelte store contract.

This means that any object that follows the Svelte store contract can be referred to as a Svelte store. As a Svelte store, there are a few syntactic sugars and built-in functions that come with it.

Before we get ahead of ourselves, let's take a look at what a Svelte store contract is.

The Svelte store contract requires an object to have a `subscribe` method and an optional `set` method:

```
const store = {
  subscribe() {},
  set() {},
};
```

I have not told you about the specific requirements for the subscribe and set methods, but I hope you can see the similarity in the subscribe and set methods in the Svelte store contract to the subscribe and notifySubscribers functions illustrated in the previous section.

But something is missing here. Where do we place the store value, or the corresponding quantity variable from the previous section?

Well, the store value is not part of the Svelte store contract, and we will soon explain why.

Let's continue with our requirements for the subscribe and set methods:

- The subscribe method has to return a function to unsubscribe from the store.

   This allows the subscriber to stop receiving updates of the latest store value.

   For example, if we use an array to keep track of the subscriber functions being called with the subscribe function, then we can use the returned function from subscribe to remove the subscriber function from the array since the subscriber function is no longer needed to receive any new updates from the store:

```
const subscribers = [];
const store = {
  subscribe(fn) {
    // add the fn to the list of subscribers
    subscribers.push(fn);
    // return a function to remove the fn from the list of
subscribers
    return () => {
      subscribers.splice(subscribers.indexOf(fn), 1);
    };
  }
};
```

- When the subscribe method is being called with a function, the function must be called immediately and synchronously with the store value.

   If the function is not called immediately, the store value is assumed to be undefined:

```
let storeValue = 10;
const store = {
  subscribe(fn) {
    // immediately call the function with the store value
    fn(storeValue);
    // ...
  },
};
```

This requirement means that to read the store value out from the Svelte store, you will need to use the `subscribe` method:

```
let storeValue;
store.subscribe((value) => {
  storeValue = value;
});
console.log(storeValue);
```

In the preceding snippet, you can see that if the callback function that's passed into the `subscribe` method is not being called immediately and synchronously, then immediately in the next statement where we console out the value of `storeValue`, you will see that the value of `storeValue` remains `undefined`.

- The `set` method of a Svelte store takes in a new store value and returns nothing:

```
store.set(newValue);
```

The `set` method is supposed to update the value of the store. Naturally, we would implement the `set` method such that it will notify all the store subscribers of the latest store value:

```
const store = {
  // ...
  set(newValue) {
    // notify subscribers with new store value
    for(const subscriber of subscribers) {
      subscriber(newValue);
    }
  },
};
```

With that, we've gone through the requirements of a Svelte store contract. Along the way, we've also seen snippets of code on implementing each requirement of a Svelte store. By putting them together, we will have a Svelte store.

Creating a Svelte store is such a common use case that Svelte has provided a few built-in functions to help us with creating one.

Creating Svelte stores with built-in functions

Svelte provides a sub-package that exports a few built-in functions for Svelte stores. You can import them from the `'svelte/store'` package.

Here is the list of built-in Svelte store functions:

- `readable()` helps create a readable Svelte store. Since the `set` method in a Svelte contract is optional, a readable store is a store that does not implement the `set` method.

To update the store value, the `readable()` function takes in a callback function that will be called when the store is being subscribed, and the callback function is called with a `set` function that can be used to update the store value:

```
const store = readable(initialValue, (set) => {
   // update store value
   set(newValue);
});
```

The `set` function in the callback function can be called numerous times. In the following example, we are calling the `set` function every second to update the store value to the latest timestamp:

```
const store = readable(Date.now(), (set) => {
   setInterval(() => {
      // update store value to the current timestamp
      set(Date.now());
   }, 1000);
});
```

- `writable()` helps create a writable Svelte store. This is similar to the readable store, except it implements the `set` method:

```
const store = writable(initialValue);
store.set(newValue);
```

- `derived()` creates a new Svelte store, deriving from existing stores.

  We will explore `derived()` in more detail in the next chapter when we talk about creating custom stores.

With `readable()`, `writable()`, and `derived()`, you can easily create a new Svelte store without having to implement the Svelte store contract yourself.

So, we have built-in methods to create a Svelte store, but do we have any built-in methods for using Svelte stores? Let's find out.

Auto-subscribing to a Svelte store

Since all Svelte stores follow the Svelte store contract, all Svelte stores have the `subscribe` method and, optionally, the `set` method. We can use the `store.subscribe()` method to subscribe to the latest store value, and `store.set()` to update the store value:

```
<script>
   import { onMount } from 'svelte';
   let storeValue;
   onMount(() => {
      // use `subscribe` to subscribe to latest store value
```

```
        const unsubscribe = store.subscribe(newStoreValue => {
            storeValue = newStoreValue;
        });
        return () => unsubscribe();
    });
    function update(newValue) {
        // use `set` to update store value
        store.set(newValue);
    }
</script>
<p>{storeValue}</p>
```

When using a Svelte store in a Svelte component, we only subscribe to the Svelte store when needed (usually as we mount the Svelte component). In the preceding snippet, we subscribe to the store exactly after the Svelte component is mounted by calling the store.subscribe method inside an onMount callback.

It is important to unsubscribe from new store value changes when it is no longer necessary. This is usually when we unmount and destroy the Svelte component. In the preceding snippet, we return a function in an onMount callback, which will be called when the component is unmounted. In the function, we call the unsubscribe function return from the store.subscribe method.

This is in accordance with the Svelte store contract, where the store.subscribe method has to return a function to unsubscribe from the store.

In a Svelte component, we need to remember to call store.subscribe during onMount, and remember to clean up by calling unsubscribe during onDestroy.

This can become verbose, so Svelte provides a way to auto-subscribe to a Svelte store in a Svelte component.

When you have a variable that references a store in a Svelte component, you can auto-subscribe to the store and access the value of the store through the $ prefixed variable name of the store variable.

For example, let's say you have a Svelte store variable named count, as shown here:

```
<script>
    import { writable } from 'svelte/store';
    const count = writable();
</script>
```

In this case, you can auto-subscribe to the count Svelte store and access the store value through $count:

```
<script>
    import { writable } from 'svelte/store';
    const count = writable();
    console.log($count);
</script>
```

This is equivalent to subscribing to the store and assigning the latest store value to the $count variable, However, when doing it this way, you no longer need to explicitly call the count.subscribe method to subscribe to the store and call the unsubscribe function to unsubscribe from it.

If you paid attention to the code, you may have noticed that we did not declare the $count variable at all. However, it is magically available, automatically declared by Svelte as Svelte builds the Svelte component code.

This also assumes that whenever you are using the variable that starts with $, the variable without the $ prefix is assumed to be a Svelte store.

Also, because of how Svelte auto declares the $ prefixed variable, it disallows any declaration of any variable with a variable name starting with the $ sign.

What happens if I assign a new value to the $ prefixed variable? Doing so is equivalent to calling the set method of the store:

```
$count = 123;
// is equivalent to
count.set(123);
```

So, now that we've learned about the Svelte context and Svelte store, let's discuss when we should use a Svelte context and/or a Svelte store.

Choosing between a Svelte context and a Svelte store

The Svelte context and Svelte store are designed for very different use cases.

Here's a recap: the Svelte context helps pass data from a parent component to all descendent components, while a Svelte store helps make data reactive across multiple Svelte components.

Although both the Svelte context and Svelte store are meant to pass data across Svelte components, they are designed for different use cases. So, choosing when to use a Svelte context and Svelte store is never an either-or situation.

You can use either a Svelte context, a Svelte store, or both to pass the same data across Svelte components.

To decide which one to use, I've come up with a 2x2 decision matrix:

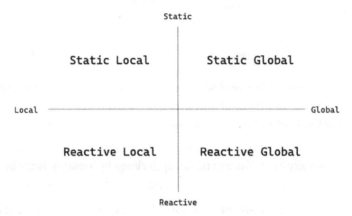

Figure 8.2: A decision matrix for choosing a Svelte store, a Svelte context, or both

In this 2x2 decision matrix, there are two dimensions: local-global and static-reactive.

Depending on the kind of data you are passing, the data should fall into one of the four quadrants. Then, we can decide on the best way of passing the data across components.

So, let's take a closer look at what each dimension means.

In the local-global dimension, we determine whether the data should have the same value globally across the entire application or have separate local versions among components that are close to each other.

For example, language preference data falls into being global instead of local. There tends to be only one piece of language preference data throughout the entire application so that the language preference is consistent in the application.

On the other hand, chart settings in a dashboard of charts could be local data. Multiple Svelte components, such as chart axis, chart data, and chart grid, within the same chart share the same data, yet different charts could have different chart settings. There's no one single piece of data throughout the entire application. So, in this case, it is more toward local in the local-global dimension.

If the data is going to be global throughout the entire application, the data can be declared in a JavaScript module and imported from anywhere within the application:

```
// language-preference.js
export const languagePreference = ...;
```

On the other hand, if the data is going to be local, the data can be declared as a Svelte context. This allows the child component to get different values, depending on where the component lives in the component tree hierarchy:

```
<!-- Chart.svelte -->
<script>
  import { setContext } from 'svelte';
  setContext('chart', ...);
</script>

<!-- ChartAxis.svelte -->
<script>
  import { getContext } from 'svelte';
  // chartSettings depending on which chart it falls under
  const chartSettings = getContext('chart');
</script>
```

In the static-reactive dimension, we determine whether the data should be static, meaning it wouldn't change through the life cycle of the application, or should be dynamic, where the value of the data will change as the user interacts with the application.

An example of static data would be the theme of an application. The value of the data could be determined based on dynamic conditions, but once the value is determined at the start of the application, the value does not change throughout the application life cycle. The application theme is a good example of such a scenario. Usually, the theme of an application is determined at the start as the application loads, and the theme stays throughout the application.

On the other hand, an example of dynamic data would be chart data. Chart data is dynamic and can be changed throughout the application's life cycle.

If the data is going to be static throughout the application's life cycle, then the data can be declared using a normal JavaScript variable:

```
let theme = 'dark';
```

However, if the data is going to be dynamic, and needs to be reactive across multiple components, the data should be declared as a Svelte store:

```
import { writable } from 'svelte/store';
let chartData = writable();
```

If we combine the two dimensions, we get the following:

- **Static global**: The data is declared as a normal JavaScript variable in a JavaScript module and exported for Svelte components to import
- **Dynamic global**: The data is declared as a Svelte store in a JavaScript module and exported for Svelte components to import
- **Static local**: The data is declared as a Svelte context with a normal JavaScript variable as the Svelte context value
- **Dynamic local**: The data is declared as a Svelte context with the Svelte store as the Svelte context value

With that, we've seen how we can use a Svelte context and a Svelte store individually, but when we pass dynamic local data across Svelte components, we use both a Svelte context and Svelte store together.

So, how do you combine both a Svelte context and a Svelte store? Let's find out.

Passing dynamic context using a Svelte store

To make Svelte context data dynamic and reactive across components, we need to pass a Svelte store as the Svelte context data instead of a normal JavaScript variable.

This is very similar to importing a Svelte store from a JavaScript module, except we are not importing the Svelte store; instead, we are sending the Svelte store through the Svelte context.

To begin, we are creating a Svelte store, and passing the Svelte store into the context:

```
<script>
  import { writable } from 'svelte/store';
  import { setContext } from 'svelte';

  // declare a Svelte store
  let data = writable(0);
  setContext('data', data);
</script>
```

Note that we are passing the store into the Svelte context directly, instead of passing the store value.

In the child component, we can read the value out from the context through `getContext()`:

```
<script>
  import { getContext } from 'svelte';
  const data = getContext('data');
</script>
```

Since data is a Svelte store, we can reference the Svelte store value using the $ prefixed variable:

```
<script>
  import { getContext } from 'svelte';
  const data = getContext('data');
</script>
<p>{$data}</p>
```

To test whether the reactivity works, we can set a new value to the data store in the parent component:

```
<script>
  let data = writable(0);
  setContext('data', data);
  function update() {
    $data = 123;
  }
</script>
```

This goes both ways. If you attempt to update the store value from the child component, the store value in the parent component will be updated too. Since you are getting the same store value through the context in all the children components, any component using the same store will be updated as well.

Summary

In this chapter, we learned what Svelte context and Svelte store are.

Although both Svelte context and Svelte store are meant for sharing data across multiple Svelte components, they are designed and used for different reasons.

Svelte context is meant for sharing the same data across all descendant components in the component tree, while Svelte store is meant for sharing reactivity across Svelte components.

Then, we explored the decision matrix on when to use a Svelte context, when to use a Svelte store, and when to use both.

This chapter served as an introduction to the Svelte context and the Svelte store. By now, you should have a good understanding of what they are and how they work, and feel confident in knowing when to use them. As we move forward, we will explore practical use cases that involve Svelte context and Svelte store, allowing you to apply these powerful concepts effectively in real-world scenarios.

In the next chapter, we will dive deeper into the topic of the Svelte store and look at how to create a custom one.

9

Implementing Custom Stores

In the last chapter, we learned that a Svelte store is any object that follows a Svelte store contract, and encapsulating data within a Svelte store allows the data to be shared and used across multiple Svelte components reactively. The Svelte component keeps the DOM up to date with the data, even though the data is modified outside of the Svelte component.

We learned about two of Svelte's built-in methods for creating a Svelte store—namely `readable()` and `writable()`, which create a readable and writable store. The two methods follow the Svelte contract and create a very basic Svelte store. However, besides using a Svelte store to encapsulate data, we can also encapsulate logic with the data, making the Svelte store modular and highly reusable.

In this chapter, we will be creating custom Svelte stores—Svelte stores that encapsulate custom data logic. We will go through three distinct examples; each example will serve as a guide, brimming with tips and tricks for creating your own custom Svelte stores.

First up, we'll examine how to turn user events into store values, specifically turning click counts into a Svelte store.

Second, we'll explore a custom store that goes beyond the basic `set` method to modify its value. We'll look at an undo/redo store, which incorporates additional methods for reverting or redoing changes to its value.

Lastly, we'll turn our attention to higher-order stores. While not a custom store in itself, a higher-order store is a function that accepts a Svelte store as input and returns an enhanced version of it. This chapter includes sections on the following topics:

- Creating a Svelte store from user events
- Creating an undo/redo store
- Creating a debounced higher-order Svelte store

So, without further ado, let's dive into creating our first custom Svelte store.

Technical requirements

All the code in this chapter can be found on GitHub: `https://github.com/PacktPublishing/Real-World-Svelte/tree/main/Chapter09`

Creating a Svelte store from user events

A Svelte store stores data, but where does the data come from?

It could be from user interaction or user input, which calls an event handler that updates the store value by calling `store.set()`.

What if we can encapsulate the user events and event handler logic into the store so that we do not need to call `store.set()` manually?

For example, we are going to have a Svelte store to calculate how many times the user clicks on the screen. Instead of manually adding an event listener on the document, if there's a way to create a Svelte store and update it every time there's a new click, how would that look? In short, how about having a custom Svelte store that can do all of that for us?

It would be great if we could reuse this Svelte store the next time we have a similar need, instead of having to manually set it up again.

So, let's try to implement this click counter custom Svelte store.

Let's first scaffold the Svelte store:

```
const subscribers = [];
let clickCount = 0;
const store = {
  subscribe: (fn) => {
    fn(clickCount);
    subscribers.push(fn);
    return () => {
      subscribers.splice(subscribers.indexOf(fn), 1);
    }
  },
}
```

In the preceding code snippet, we created a basic Svelte store based on the Svelte store contract with just a `subscribe()` method. The value of the store is stored in a variable called `clickCount`, and in the `subscribe()` method, we keep track of all the subscribers using the `subscribers` array.

Notice that we need to synchronously call `fn` in the `subscribe()` method with the value of the store; this lets the subscriber know the current value of the store.

If you use this store in a Svelte component right now (as shown in the following code snippet), you will see 0 on the screen. That is the current value of the store at this point:

```
<script>
  import { store } from './store.js';
</script>
{$store}
```

In the preceding code snippet, we import `store` into a Svelte component and display the `store` value using `$store`. Now, let's listen to the `click` events to update the `count` value of the store. Instead of listening to the `click` events at the start of our program, we should start subscribing only when there's a subscriber.

Here's the updated code:

```
const store = {
  subscribe: (fn) => {
    // ...
    document.addEventListener('click', () => {
      clickCount++;
      // notify subscribers
      subscribers.forEach(subscriber => subscriber(clickCount));
    });
  },
};
```

In the preceding code snippet, we add the `click` event listener inside the `subscribe` method, and whenever the `document` is clicked, we increment the `clickCount` value by 1 and notify all the subscribers of the latest value of `clickCount`.

If you try to use this Svelte store in multiple Svelte components right now, you will realize that every time you click, the store value increments by more than one.

Ensuring the event listener is only added once

Why is the store value incremented more than once when it is only clicked once?

If you look at the current implementation closely, you will realize that we call `document.addEventListener` on every `subscribe` method call. When you use the Svelte store in multiple Svelte components, each Svelte component subscribes to the store changes individually. If there are five components subscribed to the store, then five `click` event listeners will be added to `document`. As a result, a single click on `document` will trigger five event listeners, causing the `clickCount` value to increase by five each time. This means the `store` value will go up by more than one for every click. To fix this behavior, we can still call `addEventListener` within the `subscribe` method, but we need to only call `addEventListener` once, even though the `subscribe` method could be called more than once.

We can use a flag to indicate if we have already called addEventListener, and make sure not to call addEventListener again when the flag is set to true, as shown here:

```
let called = false;
const store = {
  subscribe: (fn) => {
    // ...
    if (!called) {
      called = true;
      document.addEventListener('click', () => {... });
    }
  },
};
```

In the preceding code snippet, we add a variable named called and use it to prevent document from adding click event listeners more than once.

This works, but there's a better way to implement this.

Instead of having a new flag to indicate whether we have called addEventListener, we can use any existing variables to determine if we should call addEventListener. We know that we should call addEventListener once the subscribe method is being called, and it should not be called subsequently when we are adding more subscribers; we can use the length of the subscribers array to determine if we should call the addEventListener method.

If there are no subscribers currently, then we know this is the first time the subscribe method is being called. In this case, we should call addEventListener. On the other hand, if there are existing subscribers—that is, the length of subscribers is more than zero, we know that the subscribe method has been called before, and therefore we should not call addEventListener again.

So, here's the updated code to use the length of the subscribers array instead of the variable called to determine if the document should add click event listeners:

```
const store = {
  subscribe: (fn) => {
    // ...
    if (subscribers.length === 0) {
      document.addEventListener('click', () => {... });
    }
  },
};
```

In the preceding code snippet , we replaced the !called condition with subscribers.length === 0.

Now that we have added a click event listener when a subscriber is subscribing to our Svelte store, we need to clean it up when all subscribers have unsubscribed from the Svelte store.

To clean it up, we are going to call `removeEventListener` to remove the `click` event listeners from `document`. The `unsubscribe` function can be called multiple times, but we should only call `removeEventListener` when there are no more subscribers in the `subscribers` array:

```
const store = {
  subscribe: (fn) => {
    return () => {
      subscribers.splice(subscribers.indexOf(fn), 1);
      if (subscribers.length === 0) {
        document.removeEventListener('click', () => {...});
      }
    };
  },
};
```

In the preceding code snippet, the `return` function of the `subscribe` method is used for unsubscribing the store. In the function, we added a check to see if the number of `subscribers` has dropped to zero; if so, we will remove the `click` event listeners from `document`.

It is common that when you are creating a Svelte store, you need to keep track of the `subscribers` list, ensure that you only set up the event listeners once, and clean it up only after there are no more subscribers.

As you've seen in this and the previous section, we've been through a lot of steps to create a Svelte store from user events, manage a `subscribers` array, and decide when to add or remove click event listeners from document. In the next section, we'll explore a simpler way to achieve the same goal using Svelte's built-in methods and using Svelte's built-in `readable()` function.

Svelte provides built-in methods such as `readable()` to make our lives easier when creating a Svelte store.

Since the store value is only updated from `click` events, and not from elsewhere, `readable()`, out of the two most important methods—`readable()` and `writable()`—is good enough for our use case.

We will use the `readable()` function to create our click event store. There are two arguments for the `readable()` function. The first argument is for the initial value of the store. The second argument of the `readable()` function takes in a function that will be called when there's a first subscriber and not be called for the subsequent subscribers. If the function returns another function, the returned function will be called when the last subscriber unsubscribes from the store. This is perfect for us to add and remove `click` event listeners on `document`.

Let's take a look at the updated code rewritten using `readable`:

```
let clickCount = 0;
const store = readable(clickCount, (set) => {
  const onClick = () => set(++clickCount);
  document.addEventListener('click', onClick);
  return () => {
    document.removeEventListener('click', onClick);
  };
});
```

In the preceding code snippet, we utilize `readable()` to handle both the creation and the cleanup of the `click` event listener, making our code cleaner and more efficient.

Comparing it with our implementation in the last section, where we managed the `subscribers` list ourselves, you can see how using `readable()` allows us to declutter away from maintaining the `subscribers` array manually and focus on implementing the logic.

It is good to know the Svelte contract and how to implement a Svelte store from scratch. But in most real-world scenarios, it is easier to create a Svelte store out of `readable()` or `writable()` and leave the nitty-gritty detail to the built-in function.

Now that you have learned how to create a Svelte store out of click events, let's practice with an exercise.

Exercise

Let's begin our exercise, where we will implement a Svelte store in which the value of the store comes from the scroll position of the document:

```
<script>
  const scrollPosition = createStore();
  function createStore() {
    // Your code here
  }
</script>
Scroll position {$scrollPosition}
```

In the code snippet, a `scrollPosition` store is set up using a function called `createStore()`. Your task is to implement the `createStore()` function to actually create a `scrollPosition` store.

You can find the solution at the following link: `https://github.com/PacktPublishing/ Real-World-Svelte/tree/main/Chapter09/02-exercise-scroll-position`

Now that we have seen how to create a Svelte store where the store value comes from an event, let's take a look at a different kind of Svelte store.

Creating an undo/redo store

Typically, we change a store's value using the set method. However, the next custom Svelte store we'll explore provides additional custom methods to update its store value. The next custom Svelte store that we are going to look at is an undo/redo store. It is similar to a writable store where you can subscribe to and set a new store value. But an undo/redo store also comes with two more methods, undo and redo, which revert the store value backward or forward, based on the history of the store value.

Here's a snippet of how you would use an undo/redo store:

```
<script>
  let value = createUndoRedoStore();
  $value = 123;
  $value = 456;
  $value = 789;
  value.undo(); // $value now goes back to 456
  value.undo(); // $value now goes back to 123
  value.redo(); // $value now turns to 456
</script>
Value: {$value}
```

In the provided code snippet, the createUndoRedoStore() function generates an undo/redo store. Initially, we set the store's value to 123, followed by updates to 456 and then 789. When we call the store's undo method, the value reverts to 456 and then to 123. Subsequently, using the redo method takes the store's value back to 456. Now that we understand how undo/redo store functions, how do we go about creating one in Svelte?

Firstly, the undo/redo store is going to have four methods: subscribe, set, undo, and redo. The subscribe and set methods are based on the Svelte store contract and are the reason an undo/redo store is considered a Svelte store. The undo and redo methods, on the other hand, are two additional methods that we define.

A JavaScript object can contain different methods and properties, but as long as it has the subscribe and set methods, with the method signature following the Svelte store contract, we consider the object a Svelte store. You can use a $-prefixed variable to auto-subscribe to the Svelte store and reference the Svelte store value.

Now, to implement this undo/redo store, we know that without the undo/redo feature, the store behaves just like a writable store. So, we are going to implement the undo/redo store based on a writable store, as shown in the following code snippet:

```
function createUndoRedoStore() {
  const store = writable();
  return store;
}
```

In the preceding code snippet, we set the stage for our `createUndoRedoStore()` function. We start by using Svelte's `writable()` function to create a writable store, which will be the base for our undo/redo store.

But as we are setting a new value into the undo/redo store, we need to keep track of the history of store values so that we can undo or redo them.

To do that, we are going to intercept the `set` method of the writable store, like so:

```
function createUndoRedoStore() {
  const store = writable();
  function set(value) {
    store.set(value);
  }
  return {
    subscribe: store.subscribe,
    set: set,
  };
}
```

In the preceding code, I return a new object. While the `subscribe` method is the same as the original writable store's `subscribe` method, the `set` method is now a new function. We still call the writable store's `set` method in the `set` function, so the behavior has not changed much.

But now, when we call the `set` method of the undo/redo store, we are calling the `set` function first, before relaying this to the `set` method of the underlying writable store. This allows us to add additional logic into the `set` function that will be run whenever we are setting a new value to the undo/redo store.

Before we get ahead of ourselves, let's not forget that we also need to add two more methods, `undo` and `redo`, into the undo/redo store. Here's how we do this:

```
function createUndoRedoStore() {
  const store = writable();
  function set(value) { store.set(value); }
  function undo() {}
  function redo() {}
  return {
```

```
        subscribe: store.subscribe,
        set: set,
        undo: undo,
        redo: redo,
    };
}
```

In the preceding code snippet, we add two additional methods, undo and redo, to the object returned by createUndoRedoStore(). We will go ahead and implement these methods in the next steps. And now, we have the basic structure of our undo/redo store.

You can treat the preceding code as a template for creating custom Svelte stores. We use a writable store as a base and return a new object. The returned object is considered a Svelte store because, by having the subscribe and set methods, it adheres to the Svelte store contract. If we want to add logic to the subscribe or set method, we can build a new function based on the original subscribe and set methods from the writable store. In addition to that, we can also add more methods to the returned object.

Implementing the undo/redo logic

Now, to implement the undo/redo logic, we are creating two arrays, undoHistory and redoHistory, to record the history of values that we can replay when we call undo() or redo().

Whenever the set function is called, we will add the value as a new entry to undoHistory so that we can replay it later on when undo() is called. When undo() is called, we will push the latest entry in undoHistory into redoHistory so that we can redo what we've just undone.

Let's go ahead and implement the logic we've just described:

```
function createUndoRedoStore() {
    const store = writable();
    const undoHistory = [];
    const redoHistory = [];
    function set(value) {
        undoHistory.push(value);
        redoHistory.length = 0; // resets redoHistory
        store.set(value);
    }
    function undo() {
        if (undoHistory.length <= 1) return;
        redoHistory.push(undoHistory.pop());
        store.set(undoHistory[undoHistory.length - 1]);
    }
    function redo() {
        if (redoHistory.length === 0) return;
```

```
        const value = redoHistory.pop();
        undoHistory.push(value);
        store.set(value);
    }
    // ...
}
```

In the preceding code snippet, we've implemented the undo and redo function using two arrays: undoHistory and redoHistory. We've also added checks to see if there are any values in these arrays before performing an undo or redo action. This ensures that we don't attempt to undo or redo when there's no history to revert to or advance from. So, you have now learned how to create a custom Svelte store that extends from a writable store and adds new behavior to the original set method, as well as adding new methods to the store.

It's time to have an exercise.

Exercise

Now that we've learned how to create a custom store that provides custom methods to manipulate the underlying store values, let's have an exercise to build another such custom store, a tweened store. A tweened store is a Svelte store that can contain only numeric values. When you set the value of a tweened Svelte store, the tweened Svelte store takes a fixed duration to update its store value to the set value.

For example, let's suppose the tweened Svelte store is set to 0 initially:

```
const store = createTweenedStore(0); // $store = 0
```

Then, you set the value of the store to 10:

```
$store = 10;
```

The store value is not set to 10 directly but increases from 0 to 10 over a configurable fixed duration—say, 1 second.

Now you've learned the behavior of a tweened store, let's implement a tweened Svelte store. You can find the code for the tweened store on GitHub at https://github.com/PacktPublishing/Real-World-Svelte/tree/main/Chapter09/04-exercise-tweened-store.

Now that we've learned how to create a custom store, let's turn our attention to another concept, a higher-order store—a function that takes in a Svelte store as an input and returns a more specialized, custom store based on that input.

Creating a debounced higher-order Svelte store

The two preceding sections that we've seen so far each created a new Svelte store. In this section, we are going to look at how we can create a higher-order store.

The concept of a higher-order store is inspired by a higher-order function, where functions are treated just like any other data. This means that you can pass functions as arguments to other functions or return them as values.

In a similar concept, we are going to create a function that treats stores just like any data, taking a Svelte store as an argument and then returning a Svelte store.

The idea of a higher-order Svelte store is to create a function that enhances an existing Svelte store. A higher-order Svelte store is a function that takes in a Svelte store and returns a new Svelte store, an enhanced version of the input Svelte store.

The example that we are going to use to illustrate this idea will create a debounce higher-order Svelte store.

The debounce function that I am going to create will take in a Svelte store and return a new Svelte store that has its store value debounced based on the input Svelte store value:

```
<script>
  function debounce(store) { ... }
  const store = writable();
  const debouncedStore = debounce(store);
</script>
Store value: {$store}
Debounced store value: {$debouncedStore}
```

In the preceding code snippet, in the fourth line, I demonstrated how to use the debounce function that we're going to implement in this section. This debounce function accepts a Svelte store as an argument and returns an enhanced version of it, which we'll call debouncedStore. To showcase the debounce functionality, the values of both the original store and debouncedStore arguments are displayed side by side.

Before we start implementing the debounce function, let's talk about what debounce is.

Debouncing store value changes

In engineering, debounce is the process of removing unwanted input noises from user input. In web development, debounce is used when there are too many user events, and we want to trigger an event handler or process the event only after the user event settles.

Here's an example of debounce. When implementing an autocomplete search, we wouldn't want to trigger the search for an autocomplete result on every character the user types; rather, we'd only start searching after the user stops typing. This saves resources as the autocomplete result may no longer be usable as soon as the user types the next character.

Applying the concept of debounce to a Svelte store, we are going to create a new debounced Svelte store based on an input Svelte store. When the input Svelte store value updates, the debounced Svelte store only updates after the Svelte store updates settle.

If we are going to create a debounced Svelte store from scratch, we can build it up based on a writable store. I showed you how to create a custom Svelte store from a writable store in the last section, so I hope you know how to do that. Do try it out yourself; when you are done, compare it with my implementation at `https://github.com/PacktPublishing/Real-World-Svelte/tree/main/Chapter09/05-debounce-store`.

But in this section, we are going to create a higher-order store. We already have a Svelte store. It could be a writable store or an undo/redo store. Our debounce function is going to take in the Svelte store and return a debounced version of the Svelte store.

Let's start with the basic structure of a `debounce` higher-order store.

The `debounce` function is going to return a new Svelte store. It is still much easier to build a new Svelte store based on a writable store than to implement it from scratch, create a subscribe function, and maintain an array of subscribers.

Here's the basic outline of the `debounce` function:

```
function debounce(store) {
  const debounced = writable();
  return {
    subscribe: debounced.subscribe,
    set: store.set,
  };
}
```

In the preceding code snippet, the returned Svelte store is going to be based on the writable store, so the `subscribe` method is going to be the writable store's `subscribe` method.

The `set` method is going to be the original store's `set` method, instead of a new `set` function. We are not going to create a separate `set` function where it sets the original store and tries to set out a debounced store with the debounce logic.

We are not going to do like it's done in this snippet:

```
function debounce(store) {
  const debounced = writable();
  function set(value) {
```

```
      store.set(value);
      // some debounce logic and call debounce.set(value);
    }
  return {
    subscribe: debounced.subscribe,
    set: set,
  };
}
```

In the preceding code snippet, we intercepted the `set` method and relayed it to both the original store and the debounced store. We are not going to do that because we want to preserve the original Svelte store logic. When a value is passed to the `set` method, it may undergo transformations, especially if the store is a custom Svelte store. The `value` argument in the `set` method may not be the same as the final store value. So instead, we let the original store handle these potential transformations and subscribe to the original Svelte store to get the final store value. We use the final store value and update the debounced store as the original store value changes, as illustrated in the following code snippet:

```
function debounce(store) {
  const debounced = writable();
  store.subscribe(value => {
    // some debounce logic and call debounce.set(value);
  });
  // ...
}
```

In the preceding code snippet, I show how to subscribe to the original Svelte store rather than intercepting its `set` method. This approach allows us to keep the original store's logic intact while still benefiting from its features. It also takes care of situations when the original Svelte store value could change by other methods. An example of this is the `undo()` and `redo()` methods of the undo/redo store. If we only intercepted the value from the `set` function, as in the preceding code snippet, then the debounced Svelte store would not change when the original undo/redo store was being undone or redone.

To implement the debounce logic, we are going to use a timeout to update the debounced Svelte store. If there are new changes to the original Svelte store within the timeout, then we are going to cancel the previous timeout and set a new timeout. If not, then we assume the changes have settled, and we update the `debounced` store.

Here's the updated code snippet with the debounce logic:

```
function debounce(store) {
  const debounced = writable();
  let timeoutId = null;
  store.subscribe(value => {
    if (timeoutId !== null) clearTimeout(timeoutId);
```

```
      timeoutId = setTimeout(() => {
        timeoutId = null;
        debounced.set(value);
      }, 200);
    });
    // ...
  }
```

In the preceding code snippet, we use the `setTimeout` function within the `subscribe` callback to set a timeout for 200 ms. During this time, if the original store's value changes again, the existing timeout will be cleared, and a new one will be set. But if there's a new value within the 200 ms time period, we will update the `debounced` store with the latest value from the original store.

Try out the `debounced` store and see that the store value is now debounced from the changes.

One thing you might notice is that we subscribed to the original Svelte store but haven't unsubscribed from it. Let's address that next.

Subscribing and unsubscribing original store on demand

Before we wrap up, there's one small issue with the `debounced` store that we've implemented so far. We subscribed to the original Svelte store at the creation of the `debounced` Svelte store and we never unsubscribed from it, even though the `debounced` Svelte store may no longer be in use. We should only start subscribing to the original Svelte store when there's already a subscriber to the debounced Svelte store and unsubscribe when there is no longer any subscriber.

We could intercept the `subscribe` method and attempt to unsubscribe from the original Svelte store when the debounced Svelte store is being unsubscribed, like so:

```
function debounce(store) {
  const debounced = writable();
  function subscribe(fn) {
    const debouncedUnsubscribe = debounced.subscribe(fn);
    const unsubscribe = store.subscribe(...);
    return () => {
      debouncedUnsubscribe();
      unsubscribe();
    };
  }
  // ...
  return {
    subscribe: subscribe,
    set: store.set,
  };
}
```

In the updated code snippet, the `subscribe` method now subscribes to both the `debounced` store and the original Svelte store. In the `return` function, which is used to unsubscribe from the `debounced` store, we also make sure to unsubscribe from the original Svelte store.

However, this is not quite right. Doing it this way means that we subscribe to the original store every time we subscribe to the debounced store and unsubscribe from the original store every time we unsubscribe from the debounced store.

We should aim to subscribe to the original store just once, regardless of how many subscribers there are. Similarly, we should unsubscribe from it only when there are no subscribers left. Does this sound familiar?

We ran into a similar conundrum in the previous section when we were trying to implement a click-counter Svelte store. We tried to maintain a list of subscribers before we found out that Svelte provides a built-in `writable()` function that neatly takes care of that for us.

So, is there a built-in function that allows us to only subscribe to another store once a store is being subscribed, and only unsubscribe from that store once there are no more subscribers in a store?

Yes—this is where `derived()` comes into play.

Deriving a new Svelte store with the derived() function

`derived()` is a built-in function from Svelte that takes in one or multiple Svelte stores and returns a new Svelte store whose store value is based on the input Svelte stores.

For example, you can use `derived()` to define a Svelte store whose store value is always double that of another Svelte store, as seen in the following code snippet:

```
import { writable, derived } from 'svelte/store';
const store = writable(1);
const double = derived(store, value => value * 2);
```

Or, this could be a Svelte store whose store value is the sum of two Svelte stores, as shown here:

```
const store1 = writable(1);
const store2 = writable(2);
const sum = derived(
  [store1, store2],
  ([$store1, $store2]) => $store1 + $store2
);
```

> **Note**
>
> You may notice that we are using a $-prefixed variable in the callback function of the `derived()` function; for example, `$store1` and `$store2`. However, it does not work the same way as the $-prefixed variable at the top level of the script, where it auto-subscribes to the store and is referenced as the store value.
>
> In this case, it is merely a convention that some people use to denote that the variable is used to reference the value of a store. It is the same as any other variable name and nothing more.

When using `derived()`, Svelte only subscribes to the input Svelte stores—for example, `store1` and `store2`—only when the returned Svelte store—for example, `sum`—is being subscribed to, and will unsubscribe from the input Svelte stores when there are no more subscribers to the returned Svelte store.

Before we rewrite our `debounce` higher-order store using `derived()`, let's dive a little bit more into the `derived()` function first.

The `derived()` function provides two approaches to determine the store value of the returned Svelte store: synchronous or asynchronous.

The synchronous approach means that as soon as any of the input Svelte store's values change, the store value of the returned Svelte store is determined synchronously. By the same token, the asynchronous approach means it is determined asynchronously, which means the store value can be set later after the input Svelte store's value has changed.

The two examples that I showed at the beginning of this section use the synchronous approach, where the store value of the returned Svelte store is synchronously calculated and set right after the input Svelte store has changed.

The asynchronous approach can be useful when the store value of the returned Svelte store is determined through some asynchronous operations.

To determine whether the derived store is using the synchronous or asynchronous approach, the `derived()` method looks at the function signature of the callback function. If it takes in one parameter, then it is considered a synchronous approach. If it takes in two, then it is an asynchronous approach. To get a better idea, check out the following code snippet:

```
derived(store, ($store) => ...) // synchronous
derived(store, ($store, set) => ...) // asynchronous
```

In both cases, the callback function will be called every time any of the input Svelte store values change.

If the derived store uses the synchronous approach, the returned value of the callback function is used as the new store value of the returned Svelte store.

If the derived store uses the asynchronous approach, then the second parameter of the callback function is a `set` function. The `set` function can be used to set the value of the returned store at any time. The returned value of the callback function, however, will be treated as a cleanup function that will be called right before the callback function is called again.

Now that we are more familiar with the `derived()` function, let's rewrite our `debounce` higher-order store using `derived()`.

Using the derived method

Here is the updated code for our `debounced` store rewritten using the `derived()` method:

```
function debounce(store) {
  const debounced = derived(store, (value, set) => {
    let timeoutId = setTimeout(() => {
      timeoutId = null;
      set(value);
    }, 200);
    return () => {
      if (timeoutId !== null) clearTimeout(timeoutId);
    };
  });
  return {
    subscribe: debounced.subscribe,
    set: store.set,
  };
}
```

Instead of creating a new `debounced` store using `writable()`, we derived it from the original store using the `derived()` method. We shifted the `setTimeout` function into the `derived()` method callback. When there's a new value from the original Svelte store, we will clear the timeout and set a new timeout.

The `derived()` function will subscribe to the original Svelte store once only when the `debounced` store is being subscribed to and unsubscribe from the original Svelte store when there are no more subscribers for the `debounced` store.

Since we are only going to update the `debounced` store asynchronously after a timeout, we pass a callback function with two parameters into the `derived()` function. We call the `set` function to set the value of the `debounced` store after the timeout. If the value of the original Svelte store changes before the timeout, then the returned function of the callback function will be called first before the callback function is called again with the updated store value of the original Svelte store. In the returned function, we clear the timeout since we no longer need it anymore.

One last thing before we conclude—sometimes, the original Svelte store may contain additional methods, such as the undo() and redo() methods in the case of an undo/redo store. These methods should also be defined in the debounced store returned by our higher-order function. This ensures that the enhanced store maintains all the same methods and behaviors as the input store while adding the debouncing feature. You can see an illustration of this in the following code snippet:

```
const value = createUndoRedoStore();
const debouncedValue = debounce(value);
$debouncedValue = 123;
$debouncedValue = 456;
debouncedValue.undo(); // $debouncedValue reverts to 123
```

To return all the methods from the original Svelte store, we use the spread operator (. . .) to spread all the methods from the original Svelte store:

```
function debounce(store) {
  const debounced = derived(...);
  return {
    ...store,
    subscribe: debounced.subscribe,
  };
}
```

In this case, we do not even need to have set: store.set since the set method will be spread into the returned Svelte store too!

That's it! In this section, you've learned another trick—creating a higher-order store, a function that takes in an existing Svelte store and returns a new Svelte store enhanced with new behavior. Instead of building a custom Svelte store with all the logic in it, we can now create smaller well-encapsulated higher-order stores and put them into a custom Svelte store that you need.

Exercise

Now, it's time for an exercise.

The undo/redo store in the previous section is created as a custom Svelte store. Can you create an undo/redo higher-order store that turns any Svelte store into an undo/redo store with two additional methods, undo() and redo()?

Here's an example of how the undo/redo higher-order store would be used:

```
import { writable } from 'svelte/store';
const originalStore = writable(100);
const undoRedoStore = undoRedo(originalStore);
$undoRedoStore = 42;
```

```
undoRedoStore.undo(); // store value now goes back to 5
```

The preceding code snippet shows how we use the undo/redo higher-order store, undoRedo. The undoRedo function takes in a store, named originalStore, and returns a new store based on originalStore that has the undo/redo capability. For example, if we set a new value and then call the undo method, the store value will revert to its original state, which is 5 in this case.

You can find the solution for this exercise on GitHub here:

https://github.com/PacktPublishing/Real-World-Svelte/tree/main/Chapter09/07-exercise-undo-redo-higher-order-store

In this section, we've explored the process of creating a debounce higher-order Svelte store using the derived() method. I look forward to you applying this knowledge in real-world scenarios.

Summary

In this chapter, we looked at three different examples and learned three different techniques with a Svelte store.

We explored how to turn any user events into a data source for a Svelte store, learned how to create a Svelte store from scratch, and also learned how to use the built-in readable() function to make the process much simpler.

After that, we explored making a custom Svelte store with additional methods, building a new Svelte store based on the built-in writable store.

Lastly, we learned to create a higher-order store, a function that takes in a Svelte store and returns an enhanced version of the input store. In the example, we see how we can turn any Svelte store into a debounced version of itself.

By understanding these techniques, you're now equipped to manage state in Svelte more effectively to craft more scalable and maintainable applications.

In the next chapter, we will look at state management in Svelte—namely, how to do state management with Svelte stores.

10

State Management with Svelte Stores

Every user interface control has a state. A checkbox has a checked-unchecked state. A textbox's state is its current input value. A table's state is the data displayed and the columns currently being sorted. Sometimes when you have multiple user interface controls present across the screen at the same time, you need to synchronize the state across them—this is where state management comes in.

In this chapter, we are going to discuss managing states in Svelte using Svelte stores. We will start with why we should use Svelte stores, and then discuss tips that will help you when using Svelte stores for state management.

Next, we will go into the topic of using state management libraries. We will talk about why and how to use them. With that, we will be going through a few examples of integrating third-party state management libraries into Svelte through Svelte stores.

This chapter includes sections on the following topics:

- Managing states with Svelte stores
- Using state management libraries with Svelte

Technical requirements

The code in this chapter can be found on GitHub: `https://github.com/PacktPublishing/Real-World-Svelte/tree/main/Chapter10`.

Managing states with Svelte stores

When building an interactive user interface, the first thing we consider is determining the necessary states to represent the various components and interactions.

For example, in the following snippet, I have a login form that has a few components, including two inputs, one checkbox, and one button:

```
<Input name="username" />
<Input name="password" />
<Checkbox label="Show Password" />
<Button>Submit</Button>
```

Each of the Svelte components has multiple states, as outlined here:

- The `<Input />` component has an input value state and an error state set during validation
- The `<Checkbox />` component has a checked/unchecked state, checked to reveal the password in the input
- The password `<Input />` component has an additional state to reveal/hide the password
- The `<Button />` component has an enabled/disabled state, disabled when the form is incomplete

Each of these states can be represented by a variable. The variables themselves can be interrelated.

Let us examine how these variables can be related to each other. For example, when the checkbox is checked, the password input needs to reveal the password. When the name and password inputs are filled, the button needs to turn into an enabled state. When the button is pressed, validation is performed, and the inputs' error state is updated accordingly.

The art of managing multiple states across components to form a cohesive experience is called state management.

It would be clearer and easier to group all these states together and manage them as one, rather than separate individual states. In the following snippet, I group all of the aforementioned variables into one variable object:

```
const state = {
  nameValue: '',
  nameError: null,
  passwordValue: '',
  passwordError: null,
  revealPassword: false,
  submitDisabled: true,
}
```

Here, you can see the related states in one place, making it easier to see and tell if something is wrong.

To illustrate this, let's say the `nameValue` and `submitDisabled` variables are kept as two separate variables in two separate components; in the `Input` component, we have the `nameValue` variable:

```
<!-- Input.svelte -->
<script>
  export let nameValue = '';
</script>
<input bind:value={nameValue} />
```

And in the `Button` component, we have the `submitDisabled` variable:

```
<!-- Button.svelte -->
<script>
  export let submitDisabled = false;
</script>
<button disabled={submitDisabled}>Submit</button>
```

From the code, you can see that it is not straightforward to tell whether the `nameValue` and `submitDisabled` variables are related. If one of the states is not updated as expected, you don't have one convenient place to inspect both states at once; you will have to inspect them in each separate component.

For example, if the `submitDisabled` state in the `<Button />` component did not change to `false` to enable the button after typing in the name input, you would need to find and inspect the `nameValue` variable in a separate component (the `<Input />` component).

If, instead, the states are grouped into a `state` object, then you can inspect the `state` object and check the `nameValue` and the `submitDisabled` properties and see if they are set correctly. Have a look at the following example:

```
const state = {
  nameValue: '',
  submitDisabled: true,
};
```

Now that we've established that we should group multiple related states into one state object, the next question is this: If we could group states using a simple JavaScript object, why would it be necessary to group states using a Svelte store?

Well, the truth is, it is not always necessary. In some cases, using a simple JavaScript object to group states can work just as effectively. However, a Svelte store offers additional benefits and functionality that can enhance your state management experience.

As we explored in *Chapter 8*, a Svelte store is useful as it can be passed around components and have its updates propagate across components. Then, in *Chapter 9*, we saw how useful a Svelte store is, being able to encapsulate logic within the Svelte store, as well as being able to define data logic right next to the data itself.

So, for the sake of the chapter, we are going to proceed with grouping multiple related states into a state object using a Svelte store. Here's a short snippet of code of how it would look:

```
<script>
  import { writable } from 'svelte/store';
  const state = writable({
    nameValue: '',
    nameError: null,
    passwordValue: '',
    passwordError: null,
    revealPassword: false,
    submitDisabled: true,
  });
</script>
```

Here, we use a `writable()` store for creating the state object because we will be modifying the state object.

The state object can be defined either inside or outside a Svelte component. Since our state object is a Svelte store, we can import the state object into any component, and any updates to the state object will be propagated across all Svelte components that use the state object—so, it doesn't matter in which file we define the state object in.

If we define our state object in a Svelte component, then we can pass our state object to the component's child component through props. Here's an example of doing so:

```
<script>
  const state = writable({ name: 'Svelte' });
</script>
<Input {state} />
```

On the other hand, if we define our state object in a JavaScript module, then we can import our state object into any Svelte components that will be using the state object. The following is a snippet of importing a Svelte store state object into a Svelte component:

```
<script>
  // import state object defined in './state.js'
  import { state } from './state.js';
</script>
```

In *Chapter 8*, we learned how to read, subscribe to, and update a Svelte store. Whether the data stored inside a Svelte store is a state object or anything else, there is no difference in terms of the operations to read, subscribe, and update the Svelte store state object like any other Svelte store.

But as the state is used more frequently in a growing project, you will have more state values inside a `state` store object. As the `state` store gets larger and more complex, your application may get slower, and you may feel the need to optimize/improve it. Therefore, I am dedicating the following subsections to sharing my tips and opinions on state management with a Svelte store.

Of course, you shouldn't apply all these methods blindly. As said by Donald Knuth, the famous computer scientist, *"Premature optimization is the root of all evil"*—you should measure and evaluate whether any of the following tips apply. As I go through the tips, I will explain what they are and why and when are they useful.

Tip 1 – simplify complex state updates with unidirectional data flow

When your application becomes more complex, with multiple components and multiple places to update your state, managing state updates becomes even more challenging.

How would you know when managing state updates becomes unmanageable? You may run into situations such as this:

- Your application state changes, and you find it hard to track down why the state changed

- You change a certain state value, but unknowingly, this causes other seemingly unrelated state values to update as well, and you have a hard time working out why

These are signs that the state updates have grown complex and become difficult to manage. In such situations, having unidirectional data flow can help simplify state management.

With unidirectional data flow, state updates are managed in a single direction, and the flow of data can be easily traced and debugged.

There are state management libraries such as Redux, MobX, and XState that help to enforce a single data flow and enable you to reason with the state changes. You may be curious about how to use these state management libraries with a Svelte store; I will be covering them later in this chapter and will use one of the libraries as an example.

Tip 2 – prefer smaller self-contained state objects over one big state object

In Svelte, when a state object changes, all components that use that state object are updated, even if the specific state value that a component uses did not change. This means that if a state object becomes larger and more complex, with many unrelated state values, updating that state object can trigger unnecessary updates to many components in the application.

Here, I am going to use a product details page of an e-commerce web application as an example. In a typical e-commerce web app, you have a page that shows the details of a product. You will see other information, such as the shopping cart and product reviews, on the same page as well.

If I use one state object for all the information on the page, it may look like this:

```
<script>
  let state = {…}
</script>
<ShoppingCart cart={$state.cart} />
<ProductDetails product={$state.product} />
<ProductRatings ratings={$state.ratings} />
```

In the preceding code, we use the same state object, $state, across three components: ShoppingCart, ProductDetails, and ProductRatings. When any part of the $state state object changes, such as changing $state.cart, all three components will be triggered to update.

This is undesirable—multiple components updating unnecessarily could lead to slower performance and a less responsive user interface.

So, it is recommended to split big state objects into smaller state objects. Using the same example, that would mean splitting the $state state object into three smaller state objects, like so:

```
<script>
  let cartState = {…};
  let productState = {…};
  let ratingState = {…};
</script>
<ShoppingCart cart={$cartState} />
<ProductDetails product={$productState} />
<ProductRatings ratings={$ratingState} />
```

This way, changing the shopping cart's state, $cartState, would not trigger an update on the <ProductDetails /> and <ProductRatings /> components.

So, if you have big state objects and you find components update unnecessarily and the performance of your application is impacted by it, then consider breaking these big state objects down into smaller state objects.

But what if the state object is still big, yet the different values in the state objects are closely related and you are unable to break it apart into smaller state objects? Well, there is still hope, which leads us to our third tip.

Tip 3 – derive a smaller state object from a bigger state object

If state values are related to each other and so you can't break a big state object into smaller state objects, we can create smaller state objects that derive from the big state object. Let me show you some code to explain this clearly.

Let's say that you have a state object, `userInfo`, that has two closely related state values, `$userInfo.personalDetails` and `$userInfo.socials`, as shown here:

```
import { writable } from 'svelte/store';
const userInfo = writable({
  personalDetails: {...},
  socials: {...},
});
```

You may realize that one part of the `userInfo` state object doesn't change as often as the other. But whenever any part of `userInfo` changes, all the components that use either the `$userInfo.personalDetails` or `$userInfo.socials` state values will be updated.

To ensure that components using only `$userInfo.socials` are updated exclusively when `$userInfo.socials` changes, one way would be to break the state object into smaller, more focused state objects, like so:

```
import { writable } from 'svelte/store';
const userPersonalDetails = writable({...});
const userSocials = writable({...});
```

As you can see, you now have two separate state objects, `userPersonalDetails` and `userSocials`.

But this would mean that places where you previously updated the `userInfo` state object would have to change since `userInfo` is now split into two separate state objects.

Here is how you would change the code:

```
// previously
$userInfo = newUserInfo;
// now
$userPersonalDetails = newUserInfo.personalDetails;
$userSocials = newUserInfo.socials;
```

So, the question now is this: Is there an alternative to not having to change this, yet being able to update the components that use `$userInfo.socials` only when `$userInfo.socials` changes?

I believe I've leaked the answer already. The alternative is to derive a new state object. In the following code snippet, I am deriving a new `userSocials` state object from the `userInfo` state object:

```
import { derived } from 'svelte/store';
const userSocials = derived(userInfo, $userInfo => $userInfo.socials);
```

The component that uses `$userSocials` will only update whenever the `userSocial` state changes. The `userSocial` state changes only when the `$userInfo.socials` changes. So, when the component uses `$userSocials` instead of `$userInfo.socials`, it will not update when any other part of the `userInfo` state object changes.

I believe that seeing is believing, and it will be much clearer to see and interact with an example to get this idea forward. So, I've prepared some demo examples at `https://github.com/PacktPublishing/Real-World-Svelte/tree/main/Chapter10/01-user-social`, and you can try them out and see what I mean.

Let's quickly recap the three tips:

- Whenever the state update logic is complex and convoluted, introduce some state management libraries to enforce simpler and unidirectional data flows

- If the state object gets too big, and state changes update more components than needed, break the state object into smaller state objects

- If you can't split a Svelte store state object, consider deriving it into a smaller state object

So, we've gone through my three general tips for managing complex stores in a Svelte application; let's now elaborate more on my first tip on how to use state management libraries with Svelte.

Using state management libraries with Svelte

If you google *State management library for frontend development*, at the time of writing, you will get list after list of libraries, such as Redux, XState, MobX, Valtio, Zustand, and many more.

These libraries have their own take on how states should be managed, each with different design considerations and design constraints. For the longevity of the content of this book, we are not going to compare and analyze each of them since these libraries will change and evolve over time and potentially be replaced by newer alternatives.

It is worth noting that some of the state management libraries are written for a specific web framework. For example, at the time of writing, the Jōtai library (`https://jotai.org/`) is written specifically for React, which means you can only use Jōtai if you write your web application in React.

On the other hand, there are framework-agnostic state management libraries. An example is XState (`https://xstate.js.org/`), which can be used by any web framework as the XState team has created packages such as `@xstate/svelte` to work with Svelte, `@xstate/react` for the React framework, `@xstate/vue` for Vue, and many more.

While the `@xstate/svelte` package is tailored for seamless integration of XState in Svelte, not all state management libraries offer this level of compatibility. Nevertheless, there are several other state management libraries that you can use in Svelte, and integrating them is straightforward. In fact, I will provide some examples to showcase how simple it is to integrate these libraries in Svelte and utilize Svelte's first-class capabilities for working with stores.

One such state management library that works seamlessly with Svelte is Valtio (`https://github.com/pmndrs/valtio`), a minimalist library that turns objects into self-aware proxy states. We are going to explore how we can use Valtio in Svelte, by turning Valtio's proxy state into a Svelte store and using the Svelte store's `$`-prefixed syntax to subscribe to the proxy state changes and access the proxy state value.

Example – using Valtio as a Svelte store

Before we start talking about how to use Valtio in Svelte, let's look at how to use Valtio on its own.

Using Valtio

Valtio turns the object you pass to it into a self-aware proxy state. In the following code snippet, we create a Valtio state named `state` through the `proxy()` method:

```
import { proxy } from 'valtio/vanilla';
const state = proxy({ count: 0, text: 'hello' });
```

To update the proxy state, you can make changes to it the same way you would to a normal JavaScript object. For example, we can increment the value of `state.count` by mutating the value directly, as follows:

```
setInterval(() => {
  state.count++;
}, 1000);
```

To be notified of modifications in the proxy state, we can use Valtio's `subscribe` method, as illustrated here:

```
import { subscribe } from 'valtio';
const unsubscribe = subscribe(state, () => {
  console.log('state object changed');
});
```

In this case, every time we modify the state, the callback function passed into the `subscribe` method will be called, and we will see a new log in the console, printing `'state object changed'`.

Valtio also allows you to subscribe only to a portion of a state. For example, in the following snippet, we subscribe only to the changes made to state.count:

```
const unsubscribe = subscribe(state.count, () => {
   console.log('state count changed');
});
```

Since in this case, we are subscribing only to the changes made to state.count, then modifying state.text would not see a 'state count changed' log added to the console as the change to state.text is not subscribed.

The Valtio proxy state is meant for tracking update changes. To read the latest value of the proxy state, we should use the snapshot() method to create a snapshot object, as follows:

```
import { subscribe, snapshot } from 'valtio';
const unsubscribe = subscribe(state, () => {
   const obj = snapshot(state);
});
```

Using Valtio as a Svelte store

Now that we've learned about basic Valtio operations and concepts, let's create a simple counter application to see how we can use Valtio in Svelte. Firstly, we create a proxy state for our counter application:

```
// filename: data.js
import { proxy } from 'valtio';
export const state = proxy({ count1: 0, count2: 0 });
```

Here, I am creating two counters, count1 and count2, which will later allow us to experiment with subscribing to a specific portion of the proxy state. This way, we can observe whether our application updates only when one of the counters changes.

Also, we are creating the proxy state in a separate file, data.js, rather than declaring it inside a Svelte component; this way, we can import the state separately in each Svelte component later on.

In addition, let's create two functions to increment the counters:

```
export function increment1() {
   state.count1 ++;
}
export function increment2() {
   state.count2 ++;
}
```

Now, let's import the proxy state into our Svelte component; I have created two buttons to increment each counter separately:

```
<script>
    import { state, increment1, increment2 } from './data.js';
</script>
Count #1: {state.count1}
Count #2: {state.count2}
<button on:click={increment1}>Increment 1</button>
<button on:click={increment2}>Increment 2</button>
```

If you try clicking on the buttons, you'll realize that they are not working as expected— the counters are not incrementing.

However, if you add the following code to data.js and click on the button, the console will print out the current value of the counters, indicating that the counters are incrementing successfully:

```
import { subscribe } from 'valtio';
subscribe(state, () => {
    console.log(state);
});
```

As you can see, the counters are updating as expected. The issue, therefore, does not lie in the inability to increment the counters, but rather in the failure to display the changes on the screen. It is possible that Svelte is not recognizing the changes to the counters, and therefore, it is not updating the elements to show the latest value of the counters.

So, what can we do to make Svelte aware of the changes to Valtio's proxy state?

One approach would be to use a Svelte store, as it provides a mechanism for Svelte components to react to changes in data. We can turn Valtio's proxy state into a Svelte store. Then, by subscribing to the store, Svelte will be aware of the changes to the state and will update the elements accordingly.

This approach of converting states from other state management libraries into a Svelte store in order to take advantage of Svelte's built-in update mechanism is very common. It allows developers to use their preferred state management solution while still taking advantage of Svelte's reactive capabilities.

So, let's see how we can turn Valtio's proxy state into a Svelte store. To start off, I am creating a function called valtioStateToSvelteStore:

```
function valtioStateToSvelteStore(proxyState) {
    return {};
}
```

Before creating the Svelte store from the Valtio proxy state, let's have a quick recap on what the Svelte store contract is. The Svelte store contract dictates that a Svelte store should have a `subscribe` method and an optional `set` method. The `subscribe` method takes a callback function as its only parameter, which will be called whenever the store's value changes, and returns an `unsubscribe` function to stop further notifications.

So, let's define the `subscribe` method in the returned object of the `valtioStateToSvelteStore` function, like so:

```
function valtioStateToSvelteStore(proxyState) {
  return {
    subscribe(fn) {
    },
  };
}
```

The initial value of the Svelte store can be defined by calling the callback function synchronously with the value of the proxy state:

```
function valtioStateToSvelteStore(proxyState) {
  return {
    subscribe(fn) {
      fn(snapshot(proxyState));
    },
  };
}
```

Our next step is to subscribe to changes in the Valtio proxy state:

```
function valtioStateToSvelteStore(proxyState) {
  return {
    subscribe(fn) {
      fn(snapshot(proxyState));
      return subscribe(proxyState, () => {
        fn(snapshot(proxyState));
      });
    },
  };
}
```

Based on the Svelte store contract, within the `subscribe` method, we need to return a function to unsubscribe the callback function from the Svelte store. In our code, the reason we return the return value of the `subscribe` function from Valtio in our `subscribe` method is that the return value of Valtio's `subscribe` function is a function to unsubscribe from the proxy state.

A function to unsubscribe from changes is just what we need. Isn't this convenient?

It's no coincidence that most state management libraries provide methods for subscribing to state changes and unsubscribing from them, just like what we need to define a Svelte store. This is because both Svelte stores and state management libraries are designed based on the Observer pattern we discussed in *Chapter 8*. In summary, to turn a state management library's state into a Svelte store, we need to understand how the library works and how its APIs translate into the Svelte store contract.

Now that we have a function to transform a Valtio's proxy state into a Svelte store, let's try to use it by running the following code:

```
<script>
  import { state, increment1, increment2, valtioStateToSvelteStore }
from './data.js';
  const store = valtioStateToSvelteStore(state);
</script>
Count #1: {$store.count1}
Count #2: {$store.count2}
```

Clicking on any button in the component, you will see that the counter works perfectly fine now.

So, this is how we turn a Valtio proxy state into a Svelte store.

The next thing I would like to explore is creating a Svelte store that subscribes only to partial updates of the Valtio proxy state. By selecting only a specific portion of the state to monitor, we can ensure that the Svelte store updates only when a particular part of the state changes.

Before we do that, let's add a few more lines to show you what I mean:

```
<script>
  // ...
  $: console.log('count1: ', $store.count1);
  $: console.log('count2: ', $store.count2);
</script>
```

As you click on either of the increment buttons, you will notice that both reactive statements are called, indicating that $store is updated whenever either count1 or count2 is updated.

As discussed in the third tip earlier in the chapter, if state changes cause unnecessary code to run, we can derive a smaller state from the original state to only subscribe to partial updates. So, let's do that:

```
<script>
  import { state, increment1, increment2, valtioStateToSvelteStore }
from './data.js';
  const count1 = valtioStateToSvelteStore(state.count1);
  const count2 = valtioStateToSvelteStore(state.count2);
  $: console.log('count1: ', $count1);
```

```
    $: console.log('count2: ', $count2);
</script>
```

Here, instead of turning `state` into a Svelte store, we are turning `state.count1` into a Svelte store. This allows us to create separate Svelte stores that only subscribe to a portion of the proxy state.

This should work, but unfortunately, it doesn't. The reason for this has nothing to do with our code but with the data structure of our state. `state.count1` is a primitive value, which Valtio is unable to subscribe to.

To work around this, I'm going to change the data type of `state.count1` from a primitive value to an object:

```
export const state = proxy({
  count1: { value: 0 },
  count2: { value: 0 },
});
export function increment1() {
  state.count1.value ++;
}
```

In the preceding code snippet, we changed `state.count1` to an object with a property called `value`. We still keep the code of deriving the `count1` Svelte store from the `state.count1` proxy state. So, now, the derived Svelte store of `count1` would be an object, and to get the value of the count, we will be referring to `$count1.value` instead of `$count1`:

```
    $: console.log('count1: ', $count1.value);
```

Now, when you click on the button labeled **Increment 1**, you will only see logs printed for `count1`. Conversely, when you click on the other button, labeled **Increment 2**, you will see new logs printed only for `count2`. The reactive statement will only run when the respective counter is incremented. That's because our `count1` and `count2` stores only update when a specific part of the Valtio proxy state changes.

So, let's conclude what we've done so far.

We explored the integration of Valtio in Svelte by converting the Valtio proxy state into a Svelte store. Step by step, we implemented the Svelte store contract by leveraging Valtio's built-in methods for subscribing and unsubscribing. Toward the end, we explored how to subscribe to partial updates of the proxy state, minimizing unnecessary reactivity.

I believe you are eager to try it out yourself by now, so let's use the next state management library as an exercise.

Exercise – transforming an XState state machine into a Svelte store

XState (`https://xstate.js.org/`) is a JavaScript library for managing states using state machines. In this exercise, you are going to transform an XState state machine into a Svelte store.

XState provides a package named `@xstate/svelte` that includes utilities specifically designed for integrating XState in Svelte. Although this package can be a source of inspiration for your task, the use of `@xstate/svelte` is, however, not permitted for this exercise. The goal here is to challenge you to implement the function to transform an XState state machine into a Svelte store without the aid of pre-existing integration utilities.

To get started with this exercise, follow these steps:

1. **Understand XState**: If you're not already familiar with XState, spend some time reading its documentation and experimenting with its features. Understand how state machines work and how XState implements them.

2. **Create a state machine**: Using XState, create a state machine that you'd like to convert into a Svelte store. This could be a simple machine with a few states and transitions, or something more complex if you're comfortable with it.

3. **Transform the state machine into a Svelte store**: Now comes the key part of the exercise. You'll need to write a function that converts your XState state machine into a Svelte store. This involves subscribing to state changes in the machine and forwarding them to the Svelte store, as well as mapping actions from the store back to transitions in the state machine.

4. **Test your implementation**: After you've completed your conversion, ensure you thoroughly test it. Change states in your store and observe whether the same changes are reflected in your state machine and vice versa.

If you're stuck, take a step back and refer to the documentation of XState and this chapter, or the source code of `@xstate/svelte`.

Summary

In this chapter, we learned about how we can manage our application states with Svelte.

At the beginning of the chapter, we discussed some of the tips for managing states in Svelte through a Svelte store. These tips will be useful to you as your Svelte application grows larger and more complex.

One of the tips that we discussed is using state management libraries to manage data changes and data flows. That's why we spent the second half of the chapter exploring how we can use state management libraries in Svelte, by transforming the state management libraries' state into Svelte stores.

In the next chapter, we are going to explore how we can use a combination of both a Svelte context and a Svelte store to create renderless components—logical components that do not render any content.

11

Renderless Components

A renderless component is an advanced concept in Svelte that allows developers to create reusable components without rendering any HTML elements within the component itself.

This technique is particularly useful when leveraging Svelte to render on a canvas or in a 3D context, where the rendering of an HTML template by Svelte is not required. Instead, the canvas and **Web Graphics Library** (**WebGL**) offer an imperative API to produce graphics on the canvas. With the renderless component technique, it becomes possible to design components that enable users to describe the canvas declaratively, allowing the component to translate it into imperative instructions.

Another use case for a renderless component is to create components that only manage states and behaviors, leaving the parent component control over what should actually be rendered. This will come in handy when developing a component library and you want to make it easy for users to customize how your component looks and lets you have control over the state and behaviors.

In this chapter, we will utilize Svelte context to create our renderless component. If you are new to Svelte context, please refer to *Chapter 8*, where we explain its meaning.

Initially, we will explore the concept of renderless components and subsequently build techniques to create them. As we develop our renderless component, we will share a few examples of renderless components.

At the end of the chapter, you should possess the ability to employ the renderless component technique to convert imperative APIs into declarative components.

The topics discussed in this chapter are as follows:

- What are renderless components?
- Building renderless components with Svelte context

Technical requirements

You can find the code used in this chapter on GitHub: https://github.com/PacktPublishing/Real-World-Svelte/tree/main/Chapter11.

What are renderless components?

A renderless component, as its name implies, is a type of component that does not render any HTML elements of its own.

You might wonder, what's the purpose of a component that doesn't render anything?

Well, despite not rendering HTML, there are still several useful things that a component can do, including the following:

- **Accepting props, processing their values, and triggering side effects as their values change**: Even though the prop values are not used directly in the template, they are still reactive. You can write reactive statements with props in the component and have them run whenever the prop values change. You can see this in the following example code snippet:

```
<script>
  export let title;
  export let description;
  $: document.title = `${title} - ${description}`;
</script>
```

Even though the `title` and `description` props are not used in the template, both `title` and `description` are used in a reactive statement. Whenever the `title` or `description` props change, the reactive statement in line 4 will rerun and update the title of the document.

Setting the document title, updating the cookie value, and modifying context are good examples of side effects.

- **Exhibiting component lifecycles, and performing actions as the component mounts and gets destroyed**: The component lifecycles, such as `onMount` and `onDestroy`, still run even if no elements are mounted and destroyed in the component.

- **Providing data to child elements via context setup or by passing data through the** `<slot>` **element**: Even though a renderless component does not render any HTML elements, it can still render a `<slot>` element that allows the user of the component to pass in child elements or components.

For example, in the following `Parent` component, we render a `default` slot:

```
<!-- Parent.svelte -->
<slot />
```

Then, the user of the `Parent` component can pass in child elements or components under the `Parent` component:

```
<script>
  import Parent from './Parent.svelte';
</script>
<Parent>
```

```
    <Child /> <!-- example of child components -->
    <div /> <!-- example of child elements -->
  </Parent>
```

The `Parent` component can pass data to the child components or elements through two avenues – setting context data and setting slot props.

You can read more about setting slot props in *Chapter 4*.

- **Communicating with the parent component using context**: Similar to any other component, a renderless component can use `getContext()` to retrieve the context value set by its parent component. Depending on the type of context value provided by the parent, we can use the context value to communicate with the parent or inform it about the existence of the child component.

  In the *Writing declarative canvas components* section later in the chapter, you will see an example of such a technique.

Throughout the upcoming sections, we will challenge ourselves by creating components that perform only the operations listed in the preceding list, without rendering any HTML elements.

In this chapter, we will explore two use cases for renderless components, which are turning reusable renderless components and declarative descriptions into imperative instructions. Let's take an in-depth look at them.

Exploring reusable renderless components

The first use case for renderless components involves creating components that solely focus on the logic of the component. These components are not your typical ones, such as buttons or text inputs. Instead, think of components with slightly complex logic, such as carousels, tabs, or drop-down menus. Although the logic of a carousel component is relatively standard, its appearance can vary significantly based on where and how it is used.

So, how can we create a reusable carousel component that can look different based on where it is used?

One solution is to create a carousel component that only contains the carousel logic, without any specific styling or HTML structure. Then, the consumer of the component can decide how the carousel should look by passing in their own styling and HTML structure. This allows for greater flexibility and customization, making the component more versatile and reusable in different contexts.

For example, the carousel component could accept props such as `items`, which would determine the list of items in the carousel. The carousel component could render a `slot` element that takes in slot props such as `currentIndex` and `setIndex`, which would be the index of the currently active item and the function to set the index. This allows the carousel component to manage the carousel item cycling logic, while leaving the consumer of the carousel component to determine the actual carousel styling and structure.

By separating the carousel logic from the specific styling and structure, we can create a more modular and reusable component that can be used in various contexts, without having to rewrite the same logic over and over again. This is the power of renderless components – they allow us to create components that focus solely on their core functionality, without being tied to any specific rendering or styling requirements.

Of course, before we proceed, it's essential to clarify when not to use a renderless component to create a carousel. If you require a fully functional carousel component, including the design and style, a renderless component may not be suitable for your needs, as its main purpose is to handle the logic and behavior of the carousel without dictating its appearance.

Ultimately, the decision to create a renderless component for a carousel depends on your specific needs and goals. Consider your project requirements and design preferences before deciding on the best approach.

In the next section, I will show you step by step how we can build a renderless carousel component.

Example – building a renderless carousel component

A carousel component is a UI component that displays a set of items in a loop. It allows users to view a collection of items in a slideshow-like format. A carousel component is usually found on websites such as e-commerce platforms, news portals, and social media platforms.

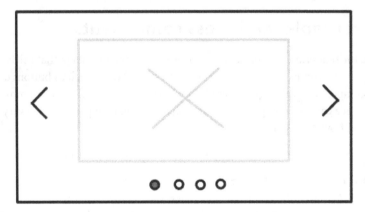

Figure 11.1: An example of a carousel component

We will create a renderless carousel component that accepts a list of items through props named `items`. The carousel component will render a `slot` element to allow customization of its appearance.

The `slot` element will take in a few slot props:

- `currentIndex`: This represents the index of the currently displayed item in the carousel.
- `currentItem`: This represents the currently displayed item in the carousel.

- `setCurrentIndex`: This is a function that can be used to update the current index of the carousel. It can be used to implement custom navigation controls.

- `next` and `prev`: These `slot` props are functions that can be used to navigate to the next or previous item in the carousel. They can be used to implement custom navigation controls or respond to user input, such as clicks or swipes.

These `slot` props allow the consumer to decide how to use them to build their own carousel UI.

To determine the appropriate `slot` props for the carousel component, we consider the essential states and functions required for users to build their own carousel UI. In this case, the key states are `currentIndex` and `currentItem`, while the necessary functions to interact with the carousel UI include `setCurrentIndex`, `next`, and `prev`, which are helpful to implement custom navigation controls.

An example of a carousel UI is one that displays the current item and has buttons to navigate forward and backward through the carousel:

```
<Carousel {items} let:currentItem let:next let:prev>
  <button on:click={prev}>{'<'}</button>
  <img src={currentItem} />
  <button on:click={next}>{'>'}</button>
</Carousel>
```

In the preceding code snippet, we use the `currentItem`, `next`, and `prev` slot props to build a simple carousel UI. We decide how to use the `slot` props and control the structure and styling of the HTML elements.

Another example of a carousel UI is displaying a list of item numbers at the bottom of it, enabling the user to quickly jump to a selected item by clicking on its number:

```
<Carousel {items} let:currentItem let:setCurrentIndex>
  <img src={currentItem} />
  {#each items as _, index}
    <button on:click={() => setCurrentIndex(index)}>
      {index}
    </button>
  {/each}
</Carousel>
```

In the preceding code, I used Svelte's `{#each}` block to create a list of buttons, labeled with a different index number. Each of the buttons has a click event listener that sets the current index of the carousel to the index number of the button. When you click on the button, the carousel will jump to the item at the index that is specified by the button.

The second carousel UI is different from the first carousel UI, and you can create and style a totally different carousel UI. You can see that the appearance of the carousel UI is entirely up to the user. The renderless carousel component focuses on the carousel logic and allows the user to decide on the UI structure and styling.

Without further ado, let's explore how to write the carousel component.

Writing a renderless carousel component

In the previous section, we decided on the props of our `Carousel` component, `items`, and decided that it should have a default `<slot>`.

Based on this information, let's create the structure of our `Carousel` component:

```
<script>
  export let items;
</script>
<slot>
```

In the preceding code snippet, the `<slot>` element will be the only element we will have in our `Carousel` component. This `<slot>` element is needed; otherwise, the child elements inside the `<Carousel>` component, indicated in the following code snippet, will be ignored and discarded if there's no `<slot>` element in the `Carousel` component:

```
<Carousel>
  <!-- content over here will be ignored if the Carousel don't have a
<slot> element -->
</Carousel>
```

In the `<slot>` element, we define the following `slot` props – `currentIndex`, `currentItem`, `setCurrentIndex`, `prev`, and `next`:

```
<slot {currentIndex} {currentItem} {setCurrentIndex} {prev} {next} />
```

However, these `slot` props are not defined in our `Carousel` component yet, so let's define them.

We initialize `currentIndex` to 0 at the start of the component:

```
let currentIndex = 0;
```

`setCurrentIndex` is used to update `currentIndex` to the value being passed in:

```
const setCurrentIndex = (value) => { currentIndex = value; };
```

currentItem will be the item in the items array at the index position of currentIndex. Here, I'll use the reactive statements so that we will have a new currentItem slot prop whenever the items array or currentIndex changes:

```
$: currentItem = items[currentIndex];
```

Finally, the prev and next functions will be used to set currentIndex, based on its current value:

```
const prev = () => setCurrentIndex((currentIndex - 1 + items.length) %
items.length);
const next = () => setCurrentIndex((currentIndex + 1) % items.length);
```

In the preceding snippet, I used % items.length so that the index is always within the bounds of the length of the items array. This way, we ensure that the carousel can loop back to the beginning of the items array after reaching the end, creating a seamless looping effect for the user.

And that's it. If you add all the preceding code snippets to the Carousel component, you'll have a working renderless component. The full code is available on GitHub at https://github.com/PacktPublishing/Real-World-Svelte/tree/main/Chapter11/01-carousel as well.

Creating a renderless component is not hard; it doesn't take us much time to create a renderless Carousel component. The key here is to figure out the props for our renderless component, then figure out the slot props needed, and finally, create a default <slot> element with the slot props.

Before we move on, let's have an exercise to create a reusable renderless component yourself.

Exercise 1 – a renderless autocomplete component

An autocomplete component is an input with an auto-suggest dropdown that shows a list of matching options as a user types in the input. It helps users quickly and easily find and select an option from a large set of choices. autocomplete components are commonly used in search bars, forms, and other areas where users need to enter data quickly and accurately.

In this exercise, we'll create a renderless autocomplete component.

The autocomplete component will take in only one prop, a search function, which takes in a search value and returns Promise, which resolves to an array of string results.

What about the slot props that our renderless Autocomplete component would provide?

We need three states for our autocomplete component:

- value: To represent the current value in the input box
- searching: A Boolean value to represent whether the autocomplete currently searches for results
- suggestions: An array of autocomplete results returned from the search function

For a user to interact with the `Autocomplete` component, we need two functions:

- `setValue`: To update the value of the input box
- `selectSuggestion`: To select the suggestion and apply it to the input box

So, the preceding three states and two functions will be the `slot` props for our `Autocomplete` component.

Here is an example of how the `Autocomplete` component could be used:

```
<Autocomplete {search} let:value let:setValue let:searching
let:suggestions let:selectSuggestion>
  <input {value} on:input={event => setValue(event.currentTarget.
value)}>
  {#if searching}Searching...{/if}
  {#if suggestions}
    <ul>
      {#each suggestions as suggestion}
        <li on:click={() =>
selectSuggestion(suggestion)}>{suggestion}</li>
      {/each}
    </ul>
  {/if}
</Autocomplete>
```

In the preceding code snippet, we use the `Autocomplete` component to render an autocomplete textbox, with an `<input>` element and an `<ul>` element in the default slot.

The `<input>` element uses the `value` and `setValue` slot props to access and modify `value`, held by the `Autocomplete` component.

The `<ul>` element uses the `suggestions` slot prop to showcase the list of suggestions provided by the `Autocomplete` component and the `selectSuggestion` slot props are used in the `click` event handler of the `<li>` element to select the chosen suggestion and apply it to the textbox.

A sample solution can be found at `https://github.com/PacktPublishing/Real-World-Svelte/tree/main/Chapter11/02-autocomplete`.

Now, let us look at the second use case for a renderless component.

Turning a declarative description into imperative instructions

The second use case for a renderless component involves allowing users to describe their needs declaratively and then translating them into imperative instructions.

A good example of this use case is when working with a canvas or WebGL.

For example, in a canvas, to create a red rectangle with a green border, you would need to use imperative APIs to create and style the rectangle:

```
ctx.fillStyle = 'red';
ctx.strokeStyle = 'green';
ctx.rect(10, 10, 100, 100);
ctx.stroke();
ctx.fill();
```

Step by step, we instruct the canvas context to set `fillStyle` and `strokeStyle` and then draw a rectangle, based on the fill color and stroke color set.

When interacting with the canvas in an imperative manner, the code focuses on how to do things rather than what to do. This can result in code that is difficult to read and maintain, with a lot of low-level details that can make it hard to see the bigger picture.

Conversely, if you write code declaratively, you describe what you want to happen, rather than how it should happen. This makes the code more expressive and easier to read, as well as more flexible and reusable.

Continuing with the example of the red rectangle, we can create a Svelte component that handles drawing the rectangle on the canvas. Instead of manually coding the instructions to draw the rectangle, we can simply describe how we want it to appear on the canvas through the component. The component then takes care of rendering the rectangle on the canvas for us.

Here's an example of code that describes the same rectangle through a Svelte component:

```
<script>
  let x = 10, y = 10, height = 100, width = 100;
</script>
<Canvas>
  <Rectangle
    fill="red" stroke="green"
    {x} {y} {height} {width}
  />
</Canvas>
```

In the preceding code snippet, we see a `Rectangle` component nested within a `Canvas` component. The `Rectangle` component has its fill, stroke, *x* position, *y* position, width, and height specified.

The following diagram illustrates how the `Rectangle` component from the preceding code renders a red square with a green border.

Figure 11.2: A red square with a green border

Even though explicit instructions to draw on the canvas are nowhere to be seen in the code, we can visualize a rectangle being drawn on the canvas based on the `Rectangle` component. This rectangle, with a width and height of 100 px each, is positioned 10 px from the left and 10 px from the top, filled with a red color and a green border.

By creating a renderless component that handles the low-level canvas instructions, we can separate the logic of drawing the rectangle from the specifics of how it should be rendered. This allows for more flexibility in how the rectangle is displayed on the canvas, as well as easier maintenance of the code.

Furthermore, by allowing a user to describe their needs declaratively, we create a more intuitive and user-friendly interface to work with the canvas and other low-level technologies. This can lead to faster development times and a more enjoyable development experience.

Let me show you an example of how declaratively describing a canvas is much faster than instructing it imperatively. If I want to animate the size of the rectangle, rather than coding the animation manually using imperative APIs, I can simply animate the `height` and `width` variables' value, just like the following code snippet:

```
<script>
  let x = 10, y = 10, height = 100, width = 100;
  setInterval(() => {
    height += 10;
    width += 10;
  }, 100);
</script>
<Canvas>
  <Rectangle
    fill="red" stroke="green"
    {x} {y} {height} {width}
  />
</Canvas>
```

Although the use of set Interval may not be the best to create an animation, the preceding code snippet attempts to demonstrate how easy it is to change the height and width of the rectangle in the canvas.

In the preceding code snippet, we update height and width on every interval. We pass height and width into the Rectangle component. As you can see, the height and width of the rectangle on the canvas increases by 10 px every 100 ms.

Conversely, if we were to animate it imperatively, we would have to clear the canvas and redraw a rectangle with a new height and width on each interval. These implementation details are now abstracted away in the declarative component, making it easier to reason about the animation and modify it in the future.

Overall, using renderless components to handle low-level imperative tasks can greatly improve the readability, maintainability, and flexibility of our code, while also making it more accessible and user-friendly.

So, how do we implement the Canvas and the Rectangle component shown in the preceding code snippet? Let's find out.

Writing declarative Canvas components

We'll start with the Canvas component.

Similar to the component structure of the Carousel component in the previous section, the Canvas component will render a <slot> element to insert all the child components.

However, what's different is that it will also render a <canvas> element, which is what we will interact with and draw on:

```
<script>
  import { onMount } from 'svelte';
  let canvas, ctx;
  onMount(() => {
    ctx = canvas.getContext('2d');
  });
</script>
<canvas bind:this={canvas} />
<slot />
```

In the preceding code snippet, we bind the reference of the <canvas> element to the variable named canvas. After the <canvas> element is mounted onto the DOM, we get the drawing context of the <canvas> element and assign it to the variable named ctx.

If you recall the previous code example, we placed the `<Rectangle>` component inside the `<Canvas>` component to draw a rectangle onto the canvas. The `<Rectangle>` component does not receive any data or slot props from the `<Canvas>` component. So, how does the `<Rectangle>` component inform the `<Canvas>` component that it is a child of the `<Canvas>` component? How does the `<Canvas>` component communicate with the `<Rectangle>` component to know what to draw and how to draw on its `<canvas>` element?

If you recall *Chapter 8*, we introduced Svelte context as a mechanism to set data and make it available to child components. Svelte context allows parent components to share data and functions with the child components without explicitly passing them as props.

We can use Svelte context for communication between the `<Canvas>` and `<Rectangle>` components.

The `<Canvas>` component can set the context with the drawing context, `ctx`:

```
<script>
  import { setContext } from 'svelte';
  // setting the context with the drawing context
  setContext('canvas', () => ctx);
</script>
```

When the `<Rectangle>` component is rendered as a child of the `<Canvas>` component, it can access the context set by the `<Canvas>` component and retrieve the `ctx` variable. In onMount, `<Rectangle>` retrieves the drawing context of the `<canvas>` element and draws a rectangle on the canvas:

```
<script>
  import { getContext, onMount } from 'svelte';
  const getCtx = getContext('canvas');
  onMount(() => {
    const ctx = getCtxt();
    // draws a rectangle onto the canvas
    ctx.fillRect(...);
  });
</script>
```

The reason we pass a function that returns `ctx` instead of directly passing `ctx` in the context is that the `ctx` value is only available in onMount after the `<canvas>` element is mounted onto the DOM, yet `setContext` has to be called during component initialization, which is before onMount. In the `<Rectangle>` component, you should only call `getCtx()` within onMount to retrieve the latest value of `ctx`.

By leveraging Svelte context, the `<Canvas>` and `<Rectangle>` components can maintain a clear and efficient communication channel. The `<Canvas>` component creates the canvas and provides the drawing context, while the `<Rectangle>` component accesses the canvas and performs the drawing tasks.

To complete the `<Rectangle>` component, we need to redraw the rectangle whenever the *x* or *y* positions or the width and height dimensions change. To do that, we will use a reactive statement:

```
<script>
  // ...
  export let x, y, width, height;
  $: draw(x, y, width, height);
  function draw(x, y, width, height) {
    const ctx = getCtx();
    ctx.fillRect(x, y, width, height);
  }
</script>
```

In the preceding reactive statement, the `draw` function is rerun whenever the `x`, `y`, `width`, or `height` values change. By using this approach, the `<Rectangle>` component can efficiently update its appearance in response to changes in position or dimensions, ensuring that the rendered rectangle always reflects the latest state.

However, you might notice that it doesn't work as expected. You'll see that the new rectangle is drawn on top of the old rectangle. This is because we need to clear the canvas before drawing another rectangle. We cannot do that with our `draw` function, as it would lead to undesirable results if we have more than one `<Rectangle>` component. Each component would clear the canvas before drawing its own rectangle, resulting in only the last `<Rectangle>` component being visible.

To fix this issue, we need the `<Canvas>` component to clear the canvas before redrawing all the child rectangles. This function can be called whenever any of the child rectangle components request an update.

Let us define a `redrawCanvas` function in the `<Canvas>` component to redraw the canvas. In the `redrawCanvas` function, we first clear the canvas through `ctx.clearRect()`. Here is the update code for the `<Canvas>` component:

```
<script>
  // ...
  function redrawCanvas() {
    ctx.clearRect(0, 0, ctx.canvas.width, ctx.canvas.height);
    // TODO: here we need to redraw all the rectangles
  }

  // Provide both the drawing context and the clearCanvas function to
  child components
  setContext('canvas', { getCtx: () => ctx, redrawCanvas });
</script>
```

In the `redrawCanvas` function, we want to redraw all the rectangles after we clear the canvas. But how do we do that? One idea is that instead of providing the drawing context, `ctx`, to all the child components and letting the components decide when and how to draw on the canvas, we could provide a function for the components to register their `draw` functions. This way, the `<Canvas>` component can call the `draw` functions when it needs to redraw the canvas.

In the `<Canvas>` component, we change the `getCtx` function into `registerDrawFunction`:

```
<script>
  const drawFunctions = new Set();
  function registerDrawFunction(drawFn) {
    drawFunctions.add(drawFn);
    return () => {
      drawFunctions.delete(drawFn);
    };
  }

  function redrawCanvas() {
    ctx.clearRect(0, 0, ctx.canvas.width, ctx.canvas.height);
    // Redraw all the rectangles
    for (const drawFn of drawFunctions) {
      drawFn(ctx);
    }
  }

  setContext('canvas', { registerDrawFunction, redrawCanvas });
</script>
```

In the preceding `redrawCanvas` function, we loop through the `drawFunctions` registered from child components and call them with the drawing context, `ctx`. This way, we don't need to provide `ctx` through Svelte context, yet the child components can get the latest `ctx` in their `draw` functions.

Finally, let us register our `draw` function in the `<Rectangle>` component:

```
<script>
  // ...
  const { registerDrawFunction, redrawCanvas } = getContext('canvas');
  function draw(ctx) {
    ctx.fillRect(x, y, width, height);
  }
  onMount(() => {
    // register the draw function
    const unregister = registerDrawFunction(draw);
    return () => {
      unregister();
```

```
        redrawCanvas();
    };
  });
  // call redrawCanvas when x, y, height, width changes
  $: x, y, height, width, redrawCanvas();
</script>
```

In the onMount callback, we register the draw function of the <Rectangle> component through Svelte context. When the component is destroyed and removed from the DOM, the <Rectangle> component unregisters itself and calls the redrawCanvas function. This ensures that the <Canvas> component is updated, and the canvas is cleared of the removed rectangle.

Moreover, by calling the redrawCanvas function in a reactive statement whenever x, y, height, or width changes, the <Rectangle> component ensures that its position and dimensions are accurately reflected on the canvas. This way, the <Canvas> component always maintains an up-to-date visual representation of its child components.

Now, the <Canvas> component has full control over redrawing the entire canvas, and the <Rectangle> components can register their draw functions with the <Canvas> component. This approach ensures that the canvas is always cleared before redrawing and allows multiple <Rectangle> components to coexist without interfering with each other's drawings.

We now have functional <Canvas> and <Rectangle> components. Throughout the process of creating these components, we have transformed imperative canvas operations into more manageable, declarative components.

To facilitate communication between parent and child components, we utilized Svelte context as the communication channel. As demonstrated in the preceding code snippets, the parent <Canvas> component maintains a list of draw functions from its child components, enabling it to invoke them as needed. This general pattern can be applied to parent components that need to track and call methods from their child components.

While the code we've written is functional, it may still require some refinements. To access the full working code, including any additional features or optimizations necessary for a polished and comprehensive implementation, please visit the GitHub repository: https://github.com/PacktPublishing/Real-World-Svelte/tree/main/Chapter11/03-canvas.

Exercise 2 – expanding shape components

In this exercise, we challenge you to create additional shape components to expand the capabilities of your existing <Canvas> component.

Examples of shapes you can create include the following:

- A `<Circle>` component that takes in x, y, `radius`, and `color` as props. The component should draw a circle on the canvas at the given coordinates and with the specified radius and color.

- A `<Line>` component that takes in x1, y1, x2, y2, and `color` as props. The component should draw a line on the canvas between the two sets of coordinates with the specified color.

- Other shape components, such as `<Ellipse>` and `<Triangle>`.

You may need to refer to the Canvas API documentation to learn how to draw different shapes.

You can find the code for the `<Circle>` and `<Line>` components at `https://github.com/PacktPublishing/Real-World-Svelte/tree/main/Chapter11/03-canvas`.

Summary

Throughout this chapter, we have delved into the concept of renderless components in Svelte and explored their various use cases. Understanding renderless components equips you with a new toolset to create reusable components. A renderless component emphasizes reusability by focusing on the core logic, state, and behavior, leaving the visual presentation flexible for customization.

By using slot props, we demonstrated how to build a renderless component that is reusable and gives users control over its appearance, while maintaining the component logic and transforming imperative operations into declarative Svelte components.

We also presented practical examples of transforming imperative operations into declarative Svelte components. We demonstrated how to create `<Canvas>` and `<Rectangle>` components that draw a rectangle on a canvas, which can change in size dynamically.

In the next chapter, we will explore how Svelte stores and animations can be combined to create fluid, animated applications.

12

Stores and Animations

In this chapter, we will delve into the world of Svelte animations, focusing on the power and versatility of the `tweened` and `spring` stores. The `tweened` and `spring` stores are writable stores in which their store value changes over time when the `set` or `update` method is invoked, enabling us to develop more complex and visually appealing animations. By effectively harnessing these stores, you can elevate the user experience and create applications that are both dynamic and captivating.

We begin this chapter by delving into the `tweened` and `spring` stores, learning how to create animations using these stores. Following that, we explore interpolation and the use of custom interpolations. Throughout the chapter, we examine various examples, such as animated graphs and image lightboxes, to illustrate the concepts. By the end of this chapter, you will have acquired the skills necessary to harness the `tweened` and `spring` stores effectively, enabling you to create intricate and engaging animations in your Svelte projects.

This chapter covers the following topics:

- Introduction to the `tweened` and `spring` stores
- Custom interpolation and its usage
- Animating with the `tweened` and `spring` stores

Technical requirements

You can find the code used in this chapter on GitHub: `https://github.com/PacktPublishing/Real-World-Svelte/tree/main/Chapter12`

Introducing the tweened and spring stores

Let us begin our journey into the world of Svelte animations by understanding the concept of `tweened` and `spring` stores.

The `tweened` and `spring` stores are writable stores that typically hold numeric values. To see the features they offer, let us compare them with a regular numeric variable.

If you are not familiar with writable stores, you can check out *Chapter 8*, where we extensively explained Svelte stores and creating writable Svelte stores using the built-in `writable()` function.

Usually, when you have a numeric variable and you update the variable, the value of the variable changes instantly. In the following example, we have a numeric variable, `height`, whose initial value is `10`. When we assign a new value of `20` to the variable, the value of the variable changes to `20` immediately:

```
let height = 10;
height = 20;
```

If we use this numeric variable to represent the height of an element or the progress in a progress bar, the height or progress jumps to the new value as soon as it is assigned. These abrupt changes can be jarring.

So, how can we ensure a smooth transition when updating the target value?

Svelte provides two built-in stores, `tweened` and `spring`, specifically designed for storing numeric values and allowing for smooth transitions to new values over a specified duration.

Let's look at an example to get a clearer idea.

In the example, we create a `tweened` store with an initial value of `10`:

```
import { tweened } from 'svelte/motion';
const height = tweened(10, {
  duration: 1000 /* 1 second */
});
```

Then, we assign a new value of `20` to the store:

```
$height = 20;
```

When that is done, the store value gradually increases from `10` to `20` over one second. If we use this store value as the height of an element, the element's height will smoothly grow or shrink toward the target value as we assign a new value to the store, resulting in a visually appealing and fluid transition.

Let us try changing the height from a `tweened` store to a `spring` store. Do not worry about the options in the `spring` function, as we will explain them in the next section:

```
import { spring } from 'svelte/motion';
const height = spring(10, {
  stiffness: 0.1,
  damping: 0.25
});
```

Now, as you assign a new value to the store, you will notice that, similar to when using the `tweened` store, the store value changes over time to the new value but at a different rate.

As you can see, the `tweened` and `spring` stores are powerful features in Svelte that enable you to create smooth animations and transitions in your applications. These stores allow for eased value changes. When used as component states, they allow state updates in a more natural and fluid manner.

The difference between a `tweened` store and a `spring` store is that a `tweened` store provides a way to smoothly transition between two values over a specified duration using an easing function, whereas a `spring` store is designed for physics-based animations, where elements behave as if they were attached to a spring.

Let us dive in and look at how we can use the `tweened` and `spring` stores.

Using the tweened and spring stores

`tweened` is a store that smoothly transitions between numeric values over a specified duration using a chosen easing function.

Here is how you can create a `tweened` store:

```
import { tweened } from 'svelte/motion';
import { cubicOut } from 'svelte/easing';
const progress = tweened(0, {
  duration: 1000,
  easing: cubicOut,
  delay: 500,
});
```

In the preceding snippet, we created a `tweened` store called `progress`, with 0 as the initial store value. When you set a new value for the `progress` store, the store value of the `progress` store stays the same for 0.5 seconds, then transitions to the new value in 1 second, using the `cubicOut` easing function.

The function signature for the `tweened` store is as follows:

```
import { tweened } from 'svelte/motion';
const value = tweened(initialValue, options);
```

`initialValue` is the initial numeric value of the store.

`options` is an object containing the following properties:

- `duration` (default: `400`): The duration of the transition in milliseconds.
- `easing` (default: `linear`): The easing function to use for the transition.

  Svelte provides various easing functions in the `svelte/easing` module, such as `linear`, `quadIn`, and `expoOut`. You can also create a custom easing function.

- `delay` (default: `0`): The delay in milliseconds before the transition starts.

On the other hand, `spring` is a store that smoothly transitions between numeric values using a spring-based physics simulation.

Here's how you can create a `spring` store:

```
import { spring } from 'svelte/motion';
const position = spring(0, {
  stiffness: 0.2,
  damping: 0.5,
  precision: 0.001,
});
```

In the preceding snippet, we created a `spring` store called `position`, with 0 as the initial store value. When you set a new value for the `position` store, this value will bounce toward the target value and oscillate around the target value for a while until it settles at it. The amplitude and duration of the oscillations depend on the `stiffness`, `damping`, and `precision` values configured.

The function signature for the `spring` store is as follows:

```
import { spring } from 'svelte/motion';
const value = spring(initialValue, options);
```

`initialValue` is the initial numeric value of the store.

`options` is an object containing the following properties:

- `stiffness` (default: `0.15`): The stiffness of the spring. Higher values result in a stiffer spring, which causes quicker and more forceful transitions.

- `damping` (default: `0.8`): The damping coefficient of the spring. Higher values result in more damping, which causes the spring to settle more quickly.

- `precision` (default: `0.01`): The threshold at which the spring is considered to be at rest. Smaller values result in more accurate simulations but may take longer to settle.

Using tweened and spring stores with arrays and objects

Both `tweened` and `spring` stores can handle not just single numeric values, but also arrays of numbers and objects with numeric properties. This makes it easy to create complex animations involving multiple values.

When you pass an array of numbers as the initial value, the stores will smoothly transition each element of the array independently. Here's an example using an array of two numbers:

```
import { tweened } from 'svelte/motion';
const coordinates = tweened([0, 0], { duration: 1000 });
// Updating the coordinates
$coordinates = [100, 200];
```

Similarly, when you pass an object with numeric properties as the initial value, the stores will smoothly transition each property independently. Here's an example using an object with two numeric properties:

```
import { tweened } from 'svelte/motion';
const position = tweened({ x: 0, y: 0 }, { duration: 1000 });
// Updating the position
$position = { x: 100, y: 200 };
```

When using arrays or objects, you can access and use the individual values in your Svelte component as follows:

```
<script>
  import { tweened } from 'svelte/motion';
  const position = tweened({ x: 0, y: 0 }, { duration: 1000 });
</script>
<div style="transform: translate({$position.x}px, {$position.y}px)"></
div>
```

This capability to handle arrays and objects makes the tweened and spring stores even more versatile and powerful, enabling you to create intricate animations with ease.

Now that we know how to use the tweened and spring stores, let us use them to create an animated graph.

Examples – creating an animated graph with the tweened and spring stores

In this section, we will explore an example that demonstrates the power of the tweened and spring stores. We will create an animated bar chart where the bars dynamically resize to reflect updated data values. By adding animation to the bar chart, we can effectively highlight data changes and provide insights into complex datasets.

Firstly, let us create a bar chart component:

```
<script>
  let data = generateData(10);
  function generateData(length) {
    const result = new Array(length);
    for (let i = 0; i < length; i ++) {
      result[i] = Math.random() * 300;
    }
    return result;
  }
</script>
<style>
```

```
  .bar {
    background-color: steelblue;
    height: 50px;
  }
</style>
<div>
  {#each data as value}
    <div class="bar" style="width: {value}px"></div>
  {/each}
</div>
```

In the code snippet provided, we initialize the data variable with an array of 10 randomly generated items, created using the generateData function. The generateData function takes a length parameter and creates an array of randomly generated data of the specified length.

With the data array, we use the {#each} block to create a <div> element for each item in the array, setting the width of the <div> element to the value of the corresponding item in the array.

As a result, we have a horizontal bar chart displaying 10 bars with randomly generated widths.

To make things more engaging, we will update the values of the bar chart at fixed intervals:

```
import { onMount } from 'svelte';
onMount(() => {
  const intervalId = setInterval(() => {
    data = generateData(10);
  }, 1000);
  return () => clearInterval(intervalId);
});
```

We initiate an interval of 1 second using setInterval as soon as the component is mounted. On each interval, we update the data by regenerating it with generateData(10).

With this new code addition, you'll observe that the horizontal bars alter their width during each interval. The width of the horizontal bars adjusts suddenly, creating a jarring visual effect.

Now, let's utilize the tweened store to make the bars grow or shrink smoothly every time the data changes:

1. First, let's import the tweened store from svelte/motion. We'll then wrap the data array with the tweened store. As shown in the previous section, we can pass an array of numbers to the tweened function to create a tweened store. This store will smoothly transition each number in the array independently when updated:

    ```
    import { tweened } from 'svelte/motion';
    const data = tweened(generateData(10));
    ```

2. Now, since `data` is a Svelte store, we need to update its value using the `$data` variable instead when making changes:

```
$data = generateData(10);
```

3. Similarly, when we want to iterate through the store value of `data` in the `{#each}` block, we need to use the `$data` variable as well:

```
{#each $data as value}
```

Putting all these changes together, you will now observe that the horizontal bars grow and shrink smoothly, greatly improving the visual appeal and user experience of the bar chart.

As you can see, creating a smoothly animating chart using the `tweened` store is quite straightforward. Before we move on to the next section, we encourage you to try this on your own: replace the `tweened` function with `spring` and observe the changes in the animation.

Exercise – creating an animating line graph

Now that you've seen how to create an animating bar chart, it's time for you to have a shot at creating an animating line graph.

You can use the `d3-shape` library (`https://github.com/d3/d3-shape`), which offers a convenient `line` method that generates an SVG path based on an array of items. Here is an example of using the `line` method:

```
const pathGenerator = line().x((d, i) => i).y((d) => d);
const path = pathGenerator(data);
```

In the preceding code snippet, we utilize the `line` method to create a `pathGenerator` function, which generates an SVG path by mapping the array's values to the *y* coordinates. You can create a line graph by using the returned SVG path with the `<path>` element in an SVG.

Once you've completed your implementation, feel free to compare your results with our example at `https://github.com/PacktPublishing/Real-World-Svelte/tree/main/Chapter12/02-line-chart`. Good luck and have fun experimenting with your animated line graph!

After familiarizing ourselves with using the `tweened` and `spring` stores with numbers, arrays, and objects, it is now time for us to incorporate non-numeric values. This will be achieved through the creation of custom tweened interpolators, which we will explore in the next section.

Creating custom tweened interpolators

Sometimes, you may want to transition between non-numeric values, such as colors. Fortunately, this doesn't prevent us from using the `tweened` store. The `tweened` function offers an option to define custom interpolation between two values.

In this section, we'll explore how to create a custom interpolation to smoothly transition between two colors.

But what is interpolation?

When transitioning between two values, interpolating means generating intermediate values between the values, to create a smooth transition.

For example, consider a `tweened` store initialized at 0, and we set it to 100. The `tweened` store generates intermediate values between 0 and 100, such as 20, 40, 60, and so on, while updating the store value with these intermediate values. As a result, during the transition from 0 to 100, the store value smoothly changes, providing a visually appealing progression from 0 to 100.

This process of generating intermediate values is known as interpolation.

The default `tweened` store is capable of interpolating between two numbers, two arrays of numbers, and two objects with numeric property values. However, it doesn't know how to interpolate between two colors. In such cases, we can pass a custom interpolation function when creating a `tweened` store.

The function signature of the `tweened` store interpolation looks like this:

```
function interpolate(a, b) {
  return function (t) {
    // calculate the intermediate value between 'a' and 'b' based on
't'
  };
}
```

In this function, a and b represent the starting and ending values, while t is a value between 0 and 1 indicating the progress of the transition. The `interpolate` function should return another function that calculates and returns the intermediate value based on t, the progress of the transition.

For example, an `interpolate` function that interpolates between two numbers linearly looks like this:

```
function interpolate(a, b) {
  return function (t) {
    return a + t * (b - a);
  };
}
```

The `interpolate` function returns another function that takes a progress value, `t`, and calculates a linear interpolation between `a` and `b` based on the `t` value. When `t` is 0, the function returns `a`, and when `t` is 1, it returns `b`. For values of `t` between 0 and 1, the result is proportionally between `a` and `b`. To create an interpolation function for colors, we could break the colors down into individual **red, green, and blue (RGB)** components and interpolate each of the components separately. After interpolating each component, we could then recombine them to form the intermediate color.

Alternatively, we could use a library that has already implemented such interpolation. A good example of such a library is `d3-interpolate` (`https://github.com/d3/d3-interpolate`). By using a well-tested library such as `d3-interpolate`, we can save time and ensure that our color interpolation is accurate and efficient.

Here's an example using `d3-interpolate`:

```
import { interpolateRgb } from 'd3-interpolate';
function interpolate(a, b) {
  const interpolateColor = interpolateRgb(a, b);
  return function (t) {
    return interpolateColor(t);
  };
}
```

In the preceding code snippet, we import the `interpolateRgb` function from `d3-interpolate`, which returns an interpolator function for the colors a and b. We then create our custom interpolate function, `interpolateColor`, which returns a function that calculates the intermediate color based on the progress, `t`.

To use our custom `interpolate` function when creating a `tweened` store, we can pass the `interpolate` function in the second argument:

```
tweened(color, { interpolate: interpolate });
```

And that's it; you can now create a `tweened` store for colors that can smoothly transition between them.

You can find a code example of using color interpolation on GitHub at `https://github.com/PacktPublishing/Real-World-Svelte/tree/main/Chapter12/04-interpolation`.

By now, you've learned how to use a `tweened` store to create animated graphs and how to transition between non-numeric values using a custom `interpolate` function.

Let's explore more examples using the `tweened` and `spring` stores to create fluid user interfaces.

Examples – creating an animated image preview

In this example, we'll create an image preview feature that allows users to view a larger, more detailed version of a thumbnail image when they click on it, enhancing the user's visual experience and allowing them to inspect images more closely.

While building this feature, you'll see how we can utilize the `spring` store to create a more fluid and natural user experience, making the transitions between images and their larger previews feel smooth and engaging.

To begin, let's create a list of images that will be displayed on our page:

```
<script>
  const images = [
    "path/to/image1.jpg",
    "path/to/image2.jpg",
    // ...more image paths
  ];
  const imgElements = [];
</script>
<div class="image-container">
  {#each images as image, index}
    <div>
      <img src={image} bind:this={imgElements[index]} />
    </div>
  {/each}
</div>
```

In this example, we create an array of images containing the paths to our image files. We use the `{#each}` block to loop through the images and create a `<div>` element containing an `<img>` element for each image.

In the preceding snippet, the `<style>` section is omitted because it is not essential for understanding how the code functions. If you would like to know what the styles look like, you can find them at `https://github.com/PacktPublishing/Real-World-Svelte/tree/main/Chapter12/03-image-preview`.

We keep the references to the `<img>` elements inside the `imgElements` variable. This will be useful later.

To preview the images and close the preview, we need to implement two functions, `openPreview` and `closePreview`, along with a variable, `selectedImageIndex`, to keep track of the currently previewed image:

```
<script>
  let selectedImageIndex = -1;
```

```
function openPreview(index) {
  selectedImageIndex = index;
}
function closePreview() {
  selectedImageIndex = -1;
}
</script>
...
    <img
      src={image}
      bind:this={imgElements[index]}
      on:click={() => openPreview(index)}
    />
```

In the preceding code snippet, we initialize `selectedImageIndex` to `-1`, indicating that no image is selected. The `openPreview` function sets `selectedImageIndex`, while `closePreview` unsets it. Lastly, we add a click event listener to call `openPreview` for the clicked image.

To create a black backdrop for our image preview, we add a `<div>`element, which will have the `.backdrop` class only when an image is selected. Clicking on the backdrop would close the preview:

```
<div
  class:backdrop={selectedImageIndex !== -1}
  on:click={closePreview}
/>
```

To display the image preview, our goal is to emphasize, enlarge, and center the image on the screen. In order to accomplish this, we must determine the target width and height for the enlarged image and calculate the x and y positions required to center it.

For simplicity, let's assume that the image has a 1:1 aspect ratio. We'll set the target width and height to be 80% of the smaller value between the window height and window width. With the target height and width determined, we can use these values to calculate the x and y positions required to center the image on the screen. Let's see how:

```
<script>
  let selectedImageIndex = -1;
  let width, height, left, top;
  function openPreview(index) {
    selectedImageIndex = index;
    width = Math.min(window.innerWidth, window.innerHeight) * 0.8;
    height = width; // same as width, assuming 1:1 ratio
    left = (window.innerWidth - width) / 2;
    top = (window.innerHeight - height) / 2;
  }
```

```
</script>
...
    <img
      src={image}
      bind:this={imgElements[index]}
      on:click={() => openPreview(index)}
      style={selectedImageIndex === index ? `
        position: fixed;
        left: ${left}px;
        top: ${top}px;
        width: ${width}px;
        height: ${height}px;
      ` : ''}
    />
```

In the code snippet, we set the style for the selected image. When an image is selected, we use `position: fixed` to position it, allowing us to set the `left` and `top` positions of the image relative to the viewport. At this point, we have a simple image preview component.

Now, let's move on to an interesting question: how can we use the `spring` store to make the preview more fluid, rather than abruptly placing the image at the center of the screen?

One idea is to use `transform: translate` instead of directly setting the left and top positions to center the image. We can keep the left and top positions unchanged, and use `transform: translate` to move the image to the center of the screen. The values for the translation offsets would come from the `spring` store.

The reason for using `transform: translate` instead of updating the left and top positions is that it allows for smoother and more efficient animations, as it doesn't trigger layout recalculations and repaints as frequently as updating positional properties such as `left` and `top`. Also, using `transform: translate` makes it much easier to reset the image back to its original position by simply resetting the translation offset back to 0.

Similarly, we can apply this idea to the width and height of the image. We can maintain the original image dimensions and utilize `transform: scale` to resize the image.

With this idea ready, let's get to the code. Here, I initialize the transformation as a `spring` store:

```
const transform = spring(
  { translate: { x: 0, y: 0 }, scale: { x: 1, y: 1 } },
  { stiffness: 0.1, damping: 0.25 }
);
```

The default value of the `transform` spring store is a 0 translation offset and 1 as the scale.

To keep the image in its original position after setting it to use `position: fixed`, we need to get the `<img>` element's current position and dimension, which can be obtained through `getBoundingClientRect`:

```
function openPreview(index) {
  // ...
  const rect = imgElements[index].getBoundingClientRect();
  left = rect.left;
  top = rect.top;
  width = rect.width;
  height = rect.height;
}
```

The previous formula we calculated for the `left`, `top`, `width`, and `height` values to center and enlarge the image will be our target `left`, `top`, `width`, and `height`. They will be used to calculate the translation offset and scale:

```
const targetWidth = Math.min(window.innerWidth, window.innerHeight)
* 0.8;
const targetHeight = targetWidth;
const targetLeft = (window.innerWidth - targetWidth) / 2;
const targetTop = (window.innerHeight - targetHeight) / 2;
$transform = {
  translate: {
    x: targetLeft - left,
    y: targetTop - top
  },
  scale: {
    x: targetWidth / width,
    y: targetHeight / height
  },
};
```

The translation offset is calculated using the difference between the target position and the actual position, while the scale is the ratio between the target width and height compared to the actual width and height.

Incorporating the transform values into the `<img>` styles looks as follows:

```
<img
  style={selectedImageIndex === index ? `
  ...
  transform: translate(${$transform.translate.x}px, ${$transform.translate.y}px) scale(${$transform.scale.x}, ${$transform.scale.y});
  ` : ''}
```

With these changes, the image will smoothly spring into the center when clicked, creating a more fluid and natural user experience.

Now it's your turn to try it for yourself. Experiment with creating an opacity value using the `spring` store and use this value to adjust the dimness of the image preview backdrop. This will further enhance the fluidity and visual appeal of the image preview component.

Summary

In this chapter, we looked at the `tweened` and `spring` stores from Svelte.

We explored how to use the `tweened` and `spring` stores to create smooth animations and transitions, enhancing the visual appeal and user experience. By working with custom interpolation functions and applying them to non-numeric values, such as colors, we've expanded the possibilities for creating dynamic and engaging user interface elements.

Throughout the chapter, we've seen multiple examples of the `tweened` and `spring` stores in action, seeing how easy it is to use the `tweened` and `spring` stores to create animations. Hopefully, you are now more comfortable using the `tweened` and `spring` stores in your Svelte projects.

This is our last chapter discussing Svelte context and Svelte stores. In the next chapter, we will look into transitions, namely, how to use transitions in our Svelte components.

Part 4: Transitions

In this final section, we will delve into Svelte transitions. We will begin by understanding how to incorporate built-in transitions in our Svelte components. Following that, we will guide you through creating your own custom transitions. To end the section, we will wrap up by emphasizing accessibility and how we can create an accessible application with transitions that caters to all users.

This part has the following chapters:

- *Chapter 13, Using Transitions*
- *Chapter 14, Exploring Custom Transitions*
- *Chapter 15, Accessibility with Transitio*n

13

Using Transitions

Transitions are essential in creating smooth and engaging user experiences. By defining how elements appear, disappear, or change within a user interface, transitions can turn ordinary interactions into captivating experiences that leave lasting impressions on users.

Over the next three chapters, we will explore the topic of transitions in Svelte, beginning with a comprehensive understanding of how to use transitions in Svelte.

In this chapter, we will start by learning how to add transitions to elements in Svelte. We will explore the different transition directives and learn how to customize the transitions.

After that, we will discuss when and how the transitions are being played. We will look at different scenarios, such as where there's a mix of elements with and without transitions, or when the elements are within nested logical blocks.

To truly master transitions, it's important to understand the inner workings of the Svelte transition system. We will conclude the chapter by examining the underlying mechanics and offering insights that will help you optimize your use of transitions in your projects.

By the end of this chapter, you will have a solid foundation in Svelte transitions, allowing you to create engaging and dynamic user interfaces with ease.

This chapter includes sections on the following:

- How to add transitions to elements
- When the transitions for the elements are played
- How transitions work under the hood

Technical requirements

You can find the code used in this chapter on GitHub: https://github.com/PacktPublishing/
Real-World-Svelte/tree/main/Chapter13.

Adding transitions to elements

Svelte provides a simple and powerful way to add transitions to your application elements. The framework offers built-in transition functions that can be easily applied to elements, allowing for smooth animations and seamless user experiences. You can also define your own custom transitions, which we will learn about in the next chapter.

Transitions in Svelte are applied to elements when the elements are mounted or unmounted from the DOM. This ensures that elements appear and disappear gracefully, rather than just abruptly popping in and out of view.

To add a transition to an element in Svelte, you can use the transition: directive with the desired transition function. Here's an example of adding a transition to an element:

```
<script>
  import { fade } from 'svelte/transition';
</script>
<div transition:fade>some text here</div>
```

In the preceding code snippet, we imported fade from svelte/transition and applied it to the <div> element.

What you will see with the preceding code is that when the <div> element is mounted onto the DOM, the <div> element will smoothly fade in. When the <div> element is unmounted from the DOM, the <div> element will smoothly fade out.

The transition: directive sets the transitions played when the element is both mounted onto the DOM and unmounted from the DOM. If you want to have finer control over which transitions are played as the element is mounted or unmounted, you can use the in: and out: directives instead:

```
<script>
  import { fade, blur } from 'svelte/transition';
</script>
<div in:fade out:blur>some text here</div>
```

In the preceding code snippet, we applied fade as the in transition and blur as the out transition. When the <div> element is mounted onto the DOM, the <div> element will smoothly fade in. When the <div> element is unmounted from the DOM, the <div> element will smoothly blur out.

Thus, the `transition:` directive is essentially a shorthand for both `in:` and `out:` transitions. In other words, the transitions applied to the two elements in the following snippet are functionally identical:

```
<div transition:blur>some text here</div>
```

So, the preceding code snippet is similar to the following code snippet:

```
<div in:blur out:blur>some text here</div>
```

From the preceding examples, we have seen two of Svelte's built-in transitions, `fade` and `blur` – let us look at more of them!

Svelte's built-in transitions

Svelte's built-in transitions are exported from the `svelte/transition` module.

The following list provides an overview of Svelte's built-in transitions:

- `fade`: This transition smoothly fades an element in or out, adjusting its opacity over time
- `blur`: The `blur` transition gradually applies or removes a blur effect on an element
- `slide`: The `slide` transition makes an element slide smoothly in or out of view
- `fly`: The `fly` transition makes an element smoothly translate from a specified x and y offset
- `scale`: This transition causes an element to grow or shrink in size while appearing or disappearing
- `draw`: The `draw` transition creates a drawing or erasing effect on SVG paths

As you go through the list of built-in transitions, you may notice that some of these transitions rely on user-specified values. For example, the `fly` transition depends on the specified x and y offset from which the element should fly when transitioning in.

Customizing a transition

To make use of these transitions with their required values, you can pass a configuration object containing the necessary properties to the transition directive:

```
<script>
  import { fly } from 'svelte/transition';
</script>
<div transition:fly={{ x: 200, y: 100 }}>Content goes here</div>
```

In the preceding code snippet, we apply the `fly` transition with the specified x and y offsets, indicating that the element will fly in from 200 pixels to the right and 100 pixels down. By providing the appropriate values, you can achieve a wide range of customized transition effects in your Svelte components.

This approach can be particularly useful when you want an element to fly to a different location as it transitions out, compared to the location from which it flies in during the transition.

Instead of using the transition: directive and having only one configuration for both in and out transitions, you can separate it into the in: and out: directives and pass different configuration objects to each directive.

An example of this can be seen in the following code snippet:

```
<script>
  import { fly } from 'svelte/transition';
</script>
<div in:fly={{ x: 200, y: 100 }} out:fly={{ x: -200, y: 50 }}>Content
goes here</div>
```

The <div> element flies in from 200 pixels to the right and 100 pixels down, while it flies out 200 pixels to the left and 50 pixels down. By separating the transition: directive into in: and out: directives, you can control the in and out transition with different configuration objects, having more intricate transition effects in your Svelte components.

In addition to custom configurations specific to each transition, all of Svelte's built-in transitions accept delay, duration, and easing as part of the transition configuration. These parameters allow you to control the timing of your animations, providing greater flexibility in designing your user interface.

The delay parameter determines the waiting time before the transition begins while the duration parameter specifies how long the transition lasts. By modifying these values, you can coordinate when a transition begins and how long each transition takes, creating more complex and engaging animations.

Here is an example of adjusting the delay and duration values of a fade transition:

```
<script>
  import { fade } from 'svelte/transition';
</script>
<div transition:fade={{ delay: 500, duration: 1000 }}>Content goes
here</div>
```

In the preceding code snippet, the fade transition will start with a 500 ms delay after it is mounted onto the DOM, and the transition will last for 1000 ms.

On the other hand, easing is a function that is responsible for controlling the pacing of the animation. By adjusting the easing function, you can create animations that start slow and end fast, start fast and end slow, or follow a custom pattern, giving you even more control over the look and feel of your animations.

Svelte comes with a collection of built-in `easing` functions, which can be imported from `svelte/easing`. These `easing` functions can then be applied to transitions, as seen in the following code:

```
<script>
  import { fade } from 'svelte/transition';
  import { quadInOut } from 'svelte/easing';
</script>
<div transition:fade={{ easing: quadInOut }}>Content goes here</div>
```

In the preceding code snippet, the `fade` transition uses the `quadInOut` `easing` function, which causes the animation to start slowly, accelerate, and then end slowly. By incorporating different `easing` functions into your transitions, you can create a variety of animations for your application.

Exercise – discovering Svelte's built-in transitions

As a practice exercise, try to visit the official Svelte documentation and identify the list of configurable properties for each built-in transition.

To get you started, here is a list of Svelte's built-in transitions:

- `fade`
- `blur`
- `fly`
- `slide`
- `scale`
- `draw`

We know that transitions are played when elements are mounted or unmounted from the DOM, but when and how exactly are the transitions played?

Let us explore the timing and manner in which the transitions are played in the next section.

When are the transitions played?

The transitions in Svelte are played when elements are added or removed from the DOM.

`in:` transitions are executed when an element is added to the DOM. This usually occurs when a component is initialized or when a condition that controls the element's rendering becomes `true`.

For example, in an {#if} block, when the if condition turns from falsy to truthy, the elements inside the {#if} block are added to the DOM. All the in: transitions applied to these elements will be **played simultaneously** as soon as the elements are inserted into the DOM:

```
{#if condition}
  <div in:fade>some content</div>
  <div transition:blur>more content</div>
{/if}
```

In the preceding code snippet, as condition turns to true, both <div> elements will be inserted into the DOM. As soon as both <div> elements are inserted, both the fade and blur transitions will start playing simultaneously. Whether both the fade and blur transitions end at the same time depends on the specified duration for each transition.

Conversely, out: transitions are executed when an element is removed from the DOM. This can happen when a component is destroyed, or when a condition that controls the element's rendering becomes false.

The transition begins as soon as the element is scheduled for removal from the DOM. After the transition is complete, the element is removed from the DOM.

Let us illustrate this with an example:

```
{#if condition}
  <div out:fade>some content</div>
  <div transition:blur>more content</div>
{/if}
```

In the preceding code snippet, when condition turns to false, both the <div> elements remain in the DOM, even though the condition is no longer true. This is because the out: transition needs to be played on both <div> elements before they are removed from the DOM. If the <div> elements were removed from the DOM immediately, they would no longer be visible to users, rendering any subsequent out: transitions ineffective and invisible.

Both fade and blur transitions will play simultaneously on both the <div> elements as out: transitions. Similar to the in: transition, the duration of each transition depends on the specified duration for each transition.

Once all the out: transitions have finished playing, both <div> elements will be removed from the DOM together, making the DOM state consistent with the updated value of condition.

In the previous examples explaining when in: and out: transitions are played, all elements within the {#if} block had transitions applied to them, resulting in the transitions being played simultaneously in all the elements in the {#if} block. But, what happens if not all elements inside the {#if} block have transitions applied? Let's discuss that next.

Handling mixed transition and static elements

When some elements inside an {#if} block have transitions applied and others do not, Svelte handles each element differently based on the specified transitions.

Let's consider an example:

```
{#if condition}
    <div in:fade>Element with fade transition</div>
    <div>Static element without transition</div>
    <div transition:slide>Element with slide transition</div>
{/if}
```

In this example, when condition becomes true, the elements with transitions applied will animate as they are inserted into the DOM, while the static element without a transition will simply appear without any animation.

Based on the preceding code snippet, the second <div> element will be inserted and visible on the DOM immediately, as the first and third <div> elements fade and slide in, respectively.

Similarly, when condition turns to false, the elements with out: transitions (in this case, only the third <div> element, since the transition: directive implies both in: and out: transition) will play their respective out transitions.

Based on the preceding code snippet, you will see that both the first and second <div> elements remain unchanged, and the slide transition is played on the third <div> element. All elements within the {#if} block will only be removed from the DOM together after all the out: transitions have finished playing.

In summary, when you have a mix of elements with and without transitions inside the same logical block, all the elements will be added into and removed from the DOM at the same time. Svelte animates only the elements with transitions applied, while the static elements without transitions will be inserted or removed without any animations.

So far, we have only seen examples using the {#if} block as a means of adding or removing elements, but there are other logical blocks in Svelte that can also be used.

Let us look at what they are.

Other Svelte logical blocks for transitions

The {#if} block adds or removes elements based on the if condition. In addition to the {#if} block, there are other logical blocks in Svelte that provide opportunities for applying transitions when adding or removing elements, such as {#each}, {#await}, and {#key}. These blocks can also have transitions applied to the elements they contain, providing a wide range of possibilities for animating your user interface.

For example, the {#each} block is used to iterate over a list of items and render elements for each item. You can apply transitions to the elements within an {#each} block in a similar way as you would with an {#if} block. Let's look at an example of that:

```
{#each items as item (item.id)}
  <div in:fade out:slide>{item.name}</div>
{/each}
```

In this example, as new items are added or removed from the items array, the elements within the {#each} block will have their respective in: and out: transitions played. When there is a new item in the items array, the new <div> element will fade into the end of the list. When an element is removed from the items array, the respective <div> element will slide out of the list. Using transitions in a list allows you to create a dynamic and engaging user experience, providing clear visual cues when items are added to or removed from the list.

Similarly, you can use transitions with {#await} and {#key} blocks to create visually appealing animations while managing the addition and removal of elements in various scenarios.

The transition:, in:, and out: directives can be applied to any elements, and elements within the same logical block will be added or removed at the same time. This also holds true for nested logical blocks.

For example, let us consider the following code snippet:

```
{#if condition}
  <p transition:blur>paragraph 1</p>
  {#each items as item (item.id)}
    <div transition:fade>{item.name}</div>
  {/each}
  <p>paragraph 2</p>
{/if}
```

When condition changes from false to true, the following happens:

- The first <p> element with the blur transition will animate as it is inserted into the DOM
- Simultaneously, for each item in the items array, the <div> elements with the fade transition will animate as they are inserted into the DOM
- The last <p> element, which does not have any transition, will simply appear in the DOM without animation

Conversely, when condition changes from true to false, the following happens:

- The first <p> element with the blur transition will animate
- Simultaneously, for each item in the items array, the <div> elements with the fade transition will animate

- The last `<p>` element, which does not have a transition, will remain unchanged

- Once all the transitions in the `<p>` element and all the `<div>` elements in the `{#each}` block have finished, both the `<p>` and `<div>` elements will be removed from the DOM together

By using transitions in combination with nested logical blocks, you can create intricate animations that enhance the user experience.

By default, transitions are only played when the nearest logical block causes an addition or removal of the element. However, we can change this behavior with the `global` modifier.

The global modifier

Transitions being played only when the nearest logical block causes an addition or removal of the element helps limit the number of simultaneous animations, making the user experience more focused and less overwhelming. This is called the *local* mode; that is, transitions are only applied for local changes.

To change this behavior, we can apply the `global` modifier. The `global` modifier, when applied to the `transition:`, `in:`, and `out:` directives, ensures that the animation is played whenever the element is added or removed.

To apply the `global` modifier, simply suffix the directive with `|global`, like this:

```
{#if condition}
   <div in:fade|global>some text here</div>
{/if}
```

As per the preceding example, before applying the `global` modifier, the `fade` animation was only being played when the nearest logical block, the `{#if}` block, triggered the insertion or removal of the `<div>` element. This means that if another parent logical block caused the addition or removal of the element, the animation would not be played. With the `global` modifier, the transition will be played whenever the `<div>` element is added or removed, irrespective of which logical block causes it.

To elaborate further, let us look at the following nested `{#if}` block example:

```
{#if condition1}
   <div transition:fade>first div</div>
   {#if condition2}
     <div transition:fade>second div</div>
     <div transition:fade|global>third div</div>
   {/if}
{/if}
```

Let us start with `condition1` as `false` and `condition2` as `true`.

When `condition1` turns `true`, the three `<div>` elements will be inserted into the DOM together. Since `condition2` has always been `true`, at this point, the `{#if}` block that causes all the `<div>` elements to be inserted is the one with `condition1`.

The first `<div>` element will fade in because its nearest logical block, `{#if condition1}`, is responsible for the insertion of the `<div>` element.

The second `<div>` element will be immediately visible on the screen without playing the `fade` transition. This is because, by default, the transition is in *local* mode, and its nearest logical block, `{#if condition2}`, is not the cause of the `<div>` element being inserted at this point.

The third `<div>` element will fade in simultaneously with the first `<div>` element. Because the `<div>` element has the `|global` modifier applied to its transition, it doesn't matter which logical block is responsible for its insertion. The transition will play regardless of the specific logical block that causes the `<div>` element to be inserted.

Now what if `condition1` turns from `true` to `false`?

The same logic applies; therefore, the second `<div>` element will remain unchanged, and only the first and third `<div>` elements will fade out. Once the fade transition has finished, all three `<div>` elements will be removed from the DOM.

In the scenarios we have walked through, the second `<div>` element's `fade` transition has not been played yet. So, when will the `fade` transition of the second `<div>` element be played?

To understand when the `fade` transition of the second `<div>` element will be played, let's consider the situation where `condition1` remains `true` and `condition2` changes from `false` to `true`.

When `condition1` is `true` and `condition2` changes from `false` to `true`, the second `<div>` element will be inserted into the DOM. Since its nearest logical block, `{#if condition2}`, is now responsible for the insertion, the `transition:fade` transition will be played.

As you can see, with the `global` modifier, we can change when transitions are played in response to changes. Instead of playing the transition only when they are relevant to specific conditions affecting the elements, we can change it to be played all the time.

> **Difference between Svelte 3 and Svelte 4**
>
> As we've explained earlier, Svelte transitions are in *local* mode by default. However, this is only changed in Svelte 4, where in Svelte 3 it is the other way around. In Svelte 3, transitions are in *global* mode by default, and you would need to apply the `local` modifier to the transition to change it to *local* mode.

So far, we have covered how to add a transition to an element, using the `transition:`, `in:`, and `out:` directives. We have learned when and how the transitions are played. Before we end the chapter, let us dive deeper into the inner workings of transitions in Svelte to better understand their mechanics.

How Svelte transition works under the hood

Before we delve into the inner workings of Svelte transitions, let us first briefly discuss the general methods for creating animations on the web. Understanding these fundamental concepts provides a solid foundation for grasping how Svelte transitions work.

In general, you can create animations using either CSS or JavaScript.

Creating animations with CSS

To create animations using CSS, you can use the CSS `animation` property along with the `@keyframes` rules. The `@keyframes` rule is used to define a sequence of styles, specifying the CSS styles at each keyframe (from 0% to 100%) during the animation.

See this, for example:

```
@keyframes example {
  0% {
    opacity: 1;
    transform: scale(1);
  }
  100% {
    opacity: 0;
    transform: scale(1.75);
  }
}
```

In the preceding code snippet, we defined an animation keyframe named `example` that changes the opacity from 100% to 0% and the scale from 1 to 1.75 simultaneously.

To apply the `example` animation to an element, we use the CSS `animation` property:

```
<div style="animation: example 4s 1s 1;">Animated element</div>
```

In the preceding code snippet, we set the animation to the `example` animation keyframe, with a duration of four seconds, a delay of one second, and only play the animation exactly once.

The `@keyframes` rule is versatile. We have fine-grained control over the intermediate steps of the animation sequence through `@keyframes` declarations. Combining it with the `animation` property, we control how the animation would look, and when and how long it will play.

The advantages of using CSS to create animations are that it does not involve JavaScript, and the browser can optimize for the CSS animation on its own. This saves JavaScript bandwidth, and as a result, the animation can run smoothly even if you have intensive JavaScript tasks running concurrently. This ensures a better performance and user experience, as the animations remain responsive and fluid even under heavy processing loads.

Creating animations with JavaScript

Creating animation using JavaScript involves manipulating the DOM elements' styles and properties dynamically.

As an example, let us write a fade-in animation using JavaScript.

To achieve this, we need to gradually change the element's opacity from 0 to 1. To set a `<div>` element's opacity to 0 in JavaScript, we set it directly through the element's `style.opacity` property:

```
div.style.opacity = 0;
```

In the preceding code snippet, we assumed that we have obtained a reference to the `<div>` element, which we have stored in the variable named `div`. We then set the opacity of the `<div>` element to 0 through the `div` variable.

To animate the opacity of an element from one value to another, you would need to update the styles at regular intervals over a specified duration of time.

Instead of setting a fixed interval through `setInterval`, the interval for updating styles is usually achieved using the `requestAnimationFrame` method. `requestAnimationFrame` is a browser method that optimizes the animation performance by calling the specified function before the next repaint occurs. `requestAnimationFrame` helps ensure that your animations run smoothly and efficiently by allowing the browser to determine the best time to update the styles, avoiding unnecessary work or redundant repaints.

Here is an example of using `requestAnimationFrame` to create an animation:

```
let start;
const duration = 4000; // 4 seconds
function loop(timestamp) {
    if (!start) start = timestamp;
    // get the progress in percentage
    const progress = (timestamp - start) / duration;

    // Update the DOM element's styles based on progress
    if (progress > 1) {
      div.style.opacity = 0;
      div.style.transform = 'scale(1.75)';
    } else {
      div.style.opacity = 1 - progress;
      const scale = 1 + progress * 0.75;
      div.style.transform = `scale(${scale})`;
      // continue animating, schedule the next loop
      requestAnimationFrame(loop);
    }
}
```

```
}
// Start the animation
requestAnimationFrame(loop);
```

In the preceding code snippet, we schedule the `loop` function in the next animation frame until the progress is finished. We calculate `progress` as the percentage of time passed over the total duration of the animation. With the value of `progress`, we calculate the opacity and the scale of the `<div>` element.

In this example, the end result of using JavaScript animation with `requestAnimationFrame` is the same as the end result achieved with the examples of using CSS animations from the previous section.

The `<div>` element starts at opacity 1 and scale 1 at the beginning of the animation and ends up with opacity 0 and scale 1.75 at the end of the animation.

Using JavaScript for animations offers more control over the animation logic, enabling you to create complex and interactive animations that can respond to user input or other events.

However, one of the downsides of using JavaScript for animations is that it can be more resource-intensive as the animations rely on the browser's JavaScript engine to process and execute the animation logic.

Now that we have learned about the two different approaches to creating animations on the web, which one does the Svelte transition use?

The answer is both.

Animating transitions in Svelte

Although all of Svelte's built-in transitions use CSS for animating, Svelte is capable of animating transitions using both CSS and JavaScript.

To animate the transition through CSS, Svelte generates a one-time-only `@keyframes` rule for each element, based on the transition and the specified configuration object.

Let us look at a `fly` transition as an example:

```
<script>
   import { fly } from 'svelte/transition';
</script>
<div in:fly={{ x: 50, y: 30 }}>Some text here</div>
```

In the preceding code snippet, the `fly` transition is applied to a `<div>` element. In response to that, Svelte generates a `@keyframes` rule that looks like this:

```
@keyframes fly-in-unique-id {
  0% {
    transform: translate(50px, 30px);
```

```
    opacity: 0;
  }
  100% {
    transform: translate(0, 0);
    opacity: 1;
  }
}
```

This generated `@keyframes` rule will be applied to the element for the duration of the transition. The `unique-id` part of the keyframe name ensures that each generated keyframe is unique and doesn't interfere with other elements.

Based on the specified `duration` and `delay` of the transition, Svelte will calculate the appropriate timing for the animation and apply the generated `@keyframes` rule to the element, using the CSS `animation` property. The element will then animate according to the specified `transition`, `duration`, and `delay`.

For example, in the following code snippet, we have a `fly` transition applied to a `<div>` element with a specified duration of 500 ms and a delay of 200 ms:

```
<script>
  import { fly } from 'svelte/transition';
</script>
<div in:fly={{ x: 50, y: 30, duration: 500, delay: 200 }}>Some text
here</div>
```

To animate the `fly` transition in the preceding code snippet, Svelte will generate the corresponding keyframe animation, and apply the generated keyframe animation to the element with the specified duration and delay:

```
div.style.animation = 'fly-in-unique-id 500ms 200ms 1';
```

It is also possible to animate a transition using JavaScript.

Svelte will schedule a loop through `requestAnimationFrame` to run the animation throughout the specified duration.

We won't delve further into the specifics of how the `requestAnimationFrame` loop works with the animation at this point. In the next chapter, we will explore the creation of custom transitions using JavaScript, which will provide a deeper understanding of how the `requestAnimationFrame` loop interacts with animations and how to effectively utilize it for smooth, engaging transitions. Stay tuned to learn more about crafting your own unique animations with Svelte.

Summary

In this chapter, we learned how to add a transition onto an element. We explored the `transition:`, `in:`, and `out:` directives, and how to customize them.

Following that, we looked at when and how the transitions are played. We discussed how the transitions are played when we have a mix of elements with and without transitions, and also how the transitions are played when used inside elements within nested logical blocks.

Last but not least, we dug deeper into how the transition animations are played by Svelte.

With this knowledge, you can now confidently apply transitions into elements when working with Svelte. This will allow you to enhance the interactivity and visual appeal of your applications, thereby providing a more engaging user experience.

In the next chapter, we will look beyond the built-in transitions and will explore the creation of custom transitions.

Exploring Custom Transitions

In this chapter, we will delve into the world of custom transitions in Svelte. So far, we have explored Svelte's built-in transitions and how they can be used to create engaging and dynamic user interfaces. However, there may be situations where the built-in transitions don't quite meet your requirements and you want to create something more unique. This is where custom transitions come into play.

Custom transitions allow you to take full control over the animations and effects that you want to achieve in your Svelte application. This chapter will guide you through the process of creating your own custom transitions, whether they are CSS- or JavaScript-based. We will explore the transition contract, which serves as the foundation for creating custom transitions, and provide practical examples to help you get started.

By the end of this chapter, you will have a solid understanding of how to create custom transitions in Svelte, and you will be equipped with the knowledge to implement them in your own projects, taking your user interfaces to the next level.

This chapter includes sections on the following topics:

- The transition contract
- Writing a custom CSS transition using the `css` function
- Writing a custom JavaScript transition using the `tick` function

Technical requirements

This chapter will be somewhat code-heavy, but don't worry—you can find all the code samples used in this chapter on GitHub at `https://github.com/PacktPublishing/Real-World-Svelte/tree/main/Chapter14`.

The transition contract

Before we dive into creating custom transitions, it's essential to understand the foundation upon which they are built: the transition contract.

If you've read *Chapter 9*, you'll be familiar with the concept of a store contract. Just as a store is an object that adheres to a specific store contract, a transition is a function that follows a transition contract. By understanding and adhering to these contracts, you can create custom transitions that integrate seamlessly with Svelte's built-in transition system.

The transition contract consists of a single function that is responsible for the transition. This function accepts two arguments:

- `node`: The target DOM element that the transition will be applied to

- `params`: An object containing configuration options

The function should return an object that describes how the transition should be executed. We will delve into the details of this returned object later in the section.

Here is an example of a custom transition that adheres to the transition contract:

```
function customTransition(node, params) {
    const config = { ... };
    return config;
}
```

In the preceding code snippet, we have created a custom transition named `customTransition`. We did this by declaring a `customTransition` function that takes in two parameters: `node` and `params`. This function then returns an object—which we'll refer to as `config`—that describes the transition.

To relate the custom transition we've just created back to the usage of a transition in Svelte, here, we see how the `customTransition` function is applied to a `<div>` element:

```
<div transition:customTransition={{ duration: 500 }}>some text</div>
```

When the `<div>` element is inserted or about to be removed from the DOM, Svelte will attempt to play the transition. Svelte does this by calling the `customTransition` function with a reference to the `<div>` element and the `config` object passed to the transition:

```
const config = customTransition(div, { duration: 500 });
```

This `config` object returned by `customTransition` will determine how the transition is played out.

Now, let's focus on the requirements for the `config` object returned by the custom transition function.

The `config` object returned from a custom transition should include at least one of the following properties or methods:

- `delay`: A number specified in milliseconds. This specifies how long to wait before the transition begins.

- `duration`: A number specified in milliseconds. The duration that the transition will play. This determines how fast or slow the animation appears to the user.

- `easing`: A function for easing the transition. This function determines the rate of change in the transition's progress over time.

- `css`: A function that is called with two parameters: `progress` and `remaining`. Here, `progress` is a value between 0 and 1 representing the progress of the transition, and the value of the `remaining` parameter is equal to 1 - `progress`.

  This function should return a string containing the CSS styles to be applied to the target DOM element.

- `tick`: A function that is called repeatedly during the transition with two parameters: `progress` and `remaining`. Here, `progress` is a value between 0 and 1 indicating the progress of the transition, and the value of the `remaining` parameter is equal to 1 - `progress`.

  This function can be used to update the DOM element's styles based on the current progress.

Here is a more complete sample of a custom transition that follows the transition contract:

```
import { cubicInOut } from 'svelte/easing';
function customTransition(node, params) {
  return {
    duration: 1000,
    delay: 500,
    easing: cubicInOut,
    css: (progress) => `opacity: ${progress}`,
  };
}
```

In the preceding code snippet, our custom transition, named `customTransition`, returns an object that describes the transition's `duration`, `delay`, `easing`, and `css` styles.

We saw `delay`, `duration`, and `easing` in the previous chapter when applying transitions to an element. Since the behavior of these properties remains the same in this context, let us focus on something new: the `css` and `tick` functions.

The css function

As you might remember from the last section of the previous chapter, *How Svelte transitions work under the hood*, Svelte animates transitions using a combination of CSS and JavaScript. It leverages CSS `@keyframe` rules along with the `animation` property for CSS animations and the `requestAnimationFrame` function for JavaScript animations.

The css function is used to generate CSS @keyframe rules for custom transitions. If the css function is defined in the returned object of a custom transition, Svelte will call this function when an element is inserted into the DOM or about to be removed from the DOM. Svelte will call the css function as many times as necessary, depending on the duration and easing of the transition, in order to generate the appropriate @keyframe rules.

The first parameter of the css function relates to the progress of the transition. progress is a number between 0 and 1, where 0 represents the element being out of view, and 1 represents the element being in its final position on the screen.

For example, when transitioning an element in after it has been inserted into the DOM, the value of progress starts at 0 and moves toward 1. Conversely, when transitioning an element out before it is removed from the DOM, the value of progress starts at 1 and moves toward 0.

You can use progress to calculate the CSS styles necessary to create your custom transition.

For example, if we want to create a transition that fades an element from transparent to fully visible, we can use progress to calculate the opacity value throughout the transition:

- When the element is out of view (value of progress is 0), we want the element to be transparent (value of opacity should be 0)
- When the element is in view (value of progress is 1), we want the element to be fully visible (value of opacity should be 1)

The relationship between progress and opacity can be represented by the diagram shown in *Figure 14.1*:

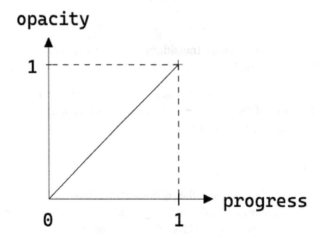

Figure 14.1: Relationship between progress and opacity

We are going to derive the value of opacity from the value of progress in the css function, like so:

```
function customTransition(node, params) {
    return {
        css: (progress) => `opacity: ${progress}`,
    };
}
```

Applying the transition in the preceding code will give you an element that fades from transparent to visible when inserted into the DOM and fades back to transparent when removed from the DOM.

Let us take another example. Let us create a transition that flies the element from the right to its final position. Here, the translation of the element changes throughout the transition, and we can use progress to calculate the translation:

- When the element is out of view (value of progress is 0), we want the element to be on the right (value of translateX is 100px)

- When the element is in view (value of progress is 1), we want the element to be at its final position (value of translateX is 0px)

Here's a diagram depicting the relationship between progress and translateX:

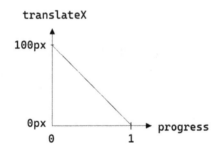

Figure 14.2: Relationship between progress and translateX

Unlike the previous example, the value of translateX is the inverse of progress: when progress is 0, translateX has a nonzero value; when progress is 1, translateX becomes 0.

So, to calculate the translateX value, we use 1 - progress times a value, as you can see in the following code snippet:

```
function customTransition(node, params) {
    return {
        css: (progress) => `transform: translateX(${(1 - progress) * 100}
px)`,
    };
}
```

When applying the `customTransition` function in the preceding code snippet to an element, as the element is added to the DOM, the element will fly in from the right to its final position. And because calculating the inverse of `progress` (`1 - progress`) is so commonly done, the value is provided as a second argument of the `css` function.

So, here is our custom transition again, but using the second argument instead to calculate the translation:

```
function customTransition(node, params) {
  return {
    css: (progress, remaining) => `transform: translateX(${remaining *
100}px) `,
  };
}
```

The `css` function returns a CSS string that can consist of multiple CSS declarations. You separate each CSS declaration with a semicolon, just as you would in a `style` attribute of an element. For example, let's create a transition that combines fading in and translating from the right simultaneously:

```
function customTransition(node, params) {
  return {
    css: (progress, remaining) => `opacity: ${progress}; transform:
translateX(${remaining * 100}px); `,
  };
}
```

In the preceding code snippet, we combine both fading in and translating from the right simultaneously. The returned CSS string contains multiple CSS declarations separated by semicolons, one for `opacity` and another for `transform`, that will be applied during the transition.

Now that we have covered the `css` function, let us look at the `tick` function.

The tick function

The `tick` function serves as an alternative to the `css` function for creating custom transitions. Unlike the `css` function, which is used to generate CSS `@keyframe` rules for the animation, the `tick` function allows you to animate a transition using JavaScript. This can provide more fine-grained control over the transition, enabling the creation of more complex animations that may not be easily achieved with CSS alone.

The `tick` function is called repeatedly during the transition through `requestAnimationFrame`. Similar to the `css` function, the `tick` function accepts two parameters: `progress` and `remaining`. The `progress` parameter is a value between 0 and 1, where 0 represents the element being out of view, and 1 represents the element being in its final position on the screen, while the `remaining` parameter is equal to `1 - progress`. These parameters can be used to modify the DOM element the transition is applied to, based on the current progress of the transition.

For example, if we want to create a fade-in transition using the `tick` function, you can update the element's opacity based on the progress value, as illustrated here:

```
function customTransition(node, params) {
    return {
        tick: (progress) => {
            node.style.opacity = progress;
        },
    };
}
```

Based on the preceding code snippet, Svelte triggers the `tick` function during every animation frame throughout the transition.

When the element starts to appear, the `progress` value is 0, and we use this `progress` value to set the initial `opacity` value of the element to 0.

As the transition continues, the `tick` function is called with `progress` values between 0 and 1, and we update the element's `opacity` value based on the `progress` value.

At the end of the transition, the `tick` function is called one last time with a `progress` value of 1. At this point, we set the element's `opacity` value to its final value of 1.

The `tick` function in the preceding code snippet operates similarly to the custom fade-in transition we created using the `css` function. Both approaches modify the element's `opacity` value throughout the transition. The key difference lies in how they are executed.

Svelte calls the `css` function multiple times with different progress values at the beginning of the transition to construct the CSS `@keyframe` rules. Once this is done, the `css` function is not called again during the transition. The newly created CSS `@keyframe` rule is then applied to the element through the CSS `animation` property. The element's `opacity` value is then updated through CSS.

On the other hand, the `tick` function is called multiple times by Svelte during each animation frame throughout the transition. On every tick call, the element's `opacity` value is modified by JavaScript.

Now that we have learned about the transition contract, let us use this knowledge to create a few more custom transitions.

Writing a custom CSS transition using the css function

The first custom transition we will be attempting to write together is an effect often witnessed in presentations, commonly referred to as the "color swipe." This effect stands out due to its dynamic sweep of color that flows across the screen, creating a sense of energy that captivates the viewer's attention.

The color swipe transition, as its name suggests, involves a sweeping change in color that takes place over an object.

Picture this: you're looking at a static screen, possibly a section of a website. Suddenly, a new color begins to surface from one edge of the screen. Like a wave, this color spreads across the screen, enveloping it. As soon as the color completely covers the screen, it starts to recede from the edge of origin, revealing new content. When the color entirely withdraws, the new content is fully unveiled:

Figure 14.3: The color swipe transition

The *swipe* can move in from any direction—it can move horizontally from left to right, vertically from top to bottom, or even diagonally.

We are going to modify the color swipe transition to apply to paragraph (<p>) elements. When a <p> element is added to the DOM, a wave of color will sweep over it, unveiling the text within the <p> element upon completion of the transition. When the <p> element is removed from the DOM, the reverse of the transition is played, concealing the text upon completion of the transition.

A visualization of the transition can be seen here:

Figure 14.4: The color swipe transition on paragraphs

In this section, we will walk through step by step how to create this captivating color swipe transition using Svelte.

Since the transition that conceals the text when the <p> element is being removed from the DOM is the same as the transition that reveals the text when the <p> element is being added but played backward, we will focus on the transition played when a <p> element is added to the DOM. This is because when a transition is applied to an element, Svelte will play the same transition when the element is removed, but in reverse. Therefore, by focusing on the transition played when an element is added to the DOM, we effectively cover both scenarios.

So, let us get started on creating a transition.

Firstly, let us create the structure of our custom transition. Recall the transition contract—a transition is a function that returns an object describing the transition:

```
<script>
    function colourSwipe(node) {
```

```
        // TODO: implement the transition here
        const config = {};
        return config;
    }
</script>
<p transition:colourSwipe>Some text here</p>
```

In the preceding code snippet, we create a `colourSwipe` transition and apply it to the `<p>` element. Our current task is to implement the `colourSwipe` transition by populating the `config` object.

The first two fields that we are going to add to the `config` object are `duration` and `delay`. As shown in the following code snippet, we set the duration of the transition to 1 second, and the transition will have no delay to start:

```
function colourSwipe(node) {
    const config = {
        duration: 1000,
        delay: 0,
    };
    return config;
}
```

However, often when creating a custom transition, you may want to allow the user of the transition to customize the duration and delay based on where the transition is being applied.

For example, a user of the transition may want to have a delay of 200 milliseconds and a duration of 2 seconds by specifying them in the `transition:` directive, as shown in the following code snippet:

```
<div transition:colourSwipe={{ delay: 200, duration: 2000 }} />
```

These custom delays and durations specified in the `transition:` directive will be passed into the `colourSwipe` transition as the second argument, which will use them in the `config` object:

```
function colourSwipe(node, params) {
    const config = {
        duration: params?.duration ?? 1000,
        delay: params?.delay ?? 0,
    };
    return config;
}
```

In the preceding code snippet, we use the values of `params.duration` and `params.delay` in the `config` object and provide a default value when these parameters aren't explicitly stated.

Now that we have specified the `delay` and the `duration` fields of the transition, let's turn our attention to the next field—`easing`.

We are going to use a `linear` easing, making the transition move at a constant speed, without any acceleration or deceleration. As we did with `duration` or `delay`, we are going to make `easing` customizable by the user. So, in the following code snippet, we set the value of `easing` based on the user-specified easing. If it is left unspecified, we fall back on our default easing—`linear` easing:

```
import { linear } from 'svelte/easing';
function colourSwipe(node, params) {
  const config = {
    duration: params?.duration ?? 1000,
    delay: params?.delay ?? 0,
    easing: params?.easing ?? linear,
  };
  return config;
}
```

Typically, in the process of creating a custom transition, the `duration`, `delay`, and `easing` fields are the simplest to set up. More often than not, we determine default `duration`, `delay`, and `easing` values, and then offer the user the flexibility to tweak these to their liking.

Having figured out the `duration`, `delay`, and `easing` values, we now delve into the crux of the transition: coming up with the CSS for the transitioning element.

If you observe the transition carefully, you will notice that the transition can be divided into two distinct stages: the initial half involves the color block expanding to envelop the entire <p> element, and the latter half corresponds to the color block retracting to unveil the text within the <p> element:

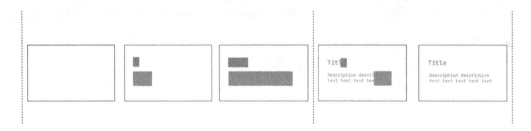

Figure 14.5: The color swipe transition split into two halves, separated by dotted lines

Let's explore how we can create these CSS rules to effectively bring to life these stages of the transition.

Before we start, let us create a `css` function in our `colourSwipe` transition:

```
function colourSwipe(node, params) {
  const config = {
    duration: params?.duration ?? 1000,
    delay: params?.delay ?? 0,
```

```
        easing: params?.easing ?? linear,
        css: (progress) => {}
    };
    return config;
}
```

We are going to fill in the css function in the preceding code snippet.

It's key to note that the progress value begins at 0 at the start of the transition and goes to 1 at the end of the transition. As we are splitting the transition into two stages, the first stage will see the progress value moving from 0 to 0.5, while the second stage advances from 0.5 to 1.

Hence, in our css function, we will implement different CSS rules for different stages of the transition:

```
css: (progress) => {
    if (progress <= 0.5) {
    } else {
    }
}
```

In the preceding code snippet, you can see that we have added an if block in the css function, which uses the progress value to determine which sets of CSS rules to apply. For the first half of the transition (progress <= 0.5), the first set of CSS rules is implemented. For the latter half (progress > 0.5), the second set of rules is used. This way, we can customize the element's appearance in distinct ways throughout the two stages of the transition.

In the first half of our transition, we need to create a growing color block. To create this, we will apply a linear gradient on the background of the element. The gradient will transition from a solid color to a transparent color. By aligning the color stop point of the solid color and the transparent color at the same location, we can create a sharp hard line in the gradient transition.

For example, if we want a solid red color block that occupies the left 25% of an element, we could apply the following CSS:

```
background: linear-gradient(to right, red 0, 25%, transparent 25%);
```

In the preceding snippet, we have a linear gradient moving from left to right, with the red and transparent colors sharing the same color stops at the 25% point. This creates a solid red block on the leftmost 25% of the gradient, while the remaining 75% is transparent.

Our choice to use a linear gradient to achieve this color block, as opposed to superimposing another element, shows the simplicity of this approach. It eliminates the necessity of creating an additional element.

Another benefit of setting a linear gradient on the background, instead of resizing the element, is to have a resizing color block effect without actually resizing an element, which would cause re-layout and layout shifts in the DOM. This way, the element with the applied CSS remains static in its original position and size throughout the transition.

So, now we've figured out the CSS to use, let's incorporate it into our transition's `css` function.

Before that, we need to do some math. We intend to use the value of `progress` to calculate the percentage of the element to be covered by the solid color block.

In the first half of the transition, the value of `progress` goes from 0 to 0.5.

Within this phase of the transition, the percentage of the element that needs to be covered should range from 0% to 100%.

Consequently, by performing arithmetic calculations, we can conclude that the percentage value is 200 times the value of `progress`:

```
const percentage = progress * 200;
```

Let's now integrate this into our `css` function:

```
css: (progress) => {
  if (progress <= 0.5) {
    const percentage = progress * 200;
    return `background: linear-gradient(to right, red 0,
${percentage}%, transparent ${percentage}%);`;
  } else {

  }
}
```

In the preceding code snippet, we use the calculated percentage to control the size of the solid color block, making it grow from the left from 0% to 100% through the first half of the transition.

Now, let's turn our attention to the second half of the transition, where the solid color block contracts from full width toward the right edge of the element.

An alternate way to envision this is by considering the expansion of the transparent portion from the left edge, covering from 0% to 100% of the element. This mirrors the first half of the transition, with the key difference being that it's now the transparent color, not the solid one, that grows to fully envelop the element.

The formula for calculating the `percentage` value remains the same, but since the `progress` value now ranges from 0.5 to 1, we need to subtract 0.5 from the `progress` value before multiplying it by 200. So, the equation becomes this:

```
const percentage = (progress - 0.5) * 200
```

With this modification, our `css` function now becomes this:

```
css: (progress) => {
  if (progress <= 0.5) {
    const percentage = progress * 200;
```

```
      return `background: linear-gradient(to right, red 0,
${percentage}%, transparent ${percentage}%);`;
    } else {
      const percentage = (progress - 0.5) * 200;
      return `background: linear-gradient(to right, transparent 0,
${percentage}%, red ${percentage}%);`;
    }
}
```

In this updated function, the solid color block and transparent areas dynamically resize according to the calculated percentage during the transition, effectively creating the visual illusion of a color swipe.

Applying the transition to an element now, you might notice that although we have a functional solid color swipe transition effect, there are a few elements that could be refined for a smoother visual experience.

One prominent aspect is that the text within the element remains visible throughout the entire transition. Ideally, it should stay hidden in the first half of the transition, when the solid color block is expanding, and only be revealed in the second half as the color block shrinks.

The following screenshot illustrates this issue:

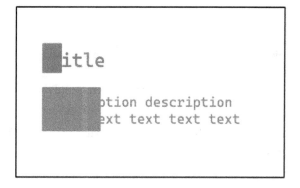

Figure 14.6: The text is not hidden in the first half of the transition

To address this, we can set the text color to transparent during the first half of the transition, as shown in the following code snippet:

```
css: (progress) => {
  if (progress <= 0.5) {
    const percentage = progress * 200;
    return `background: linear-gradient(to right, red 0,
${percentage}%, transparent ${percentage}%); color: transparent;`;
  } else { /* ... */ }
}
```

Another issue is that the solid color block remains red, regardless of the text color. Because we are using the CSS background property to create a swipe effect, the text remains at the forefront, while the solid color block is in the background.

This affects the text-revealing effect from the color block since the full text content becomes fully visible in the second half of the transition. If the solid color block shared the same color as the text, the text would blend with the background. This would create a visual illusion, giving the appearance that the text is being revealed as the color block contracts.

The following screenshot illustrates this issue:

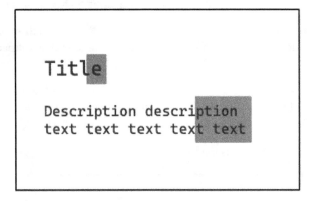

Figure 14.7: The text and block color do not match

To resolve this, we need to find a way to obtain the color of the text and incorporate it into our linear gradient background.

The window.getComputedStyle() function allows us to fetch the styles applied to an element. We can use this function to get the color of the text at the beginning of the transition and use that color for our gradient background:

```
function colourSwipe(node, params) {
  const { color } = window.getComputedStyle(node);
  const config = {
    css: (progress) => {
      if (progress <= 0.5) {
        const percentage = progress * 200;
        return `background: linear-gradient(to right, ${color} 0,
${percentage}%, transparent ${percentage}%); color: transparent;`;
      } else {
        const percentage = (progress - 0.5) * 200;
```

```
            return `background: linear-gradient(to right, transparent 0,
  ${percentage}%, ${color} ${percentage}%);`;
        }
      }
    };
    return config;
  }
```

In the preceding revised code snippet, we replace red with the text color we fetched from the node element's computed style.

And there you have it—a customized color swipe effect, implemented as a Svelte transition. The complete code can be found at `https://github.com/PacktPublishing/Real-World-Svelte/tree/main/Chapter14/01-css-transition`.

We went step by step through creating a custom Svelte transition using CSS. Throughout the process, we learned how to implement user-customizable attributes into our transition, such as `duration`, `delay`, and `easing`. In our color swipe transition, we learned how to craft a multi-staged transition and how to segment the `progress` parameter into various stages, utilize its value to compute the CSS rules, and apply it to the element.

Hopefully, you are now equipped to create your own custom Svelte transition using CSS.

At the start of this chapter, we learned that a transition contract can include not only a `css` function but also a `tick` function. The `tick` function allows us to modify elements during the transition. We've explored how to use the `css` function to create a color swipe transition; in the next section, we'll delve into creating another custom transition, this time using the `tick` function.

Writing a custom JavaScript transition using the tick function

The custom transition we will attempt to write in this section is a flipboard transition. The transition emulates the mechanics of vintage airport departure boards. During this transition, each letter of the text *flips*, cycling through characters until it finally lands on the correct one. The transition ends when all the letters have settled into the right character.

The following diagram illustrates how the flipboard transition works to reveal the phrase *Hello Svelte*, with the vertical axis representing the flow of time from top to bottom:

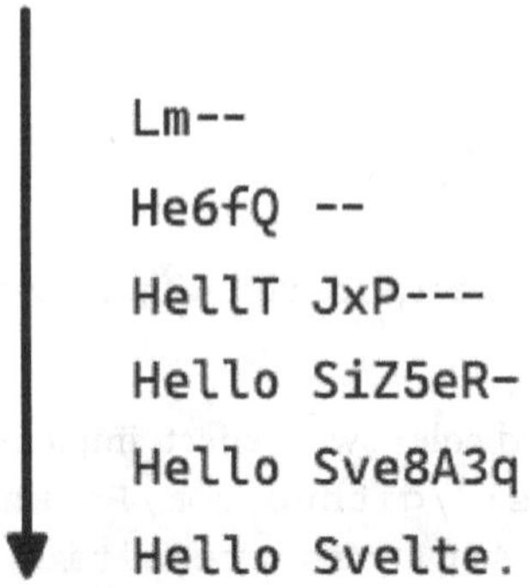

```
Lm--

He6fQ --

HellT JxP---

Hello SiZ5eR-

Hello Sve8A3q

Hello Svelte.
```

Figure 14.8: Flipboard transition visualized

At the onset of the transition, letters begin to appear from left to right, starting as a dash (-) and then flipping through random characters before settling on the correct one. This flipping motion continues from left to right until all letters have aligned with their corresponding characters, unveiling the intended phrase.

The entire transition process involves modifying characters within the element, transitioning from a blank state through jumbled characters, and finally to the correct text. Since there are no style or layout changes needed, we are not using the `css` function to implement this transition. The `tick` function is the perfect candidate to implement this transition in Svelte.

Now that we've defined how the flipboard transition would look, let us start implementing this transition.

Building on what we learned with the color swipe transition in the previous section, the flipboard transition begins in a similar way. Here is the basic code structure for our flipboard transition:

```
<script>
  function flipboard(node, params) {
    const config = {
      duration: params?.duration ?? 1000,
      delay: params?.delay ?? 0,
      easing: params?.easing ?? linear,
      tick: (progress) => {
        // TODO: implement the transition here
      },
    };
    return config;
  }
```

```
</script>
<p transition:flipboard>Hello Svelte.</p>
```

In the preceding code snippet, we have defined a flipboard function that adheres to the transition contract. It takes in two arguments, node and params, and returns a transition configuration—an object that describes the transition. As such, we are able to apply the flipboard function as a transition using the transition: directive on a <div> element.

Within the flipboard transition, we've set up the basic parameters, such as defining the duration, delay, and easing values, while leaving a placeholder for the tick function, where we will implement the transition.

To create a flipboard transition, we start by obtaining the text content of the element that will be transitioning. Then, each time the tick function is called, we determine the text to display based on the progress value and update the element accordingly.

We can retrieve the text of an element using the following API:

```
const text = node.textContent;
```

Similarly, to set the text content of an element, we assign it through the same property:

```
node.textContent = text;
```

Incorporating these into the flipboard transition, here's what we get:

```
function flipboard(node, params) {
  const text = node.textContent;
  const config = {
    // ...
    tick: (progress) => {
      let newText;
      // TODO: compute the newText based on `text` and progress value
      node.textContent = newText;
    },
  };
  return config;
}
```

In the preceding code snippet, we retrieve the text content of the element at the beginning of the flipboard function, right before the transition starts to play on the element. The tick function, called repeatedly on every animation frame, computes the new text value for the element, based on the original text value and current progress value.

The `tick` function's task is to determine how each letter should be displayed, based on the `progress` value. Some letters might appear as a dash, some as random characters, some as their original value, and others might be hidden.

For each letter, its display depends on its position relative to the full text's length and the current `progress` value. For instance, if a letter is positioned at 30% from the left, and the current `progress` value is 0.5 (or 50%), then that letter should be displayed as is.

How do we determine these rules? What leads us to the conclusions just drawn?

We want the element to reveal all its original characters at the end of the transition. This means that when the `progress` value reaches 1 (or 100%), all letters should display their original character. At the midpoint, with a `progress` value of 0.5 (or 50%), 50% of the letters from the left should show their original character, while the remaining 50% on the right should show either a dash, a random character, or nothing at all.

To generalize, if a letter's position from the left is less than the `progress` value, it should display its original character. Otherwise, it may display a dash, a random character, or nothing.

The following diagram illustrates how the `progress` value and the displayed text are related:

```
progress = 0       Lm--
progress = 0.2     He6fQ --
progress = 0.3     HellT JxP---
progress = 0.5     Hello SiZ5eR-
progress = 0.7     Hello Sve8A3q
progress = 1.0     Hello Svelte.
```

Figure 14.9: The red box shows which letters are displaying the original character at each progress value

The preceding diagram illustrates how the original characters are revealed at different values of `progress`. As the `progress` value increases, more letters in the word display their original characters.

To implement the flipboard effect just described, we will loop through each character, determine its relative position, and then decide whether it should be displayed. For characters whose position is beyond the current `progress` value, we will display a blank space.

Here is the updated code:

```
tick: (progress) => {
  let newText = '';
  for (let i = 0; i < text.length; i++) {
    const position = i / text.length;
```

```
    if (position < progress) {
      // display the original character
      newText += text[i];
    } else {
      // display a blank space instead
      newText += ' ';
    }
  }
  node.textContent = newText;
},
```

With this code, the flipboard transition now either shows the original characters or a blank space based on the progress value. When playing the transition, you will see the characters appear one by one from left to right.

Having figured out when to show up the original characters, let us continue to determine when the text should display dashes or random characters.

Using a similar idea, we can determine whether a letter should display a random character, a dash, or nothing at all. We will introduce a constant number to manage the timing of these changes. If the letter's position is beyond this constant multiplied by the progress value, it will show up as nothing. I've chosen a value of 2 for this constant, based on trial and error. It's a value greater than 1 but not too large, to create the effect of characters appearing gradually from the left.

Similarly, we could also introduce another constant to manage the display of dashes or random characters. If the letter's relative position is greater than this new constant times the progress value, but less than 2, the letter will appear as a dash. Otherwise, it will be a random character. For this purpose, I have chosen 1.5, positioning it midway between 1 and 2.

The following diagram visually represents these two constants and their effect on the transition:

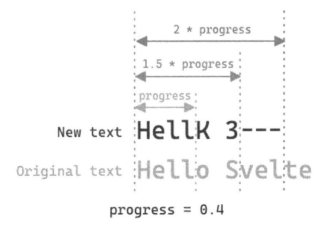

Figure 14.10: Relationship between the new text and the original text

In the preceding diagram, you can observe how the characters change during the transition. When the progress value is 0.4, for example, letters at the 40% position are showing original characters, letters at 40% - 60% (progress * 1.5) are showing random characters, letters at 60% - 80% (progress * 2) are showing dashes, and anything beyond is not shown.

Here's how the updated code for our flipboard transition looks:

```
tick: (progress) => {
  let newText = '';
  for (let i = 0; i < text.length; i++) {
    const position = i / text.length;
    if (position < progress) {
      // display the original character
      newText += text[i];
    } else if (position < progress * 1.5) {
      // display random characters
      newText += randomCharacter()
    } else if (position < progress * 2) {
      // display dash
      newText += '-';
    } else {
      // display a blank space instead
      newText += ' ';
    }
  }
  node.textContent = newText;
},
```

In the preceding code snippet, I've added two additional conditions to determine when to display dashes or random characters.

The randomCharacter() function returns a randomly selected character, implemented as follows:

```
const chars =
'ABCDEFGHIJKLMNOPQRSTUVWXYZabcdefghijklmnopqrstuvwxyz1234567890'
function randomCharacter() {
  return chars[Math.floor(Math.random() * chars.length)];
}
```

With this code, you have a flipboard transition! Try it out with an element and observe the effect. The characters slowly appear one by one from left to right, starting as a dash, flipping through characters, and finally settling with the correct character.

You may notice one small issue: not all characters are the same width, so the overall width of the text grows and shrinks. Since each letter is not aligned with its previous position, the flipping effect may not be immediately obvious.

To fix this, you can use a monospace font. Monospace fonts, also known as fixed-width fonts, ensure that each letter occupies the same horizontal space. Applying a monospace font to an element enhances the flipping effect, making it more visually distinct.

For example, you can set the font as follows:

```
font-family: monospace;
```

In this section, we've explored how to create a flipboard transition, emulating the appearance of vintage airport departure boards. We've learned how to control the appearance of characters based on the progress of the transition, using random characters, dashes, and original text. And through modifying the text of an element, we created a transition that is visually engaging.

The complete code for this section can be found at here:https://github.com/PacktPublishing/Real-World-Svelte/tree/main/Chapter13.

Summary

In this chapter, we have explored how to create custom transitions in Svelte. We went through two detailed examples that utilize the `css` function and the `tick` function.

Hopefully, you now feel well equipped to write your own custom transition in Svelte, enabling you to craft a more engaging and unique user experience in Svelte.

In our next and final chapter, we will delve into how transitions can impact the accessibility of your Svelte application, guiding you in the creation of an engaging and inclusive experience for all users.

Accessibility with Transitions

In the past two chapters, we learned how to use transitions in Svelte. Transitions, when used correctly, can enhance the user experience, guiding a user's attention, providing feedback, and adding a layer of polish to the interface. However, for users with vestibular disorders, these animations can be uncomfortable or even debilitating. Therefore, it is essential to strike a balance between creating engaging animations and ensuring that they do not negatively impact users with specific needs.

In this chapter, we will dive into the techniques available to make web transition more accessible for users with a vestibular disorder, exploring CSS and JavaScript approaches to respect a user's preferences regarding motion.

By the end of this chapter, you will have a better understanding of web accessibility and how to create more inclusive web applications that cater to all users, regardless of their specific needs or preferences.

In this chapter, we will cover the following:

- What is web accessibility?
- Understanding user preference with `prefers-reduced-motion`
- Reducing motion for a Svelte transition
- Having an alternative transition for inaccessible users

Let's start by exploring what web accessibility is.

Technical requirements

All the code in this chapter can be found at the following link: `https://github.com/PacktPublishing/Real-World-Svelte/tree/main/Chapter15/01-accessible-transition`

What is web accessibility?

Accessibility is the design of products, devices, services, or environments to be usable by as many people as possible, regardless of any physical, sensory, or cognitive disabilities they may have.

It is vital to ensure that websites are accessible to all users. There are many disabilities that can potentially affect a user's experience on a website. Ensuring a website's accessibility allows everyone, regardless of their abilities, to have equal access to the same services and information that are available to everyone.

One of the many disabilities that can hinder a website's user experience is a vestibular disorder. In this chapter, we will specifically focus on enhancing accessibility for individuals with vestibular disorders.

Vestibular disorders are conditions that affect the inner ear and brain, and they can cause difficulties with balance, spatial orientation, and movement perception. Imagine that your body's natural sense of balance isn't working right. It's like being dizzy or feeling tipsy. The ground under your feet doesn't feel stable, and the things you see around you seem to move on their own, even if you're standing still.

For individuals with vestibular disorders, certain visual stimuli, such as moving or flashing content on a web page, can trigger symptoms such as dizziness, nausea, or migraines.

We learned how to add transitions in *Chapter 13* and *Chapter 14* to make our application more engaging for users. However, for users with vestibular disorders, these transitions can inadvertently provide a negative experience. Most operating systems provide accessibility settings, enabling users with vestibular disorders to reduce or remove animation. These accessibility preferences can be used by web applications to create an inclusive user experience.

So, let's explore how a web application accesses a user's accessibility preference.

Understanding user preference with prefers-reduced-motion

Most operating systems offer accessibility settings that allow users to disable animation effects. For instance, in Windows 11, you can navigate to **Settings** | **Accessibility** | **Visual Effects** | **Animation Effects** and uncheck the **Animation Effects** option to turn off animations.

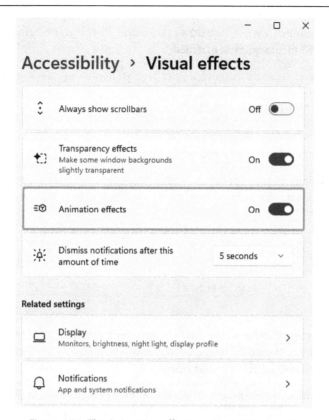

Figure 15.1: The Animation effects option in Window 11

In web applications, you can use the prefers-reduced-motion CSS media query to determine whether a user has activated a setting on their device to reduce or eliminate non-essential motion.

Here is an example of how to use the prefers-reduced-motion CSS media query:

```
@media (prefers-reduced-motion: reduce) {
  div {
    /* Removes animation */
    animation: none;
  }
}
```

In the preceding code snippet, if a user has indicated a preference for reduced motion, we set the CSS animation property to none to remove animation from the <div> element.

Alternatively, besides using CSS, you can also use JavaScript to determine a user's preference for reduced motion. The window.matchMedia method lets you check whether the web page matches a given media query string.

In the following code snippet, we use `window.matchMedia` to test whether the `prefers-reduced-motion` CSS media query is matched:

```
const mediaQuery = window.matchMedia('(prefers-reduced-motion:
reduce)');
const matches = mediaQuery.matches;
```

If the user prefers reduced motion, then the value of `matches` in the preceding code snippet will be `true`; otherwise, the value of `matches` will be `false`.

A user might change their accessibility preferences while browsing a web page. To get notified whenever the user alters their preference for reduced motion, we can listen to the `change` event of the media query. Here's how:

```
const mediaQuery = window.matchMedia('(prefers-reduced-motion:
reduce)');
mediaQuery.addEventListener('change', () => {
  let matches = mediaQuery.matches;
});
```

In the preceding code snippet, whenever a user changes their preference for reduced motion, the listener function passed into the `change` event handler will be invoked. It will evaluate the updated user preferences through `mediaQuery.matches`.

Now that we've learned how to determine user preferences for reduced motion through `prefers-reduced-motion`, let us take a look at how we can use it to reduce Svelte's transition for users with vestibular disorders.

Reducing motion for Svelte transition

After learning how to obtain a user's preference for reduced motion, let's now respect that preference by reducing unnecessary motions in our transitions, which could potentially trigger vestibular discomfort.

In the following code block, there is an example of our Svelte component, which has a `fly` transition applied to the list items:

```
<script>
  import { fly } from 'svelte/transition';
  export let list = [];
</script>
<ul>
  {#each list as item}
    <li transition:fly={{ x: 40 }}>{item}</li>
  {/each}
</ul>
```

In the preceding code, whenever a new item is added to the list, a new <li> element will fly in from the right and be inserted into the list. This flying motion could be a trigger for users with vestibular disorders.

However, the flying transition is not essential because the application will still function correctly without it. Therefore, if a user has indicated a preference for reduced motion in the system settings, we should respect that preference by reducing or removing the flying transition.

One way to achieve this is by setting the duration of the fly transition to 0. This way, the transition will take no time to play and complete and, in effect, will not be played at all.

Here's the modified version of the previous Svelte component, which does not play the fly transition if the user prefers reduced motion:

```
<script>
  import { fly } from 'svelte/transition';
  export let list = [];
  const mediaQuery = window.matchMedia('(prefers-reduced-motion:
reduce)');
  let prefersReducedMotion = mediaQuery.matches;
  mediaQuery.addEventListener('change', () => {
    prefersReducedMotion = mediaQuery.matches;
  });
</script>
<ul>
  {#each list as item}
    <li transition:fly={{
      x: 40,
      duration: prefersReducedMotion ? 0 : 400,
    }}>{item}</li>
  {/each}
</ul>
```

In the preceding code snippet, we determine whether a user prefers reduced motion by checking whether the CSS media query, prefers-reduced-motion: reduce, is matched, and we store this information in a variable named prefersReducedMotion. If prefersReducedMotion is true (meaning the user prefers reduced motion), then we set the duration of the fly transition to 0. The user will not see any flying motion when a new item is added to the list.

On the other hand, if the user does not have a vestibular disorder and has not expressed a preference for reduced motion effects, then prefersReducedMotion will be false. In this case, the duration for the fly transition will be set to 400 ms, and a flying transition will be displayed for every new item added to the list.

However, not all transitions act as triggers for vestibular motion disturbances. For instance, the `fade` transition, being a subtler animation, isn't as disruptive to users with vestibular disorders. Instead of entirely eliminating transitions by setting their duration to `0`, we can opt to replace more intense transitions with milder ones. We'll delve into this approach in the following section.

Having alternative transitions for inaccessible users

Users with vestibular disorders may feel discomfort when exposed to motion-based animations, such as scaling or panning large objects. However, they are generally less affected by subtler animations, such as fading.

Switching all transitions to fading for users with vestibular disorders is not a one-size-fits-all solution. It is always better to seek feedback from the users themselves.

We will continue using the same example from the previous section and explore how we can switch from the `fly` transition to a `fade` transition when a user prefers reduced motion.

One thing to note is that, in Svelte, you are not allowed to apply more than one transition to an element.

For example, the following code is invalid and will result in a build error:

```
<div transition:fade transition:fly />
```

This means we can't apply two transitions to an element and then decide which one to use. We must find a way to switch between different transitions while applying only one transition to an element.

As we learned in *Chapter 14* about creating custom transitions, a transition in Svelte is a function that follows a transition contract. The return value from the function determines how the transition will play out.

So, one approach to having a transition that switches between two transitions, based on a condition, is to create a custom transition that returns different transition configurations, based on the condition.

Our custom transition would look something like the following code, returning different transition configurations based on whether a user prefers reduced motion:

```
<script>
  function accessibleFly(node, params) {
    const mediaQuery = window.matchMedia('(prefers-reduced-motion:
reduce)');
    const matches = mediaQuery.matches;
    if (matches) {
      // user prefers reduced motion
      // return a fade transition
    } else {
      // return a fly transition
```

```
      }
    }
</script>
<ul>
  {#each list as item}
    <li transition:accessibleFly={{ x: 40 }}>{item}</li>
  {/each}
</ul>
```

In the preceding code snippet, we defined an `accessibleFly` transition, which is a more accessible `fly` transition that will switch to a `fade` transition if a user prefers reduced motion.

Now, we need to determine what to return in each of the conditional cases within our custom `accessibleFly` transition.

It's important to recall that a transition in Svelte is a JavaScript function. Therefore, we can call both the `fly` and `fade` transitions as functions, and the return value will be the transition configuration for each respective transition. By doing this, we can return these values from our `accessibleFly` transition, effectively allowing our transition to be either a `fly` or `fade` transition, based on a user's preference.

Here's the updated `accessibleFly` transition:

```
<script>
  function accessibleFly(node, params) {
    const mediaQuery = window.matchMedia('(prefers-reduced-motion:
reduce)');
    const matches = mediaQuery.matches;
    if (matches) {
      // user prefers reduced motion
      return fade(node, params);
    } else {
      return fly(node, params);
    }
  }
</script>
```

In the preceding code snippet, we return the value either from the `fade` or `fly` transition, depending on a user's preference. We pass the `node` and `params` values that are given to our `accessibleFly` transition into both the `fade` and `fly` transitions. The `node` and `params` values specify which element the transition is applied to and provide user parameters, such as `duration` and `delay`. These are useful for the `fade` and `fly` transitions to determine how the transitions should be executed.

With the preceding code changes, we now have an accessible `fly` transition named `accessibleFly`, which, by default, will cause an element to fly as part of the transition. However, the `accessibleFly` transition will cause the element to fade if a user has indicated a preference for reduced motion.

And there you have it–a transition that is engaging and appealing to most users, while still being considerate of those who prefer reduced motion.

You can find the code for the `accessibleFly` transition at `https://github.com/PacktPublishing/Real-World-Svelte/tree/main/Chapter15/01-accessible-transition`.

Summary

In this chapter, we explored the importance of accessibility in web design and how to implement transitions that consider the preferences of users with vestibular disorders. By understanding the impact of motion-based animations on users with vestibular disorders, we can create more inclusive and user-friendly web applications.

We learned about the `prefers-reduced-motion` media query, which allows us to detect whether a user has indicated a preference for reduced motion in their system settings. Using this media query, we can adjust our transitions to be less motion-heavy or remove them altogether for users who prefer reduced motion.

We also discussed how to create custom transitions in Svelte for accessibility. We looked at an example of a custom transition, named `accessibleFly`, that switches between a `fly` and a `fade` transition, based on a user's preferences for reduced motion. This custom transition is considerate of users with vestibular disorders while still providing engaging and interesting transitions for other users.

In summary, accessibility is crucial in web design, and transitions are no exception. By considering the preferences and needs of all users, including those with vestibular disorders, we can create more inclusive and user-friendly web applications.

Index

X

www.packtpub.com

Subscribe to our online digital library for full access to over 7,000 books and videos, as well as industry leading tools to help you plan your personal development and advance your career. For more information, please visit our website.

Why subscribe?

- Spend less time learning and more time coding with practical eBooks and Videos from over 4,000 industry professionals

- Improve your learning with Skill Plans built especially for you

- Get a free eBook or video every month

- Fully searchable for easy access to vital information

- Copy and paste, print, and bookmark content

Did you know that Packt offers eBook versions of every book published, with PDF and ePub files available? You can upgrade to the eBook version at packtpub.com and as a print book customer, you are entitled to a discount on the eBook copy. Get in touch with us at customercare@packtpub.com for more details.

At www.packtpub.com, you can also read a collection of free technical articles, sign up for a range of free newsletters, and receive exclusive discounts and offers on Packt books and eBooks.

Other Books You May Enjoy

If you enjoyed this book, you may be interested in these other books by Packt:

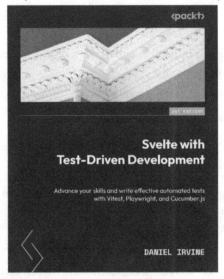

Svelte with Test-Driven Development

Daniel Irvine

ISBN: 978-1-83763-833-8

- Create clear and concise Vitest unit tests helping the implementation of Svelte components
- Use Playwright and Cucumber.js to develop end-to-end tests that simulate user interactions and test the functionality of your application
- Leverage component mocks to isolate and test individual components
- Write unit tests for a range of Svelte framework features
- Explore effective refactoring techniques to keep your Svelte application code and test suites clean
- Build high-quality Svelte applications that are well-tested, performant, and resilient to changes

SvelteKit Up and Running

Dylan Hildenbrand

ISBN: 978-1-80461-548-5

- Gain a comprehensive understanding of the core technologies of SvelteKit
- Dive deep into SvelteKit's file-based routing system and uncover basic and advanced concepts
- Master code organization in SvelteKit through effective data-loading techniques
- Elevate your application's visibility by incorporating SEO and accessibility
- Streamline the deployment process of your SvelteKit apps by using adapters
- Optimize your SvelteKit app by exploring various configuration and tooling options

Packt is searching for authors like you

If you're interested in becoming an author for Packt, please visit `authors.packtpub.com` and apply today. We have worked with thousands of developers and tech professionals, just like you, to help them share their insight with the global tech community. You can make a general application, apply for a specific hot topic that we are recruiting an author for, or submit your own idea.

Hi!

I am Tan Li Hau, author of *Real-World Svelte*. I really hope you enjoyed reading this book and found it useful for increasing your productivity and efficiency.

It would really help me (and other potential readers!) if you could leave a review on Amazon sharing your thoughts on this book.

Go to the link below or scan the QR code to leave your review:

`https://packt.link/r/1804616036`

Your review will help us to understand what's worked well in this book, and what could be improved upon for future editions, so it really is appreciated.

Best wishes,

Tan Li Hau

Download a free PDF copy of this book

Thanks for purchasing this book!

Do you like to read on the go but are unable to carry your print books everywhere?

Is your eBook purchase not compatible with the device of your choice?

Don't worry, now with every Packt book you get a DRM-free PDF version of that book at no cost.

Read anywhere, any place, on any device. Search, copy, and paste code from your favorite technical books directly into your application.

The perks don't stop there, you can get exclusive access to discounts, newsletters, and great free content in your inbox daily

Follow these simple steps to get the benefits:

1. Scan the QR code or visit the link below

https://packt.link/free-ebook/9781804616031

2. Submit your proof of purchase
3. That's it! We'll send your free PDF and other benefits to your email directly

www.ingramcontent.com/pod-product-compliance
Lightning Source LLC
Chambersburg PA
CBHW080631060326
40690CB00021B/4894